ARBITRATION 1989
THE ARBITRATOR'S DISCRETION
DURING AND AFTER THE HEARING

ARBITRATION 1989
THE ARBITRATOR'S DISCRETION
DURING AND AFTER THE HEARING

PROCEEDINGS OF THE FORTY-SECOND
ANNUAL MEETING
NATIONAL ACADEMY OF ARBITRATORS

Chicago, Illinois

May 28-June 3, 1989

Edited by
Gladys W. Gruenberg
*Professor Emerita of Economics
and Industrial Relations
St. Louis University*

The Bureau of National Affairs, Inc.

Washington, D.C.

Copyright © 1990
The Bureau of National Affairs, Inc.

Published by BNA Books, 1231 25th St., N.W., Washington, D.C. 20037

Printed in the United States of America
International Standard Book Number 0-87179-627-9
International Standard Serial Number 0148-4176

 302-l

PREFACE

Advocates played a major role in the Academy's 42nd Annual Meeting held in Chicago, Illinois. Thomas T. Roberts set the tone in his Presidential Address by regaling the Thursday luncheon audience with stories about advocates he has known (Chapter 1). This camaraderie was seconded by former UAW President Douglas A. Fraser, the Distinguished Speaker at the Friday luncheon. He emphasized that the labor movement is on the right course precisely because there is more cooperation between management and labor in solving mutual problems (Chapter 2).

It wasn't all sweetness and light, however, especially when the subject of arbitral discretion came up in the context of just cause (Chapter 4), and advocates showed varying degrees of displeasure with arbitral implications based on "sounds of silence" in the collective bargaining agreement (Chapter 5).

Arbitral advocacy came in for its lumps, but there was consensus that arbitrators should control the hearing with a firm hand (Chapter 5). Application of the Code of Professional Responsibility to hearing and posthearing conduct was stressed at a members-only session (Chapter 6). The most recent opinion (No. 20) of the Committee on Professional Responsibility and Grievances, interpreting the advertising and solicitation ban in the Code, appears in Appendix B.

Participation in permanent umpireships affords unique experiences, according to Academy members who have been selected and then unselected, to lend credence to the oxymoronic nature of these appointments (Chapter 8). To permit arbitrators and advocates a shared evaluation of different arbitration tribunals, neutrals and representatives of labor and management in five specific arbitral environments conducted concurrent workshops on arbitration in the airlines (Chapter 9), the federal sector (Chapter 10), the steel industry, the postal service, and the railroads (Chapter 11).

In accordance with the charge of the Academy's Board of Governors to make members' research and presentations at the Continuing Education Fall Conference available to a wider audience, we have included some of those papers in appropriate places (Chapters 5, 7, and 10), depending on the subject matter.

In a continuing tradition of excellence and cooperation, Program Committee Chairman I.B. Helburn and Arrangements Committee Chairman Arthur A. Malinowski deserve the Academy's thanks and appreciation for a job well done. The editor relied on their assistance on many occasions, and we again thank Camille Christie, BNA Senior Editor, for her professional guidance and patience.

August 1, 1989   Gladys W. Gruenberg
                                                      Editor

CONTENTS

CHAPTER 1

THE PRESIDENTIAL ADDRESS: ADVOCATES
I HAVE KNOWN

THOMAS T. ROBERTS*

It is strange how forces we do not understand assert subtle influences upon our lives and at times bring us to moments of personal fulfillment. My daughter, who is sensitive to such things, would ascribe this phenomenon to the gentle hand of God, while my son, the attorney, might declare that upon reflection and analysis a more secular explanation is to be found. For myself, I join with my wife Kathy in accepting, with such grace as we are able to muster, the turns and twists that inevitably intrude upon both the personal and professional life of every arbitrator.

These philosophical thoughts are generated by the extraordinary coincidence that some time ago the Board of Governors of the Academy selected Chicago as the location for our 42nd Annual Meeting, and about two years later I was honored by being asked to serve as President of the Academy during the year we were in Chicago.

Let me tell you something of the reach of that coincidence. To begin at the beginning, I was born in the old St. Luke's Hospital, then located about six blocks from where I am standing at this very moment. We lived, during the depths of the Depression, in Highland Park, a city a few miles north of downtown Chicago. At the age of 10, I sold magazines in the adjoining Chicago-Northwestern and North Shore Electric Line railroad stations. It was our joke in the family that the soles of our shoes were worn so thin that, if we happened to step on a coin, we could tell if it was heads or tails.

Following the death of my father in 1934, my mother took my sister and me to the Los Angeles area to be near a family member who was employed. To this day my family and I continue to

---

*President, 1988–89, National Academy of Arbitrators.

1

reside in Southern California. Yet the fortunes of war, both between nations and between industrial combatants, have brought me regularly back to this vibrant city on the shores of Lake Michigan—and always with genuine pleasure.

But enough of these sentimental musings. I turn now to my remarks, remarks to which I have assigned the title "Advocates I Have Known." The anecdotes I am about to relate are factual; only the identity of those proponents of justice and equity who have appeared before me over the years has been shielded. I have, of course, in particular deleted any reference to all individuals present at this luncheon, except perhaps some of those I spotted leaving early.

Advocates are sometimes lawyers and sometimes not. We are all aware that the skill and force of an arbitral presentation does not necessarily turn on the possession of a legal credential. In the General Motors-UAW umpire system, for example, nonlawyers present all of the cases in a very effective and forceful manner. They like it that way and their process has met the test of time.

Perhaps the view of at least one former resident of our host state introduces a valuable perspective regarding lawyer versus nonlawyer advocacy. I refer to a story told of U.S. President Ulysses S. Grant, a man who took no apparent care of his appearance. It seems, the story goes, that on a particularly stormy winter night Grant sought the comfort and warmth of an inn located in Galena, Illinois, a town in the northwest corner of this state and, again by coincidence, the birthplace of my paternal grandparents.

Grant entered the inn that cold and stormy night and took a table next to a group of lawyers who were in town for a session of court and who happened to be clustered around the fire for warmth. One of the attorneys spotted Grant dressed in his normally unkempt attire and made even more disheveled by the storm. The lawyer, having some sport with Grant, loudly declared to his colleagues, "Gentlemen, by the looks of this stranger he's traveled through Hell itself to get here." Grant, responding to the challenge, rather cheerfully said, "You are right, I have!" The lawyer thereupon asked, "And how did you find things down there?" Grant replied, "Just as they are here. The lawyers are all placed closest to the fire."

Now for a few recollections of advocates I have known. At the very dawn of my career as an arbitrator, I was invited to sit as chairman of a board of arbitration convened to consider the merits of the discharge of a bus driver employed by a transit district serving one of the major suburbs of Los Angeles. The unhappy coach operator had been terminated upon a charge that he had pocketed a portion of the fares paid by three of his passengers.

When I convened the hearing, the advocate for the transit district noted that the charge against the grievant involved moral turpitude, and he suggested that I should therefore begin the proceedings with a call upon the Almighty to provide me with the necessary perception and wisdom to do justice. You can see what confidence he had in me! I have not since been asked to seek divine guidance at the arbitration table, although many of you for whom I have worked may feel I could use any form of help, be it divine or otherwise. In any event, this good and sincere advocate concluded his pious request with this entreaty, "Please lead us in a few words of silent prayer."

The advocate then stated that the testimony of his first and only witness, the security agent-spotter who claimed to have observed the grievant, would necessarily have to be in the form of a written statement because, if the spotter were to take the witness stand, his identity would be revealed and his cover blown. The union objected, complaining that such procedure would not permit an opportunity for cross-examination. I sustained the objection. My friend, the transit district advocate, thereupon walked to the door of the hearing room and ushered in the spotter-witness, who was wearing a paper bag over his head. The bag had two holes for eyes, much in the fashion of New Orleans Saints fans of a few years ago. It was the intent of counsel to have the agent testify and submit to cross-examination from behind the shield of this mask. The union representative immediately protested and stated to me, "You can't permit ghosts to testify!" I asked, "You don't believe in ghosts?" The union advocate replied, somewhat hesitantly, "No, I don't believe in ghosts, but nevertheless I'm afraid of them."

On another occasion an innovative advocate came before me representing a baggage handler who had been terminated by an international air carrier. The grievant he represented was accused of stealing an African gray talking parrot named Harvey from the aft cargo compartment of a Boeing 747 being loaded at the San Francisco International Airport. The parrot had been reported missing upon the arrival of the plane in London. The African gray parrot is a particularly rare and valuable breed, and the theft therefore generated the interest of Interpol. Some six months after its disappearance, the FBI managed to track the errant creature to Atlanta, Georgia, where it was found in the home of the grievant's ex-wife. The parrot was then reunited with its owner in London. Presumably each had much to relate to the other!

At the arbitration hearing, the grievant's representative argued that no proof of his client's guilt existed because the parrot had not been produced to be identified by its owner. To this the lawyer representing the airline replied, "We can't interfere with the lives of our passengers by asking them to return to the United States with their parrots." The grievant's representative rather indignantly responded, "Why not, this is the greatest country in America." He then added, "If the parrot won't talk, neither will my client." Faced with that procedural impasse, I ruled that the parrot and its owner could remain in London, but the grievant was entitled to a presumption that the testimony of the missing bird would in all probability not fly.

I will never forget the oppressive heat that settled over an arbitration I once convened in the middle of the summer in the historic mining town of Globe, Arizona. The proceedings took place in a room rented for that purpose at the local YMCA, a building of considerable antiquity erected long before the availability of air conditioning. In a word, it was just plain hot, and all of us were demonstrating our individual discomfort in a variety of ways.

One of the potential witnesses removed his shirt, while another wore a dampened bandana about his forehead. We were all squirming in discomfort. Finally, in midafternoon the grievant, who had been discharged for purportedly stealing a drill bit, was called to the stand to give his version of what had actually occurred. He accepted the customary arbitral oath dressed in a starched white shirt and tie, with his pants recently pressed. The grievant thereupon proceeded to recount the events of the day of his termination in exquisite detail and with great precision. Beyond that, he fielded each and every one of the questions prepared by his union representative with calm self-assurance. It was a truly remarkable performance carried out in the face of trying environmental circumstances.

Finally, the grievant-witness was turned over to the company advocate for cross-examination. The exchange that followed began with the following sally (and I quote from the transcript):

The advocate for the employer: "Under all of the circumstances—the heat and the fact that your job is at stake—you seem
remarkably cool on the witness stand." Without a pause, the
grievant replied, "Thank you. You don't look so hot yourself."

In another case an airport policeman at the Los Angeles
International Airport was placed on disciplinary suspension
after being discovered asleep in his black-and-white cruiser
while on duty. This dereliction was compounded by the fact that,
at the time he was found asleep, he was stationed alongside an
active runway with specific orders to guard a DC-10 that was the
subject of a bomb threat. The aircraft was in danger of being
blown to smithereens and yet the good officer assigned to keep
the area secure had fallen asleep at his post!

At arbitration the officer denied being asleep and added, "I
have nothing further to say, and I'll only say it once." There
followed an extensive evidentiary presentation placed in the
record by the Deputy County Counsel assigned to represent the
Department of Airports at the hearing. She produced a number
of witnesses, all of whom testified to the somnolent appearance
of the grievant on the afternoon in question, even in the presence of emergency vehicles with their sirens blaring. At the close
of her case, the Deputy County Counsel suddenly announced,
"There is so much paperwork in my file I overlooked a document I wish to introduce in evidence." With that, and in the
nature of a reflex reaction, the grievant-sleeper blurted out,
"You have to stay alert!"

An off-duty airline mechanic was walking about the terminal
at Kennedy Airport when he came upon an attractive young lady
I shall call Shirley. Shirley was seated on a bench crying her eyes
out. She had been deposited there by a disenchanted suitor who
had left her with nothing more than a broken heart and a return
ticket to her home in New Orleans. The grievant-mechanic
engaged her in conversation and offered his sympathy for her
predicament. Soon they found themselves in a nearby tavern.
After Shirley had consumed—in only one hour—and I quote
from the transcript, "five scotch and sodas chased by three
martinis," the two adventurers returned to the terminal parking
lot in the automobile of the grievant. To put it in his words, "One
thing led to another and we had sexual intercourse." Almost
immediately thereafter, however, Shirley bolted from the automobile shouting that she had been raped. The police were
summoned; the grievant was placed in custody and thereafter

arraigned on a felony count of forcible rape. To add to these difficulties, he was forthwith summarily terminated by his employer.

When the matter of the propriety of the discharge came before the system board of adjustment, counsel for the carrier argued that the grievant had engaged in conduct unbecoming an employee of the airline and thus had been properly discharged. In his summary on behalf of the grievant, the advocate for the union declared, "The conduct of which the grievant stands accused took place away from the premises of the company and while he was off the clock. You cannot attach guilt to that for which he was not being paid. Nor can you sustain the discharge of an otherwise satisfactory employee who engaged in but a single indiscretion, permitting the girl in question to mix her brand of drinks."

Advocates are no different from the rest of us in that they sometimes garble a phrase or reverse a sentence while in the forensic heat of their presentation. Things of this sort seem particularly common in the world of Major League Baseball. To set the background, permit me first to recall two such slips of the tongue perpetrated, not by the much-maligned Yogi Berra, but by Tex Richards, the former public address announcer for the Dodgers—Brooklyn, that is, not Los Angeles. Richards once proclaimed over the public address system with great solemnity, "A little boy has been found lost." On another occasion when the fans sitting in the left field bleacher seats had draped jackets and other articles over the railing he called out, "Would the fans along the outfield rail please remove their clothes?"

Well, enough of that. Let us turn now to some encounters of my own with advocates representing either clubs or players in that unique form of interest arbitration known as baseball salary arbitration. I begin with an encounter I had several years ago with an agent who elected to represent his player-client in a dispute with the club-employer over the salary to be paid during the forthcoming season. The player in question was a left-handed pitcher, and the agent was attempting to inflate his worth by arguing that he was the most versatile player in the game since he could serve the club as both a starting pitcher and a relief pitcher. As the agent put it, "The club can have confidence in the abilities of my man both when he is a member of the starting rotation and when he is throwing up in the bullpen."

In compiling the statistical data to support the foregoing contention, the agent proffered an exhibit that mistakenly listed the player he represented as having started on the mound and having been called from the bullpen in the same game. When the advocate for the club recognized this anomaly, he interrupted and asked, "Are you saying he relieved himself on the mound?"

If you have concluded from my remarks that baseball salary arbitrations involve a great deal of statistical evidence and comparisons, you are absolutely correct. Each side has one hour to present its case, followed by only one-half hour for rebuttal and summation. There is a great deal of money at stake. This factor, coupled with the tight time constraints, sometimes causes the advocates to mix metaphors or otherwise trip over syntax. Consider, for example, the agent for an American League outfielder who submitted in evidence a detailed set of data in support of his salary request. Hurrying to complete his presentation, the agent stated, "I have arranged for purposes of comparison all comparable players aligned by salary paid alphabetically." The advocate for the club rapidly glanced over the assembled performance figures and solemnly remarked, "Their similarities are different." The agent replied, "Well, the club may have overpaid him this year but he is worth every penny of it."

One final baseball story. I will always remember the lawyer who represented the New York Mets and on one occasion reacted in astonishment to the exaggerated claims of a player representative engaging in a considerable degree of puffery on behalf of his client. This particular presentation began with questionable statistical comparisons and gradually but steadily built to an emotional climax, in which the agent compared the talents of his player with those of a number of the revered Mets heroes of the past. With the calling out of the name of each such retired Met star, the lawyer became increasingly discomforted, if not distraught. Finally, he could contain himself no longer and he shouted, "If Casey Stengel were alive today to listen to this nonsense, he would be spinning in his grave."

It is time now to leave baseball and briefly recall some other advocates I remember, in some instances with admiration, in others with affection and, in a few situations, with total astonishment. All have appeared before me; some have even survived pretty much in one piece! They include:

- The movie and television actress-advocate who later rose to the high office of president of an international union.
- The advocate who led me in prayer, expressed in the rhymes of ancient yet new Hebrew, when the two of us flew in a light plane through a midnight blizzard between Fairbanks and Anchorage during the period of the construction of the Alaska pipeline.
- The advocate-to-be who worked on high voltage utility lines during the day and went to law school at night in order to sharpen his representational skills. He is now a member of the California Bar and a very effective union officer.
- The advocate who brought two City of Memphis police officers to the hearing room to arrest and drag off to jail a grievant he had accused of stealing company property.
- The advocate who went on to become the Attorney General of the United States.
- The advocate who is now in jail.
- The advocate who is in training to become a Major League Baseball announcer.
- The advocate who responded in kind to a rhetorical question posed by opposing counsel. He was asked, "What will you tolerate the least—ignorance or indifference?" He answered, "I don't know and I don't care!"
- And dearest to my arbitrator's heart, the three advocates I have earlier encountered in hearings, all of whom have since become neutrals and, beyond that, distinguished members of the National Academy of Arbitrators, as well as a fourth former advocate who now works with me as an arbitrator and who is teaching me a great deal in the process.

Finally, I wish to pay my respects to the one advocate I have most admired over the years. In doing so, I will in this one instance identify the individual by name. I speak of the late Juan Chacon.

Juan Chacon was the son of Indian-Mexican parents who resided in the Southwest. As Juan entered his teen years, he went to work in an open pit copper mine at Santa Rita, New Mexico. In the crucible of that physically demanding job, performed in the searing heat of the high desert summers and the bone deep chill of winter storms, Juan matured into an adult with a commanding presence, reflecting leadership qualities enhanced by a staunch personal integrity. He was not a large man, but he was all man!

At an early point in his tenure in the mines, Juan became active in the conduct of the affairs of his local of the Mine, Mill and Smelter Workers Union, a labor organization now succeeded by the United Steelworkers of America. The personal-human characteristics reflected in his understanding of the needs of his constituency soon caused Juan to become something of a legend among the workers and their families, all of whom lived in and around the company town situated between Hurley and Silver City, New Mexico.

Juan rose rapidly through the various levels of responsibility within the local union, and ultimately he was elected its president. At about this same time he met and fell in love with an attractive young woman, the daughter of a fellow mine worker. Following an appropriate period of courtship, Juan and Lupe were married, and they took residence in a small wooden bungalow owned by the company. The bride and groom were subsequently blessed with two children. There was, however, a dark cloud of labor-management unrest on the horizon.

When the collective bargaining agreement at the mine expired by its terms, the parties were unable to reach agreement on the provisions of a successor contract. This caused Juan ultimately to lead the members of the local out of the pit and smelter to protest in the streets of their tiny town. Tragically, strife followed, marked by violent clashes between the miners and company-employed guards. The homes of the miners came under siege, and in some instances they were burned to the ground. Casualties were suffered by both sides. Many of the partisans were injured and regrettably others were killed, some might say murdered. Juan and his supporters nevertheless stood their ground throughout this travail, and ultimately they were rewarded by the granting of a few pennies in increased wages and some improved fringe benefits.

After the men went back to work, the price they paid in lost wages (to say nothing of injured or dead brothers and fathers) came to the attention of socially conscious observers across the land. One such "seed" of interest germinated within a group of motion picture writers, directors, and producers who were at the time themselves the victims of the economic and political havoc wrought by the spectre of McCarthyism then so prevalent, not just in Hollywood but across the land. The motion picture studios were terrified of becoming identified with this group of artists. Yet, although blacklisted as "commies" or worse, they somehow managed to produce a documentary black and white film. It told the story of the tragedy and triumph of the strike as experienced by Juan Chacon and his friends. Indeed, although a professional actress played the part of Mrs. Chacon, Juan and most of the others played themselves!

Somehow, the strength and principles of this remarkable man were captured for the screen. The film was at once both beautiful and gut wrenching. The message it represents has stayed with me to this day. It was an extraordinary performance by a man who consented to assume the unfamiliar role of film actor only after he was convinced that others might gain through the telling of his story. With the same talents he had employed as an advocate at the arbitration table, Juan projected on film the dignity and strength of his cultural, religious, and earth-oriented heritage. He was, in a word, magnificent!

The film of which I speak was entitled, "Salt of the Earth." Unhappily, most movie theaters refused to exhibit "Salt of the Earth" out of fear of being tarred by the black brush of anticommunism. Through a happy fortuity, however, the operator of a small theater in Hollywood chose not to be intimidated and the film was shown. I was at the time "courting" my wife Kathy, and on one of our dates I took her to see "Salt of the Earth." We were both touched by the story—a real life story—of Juan Chacon, his family, and his friends. This emotion remained in our hearts even after our picture was snapped by a government surveillance team as we left the theater, presumably to assist in any future inquiry into the purity of our political affiliations. The lesson of the misplaced suspicions of the inquisitorial climate of those times remains with me even today. I learned that it is wrong and evil to permit yourself to judge someone simply on the basis of innuendo, transitory public hysteria or, the worst of all, group association.

If you happen to find yourself in the vicinity of Hurley, New Mexico, I recommend a visit to the old Mine, Mill and Smelter Workers hall located on a two-lane highway at the edge of town. There you will find on all four walls of the meeting room a mural painted by an extraordinarily talented local artist. The mural depicts the history of the people of the area as their lives have been affected by the presence of the Santa Rita mine. You will, of course, find Juan Chacon, his family, his priest, his friends, and fellow workers in much of the story. The presence of Juan Chacon and his remarkable accomplishments continue to be a force in that otherwise modest union hall.

I think of Juan Chacon often. He brought to the arbitration hearing room in a most compelling manner the truth that every man and woman who works for a living is entitled to respect and dignity no matter how humble their origins or how routine their employment function. Juan Chacon taught me this long ago, and it is appropriate from time to time to restate the lesson, particularly in this city of my own origins. Thank you for permitting me this opportunity to do so.

CHAPTER 2

IS THE LABOR MOVEMENT ON THE RIGHT COURSE?

DOUGLAS A. FRASER*

In introducing me, Jim [Stern] neglected to tell you about my latest credentials. I am now an arbitrator of sorts. In 1986 the Executive Council of the AFL-CIO decided to establish an arbitration procedure by which, in any contested election of two or more unions trying to organize the same group of workers, unions could avail themselves of the arbitration process. Glenn Watts, former president of the Communications Workers of America, and I were named arbitrators.

You know how unions jealously guard their jurisdictions— more jealously than nations guard their sovereignty. The Executive Council unanimously agreed to proceed with this new arbitration process. It was established in March 1986. By the end of the year, we had heard five cases. In 1987 we heard 10 cases; in 1988, 13 cases. The step before arbitration is a mediation process. Over 40 percent of the cases are settled in mediation. I think the system has worked well. The unions have accepted it. The Executive Council reviews the procedure every February to see how it is working. The arbitrator operates within the criteria established by the Council.

I get a great deal of satisfaction out of this work. When you think of the savage campaigns unions have conducted against one another in this country in the past, certainly arbitration is the sensible, rational, civil way of handling these disputes.

Now I'd like to move on to something else I'm greatly interested in. It's the new labor-management meetings that are going on in the United States today. As you know, the new buzz word is "quality," not only in the manufacturing sector but also in the

---

*Professor of Labor Studies, Wayne State University, Detroit, Michigan; formerly International President, United Automobile Workers of America.

12

service sector. Sometimes there is a lot of confusion about exactly what that concept means.

It reminds me of a story about a woman who was shipping her dog from Chicago to Detroit. It was a German shepherd. When the dog arrived at the airport in Detroit, the baggage handler came up to the cage and saw that the dog lay dead. He alerted the customer service agent, who came out and looked at the dog. He said, "No matter how we try to explain this, we're going to be blamed. I'll tell you what we'll do. You get a Polaroid camera and take a picture of the dog, then go to the nearest pet store and buy a dog that looks exactly like this one and we'll substitute it. Then the owner won't know the difference."

So they took a picture of the dog, and before the woman was due to pick up the dog, they had plenty of time to carry out their plan. The agent warned the baggageman to get a friendly dog so that it would be wagging its tail when the owner came. Well, they got an identical dog, and when the woman came to get her dog, she was very perturbed. The agent said, "But, madam, we've taken very good care of your dog; see how he's wagging his tail." She angrily replied, "I know that's not my dog! My dog is dead; I was shipping it back here to bury it." Sometimes all attempts to cover up the real image don't do much good. So it is sometimes with the work we do.

Jim didn't mention one of the other responsibilities I have, teaching at the Graduate School at Columbia University, two days every other week. This is my third and final year. You can imagine that the students are conservative and have a dim view of the labor movement and an even dimmer view of labor leaders. Some of the faculty organized a seminar from four to six o'clock; they had a big turnout—about 250 students—and we discussed different matters for about two hours, such as the domestic economy, the international economy, questions of national and international policies, the relation between currencies (the yen, the deutschmark, and the dollar), arms control. At the very end a young man at the back of the room got up and said: "I have to admit that I had this stereotype of a labor leader, overweight, cigar-smoking, using a lot of profanity." And I replied: "Young man, you've just described Lee Iacocca." I've told that story so many times that I've got Iacocca telling it now.

Let me raise the issue today that lots of people are asking about, namely, is the labor movement on the right course? First of all, we all recognize that the labor movement is not a monolith. There are great labor unions, there are mediocre labor unions, and a couple are quite bad. The unions that are on the right course, in my judgment, are those with leadership and membership that recognize the necessity, the inevitability of change. The task of unions is to bring about that change so that the workers don't have to accept a disproportionate burden of that change, so that the changes are made in a rational, civil, and compassionate way. I believe it is unions with leaders who have the capacity to change with events that are on the right course.

Of course, there are political risks involved with advocating change, but that's the price we have to pay. On the other hand, the protectors of the status quo, in my view, lack foresight. But they know that people and groups are comfortable with the status quo, and bringing about change is sometimes exceedingly difficult. Those for the status quo pander to those who do not wish to change. They are wedded to the past, creatures of habit, prisoners of history, and they approach each problem with an open mouth.

I hear people in my union, some of them my dear friends, say they yearn for the 50s and 60s, when we had a monopoly in the auto industry. They ask, "When are we going back to those times?" and I tell them, "Never, never, never!" It's a new world, a changing world. We're going to face ever more international competition, and we have to adjust to that inevitability. Those who say that we can go back to those glory days are either guilty of deception or they are fools.

What is this debate all about? And let me remind you that just because we have debate in our union doesn't mean that we have a fragile union or that it's going to come apart. If you have enough democracy in an organization, there is bound to be debate and discussion of issues, with the administration being attacked and ideas being attacked. Such debate doesn't mean that the union is a failure or is weak.

I happen to think that in the long run these challenges are healthy, and they will turn out that way for our union. In a democratic union there's always a mechanism whereby you can test new ideas—it's called an election. In our union in about three weeks from now, we'll have an election. Those who believe in the inevitability of change will win because they have the support of the membership.

The debate is really about different points of view of two groups of people, both well intentioned. Those who call themselves the New Directions (I call them the Old Directions or No Directions) believe that the union leadership is being co-opted because they're embarking upon mutual programs with management called labor-management cooperation (at General Motors they call it "quality of work life"; at Ford they call it "employee involvement"). What these programs mean essentially is that companies, particularly large companies, are finally coming to recognize what I knew 50 years ago, that the women and men in the workplaces of America are intelligent and innovative, that they have a great deal of ingenuity. If you give them an opportunity to make a contribution, they will make a contribution.

Labor and management might have different motives for supporting these programs. I remember Jim McDonald, former president of GM, once said: "We have to change the way we work and we have to give workers a greater voice in the decision-making process and how work is organized, because that is the only way we can compete on an international level. That is the only way we can improve our quality and efficiency." From my point of view, I was in favor of the concept because I believe it democratizes the workplace. Workers feel good about themselves; they feel that their intelligence is finally being recognized. They have a greater sense of satisfaction, of achievement, of accomplishment. So, while we have different motives, we arrive collectively at the same conclusion—that these new approaches are a good idea.

There are several things that have to be considered when embarking on these programs. It has to be voluntarily entered into. You can't force-feed union people on a program like this; neither can you force management into it. In any human relationship between two persons or between two groups, the relationship is fragile and must be based on mutual respect and mutual trust. When one side or the other loses that trust and respect, the program is in jeopardy.

Much has been said and written about the NUMMI (New United Motors Manufacturing Corporation) plant in California. That is the joint venture between General Motors and Toyota. When GM ran that plant, they used to average 22 percent absenteeism. Obviously with that kind of absenteeism, shifting people around to strange jobs to fill the gaps, they built a pretty lousy car. It was the worst car built in the GM system. But after the work force was reorganized under Toyota management, absenteeism was cut to about two percent. The car they produced, the Nova, was the best car produced in the United States, according to Consumers Union reports.

I was in that plant recently, and I want to assure you that there's nothing out of the ordinary about that plant. It doesn't have any unusual technology. In fact, there are plants in both Japan and the United States that are technically superior to the NUMMI plant. But the difference is that they handle their human resources better. The very fact that the workers' intelligence is finally recognized makes them feel good about their job and they perform in an extraordinary way.

I know that there are critics of this program and the programs at other plants. They say that the atmosphere is very oppressive at the NUMMI plant, that the work is very demanding. But a lot of those who criticize it have never been there. That reminds me of a story about a Columbia professor, with whom I was discussing this program. He finally told me what he thought the problem was. He said, "It may work out in practice but it'll never work in theory."

Most of the people who criticize this program, whether in the union or outside the union, have never been inside the plant. Those who support the new approach do not believe that union officers should be making the decisions for the members as to what is good for them. They feel that only the men and women on the line are entitled to make those decisions about whether or not to stick with the new system or to go back to the old system.

But at the NUMMI plant we have had two contracts ratified. The members have had the opportunity to go back to the old system with its multiplicity of classifications and other conditions. In each case they ratified the agreement by an overwhelming majority—in one case by 81 percent, in the other by 82 percent. That is the convincing argument that the new system is better than the old one. Maybe in the future they'll vote to go back to the old approach. I doubt it, but that's their right.

People also say that the union made a mistake when they granted concessions to the companies. But any concessions should be based on what the economics of the bargaining relationship dictate. You shouldn't give concessions when the company is prosperous, where there are no economic problems. And sometimes after you give concessions, you have to get them back. Recently the steelworkers got back some of the concessions they made earlier because the companies they deal with are back making a profit.

In the auto industry we made concessions for the first time in 1982. We had never done it before except with Chrysler. We went to the membership and got it ratified. Now in 1989 the opposition is still screaming about what we did in 1982. The UAW hasn't made any concessions since 1982. In 1990 we're not going to make any concessions because the economic facts don't justify it. GM made over four billion dollars last year; Ford made over five billion dollars. There is no justification for making economic concessions under those conditions.

But this wasn't the first time labor leaders have been asked to make concessions. Let me read a quotation from one labor leader:

> All industries and all companies within an industry do not enjoy the same economic advantages and profit ratios. We cannot blind ourselves to the fact at the bargaining table that, when the employer prospers, we expect a fair share. When he faces hard times, we expect to cooperate. Many of our unions have foregone wage increases, cooperated in the improvement of production schedules, raised money for the purchase of new equipment, and helped the hard pressed employer market his product. Chrysler, American Motors, Mack Truck, Tool and Die Association of Detroit, and countless smaller companies, have benefited from the sensible decisions of the UAW membership to make the concessions required by temporary business adversities. Our basic philosophy towards the employers whom we meet at the bargaining table is that we have a lot more in common than we have in conflict, and that instead of waging a struggle to divide up scarcity, we ought to devise ways of cooperating to create abundance and then intelligently find a way to share in that abundance.

That quotation comes from a speech by Walter Reuther, president of the UAW, at the University of Virginia Law School in 1964.

That's part of our history, part of our tradition, but nobody paid any attention to it. With small companies that were marginal and hard pressed, we were doing exactly what we did with General Motors and Ford in 1982.

In addition to the joint action at the bargaining table, we're criticized for our joint committees. But to those who attack us, to those who say that we're being co-opted by management, I raise the question about what committees they would like to eliminate. I'll mention just a few.

What about the health and safety committees? Would they like to do away with those? I remember what it was like when I was in the shop. The employer made all the decisions about what was safe and what was unsafe, what puts a worker's life and limb in jeopardy and what does not. The only recourse we had was to file a grievance. And by the time the grievance was resolved, someone may have lost his or her life or been seriously injured. I worked in a stamping plant, and they used to run the press on the hop, so that you didn't have to press any buttons. You had to feed in that metal and get your hands out of the way fast before that ram and die came down. I can't tell you how many times we had amputations. In 1973 we negotiated joint health and safety committees. As late as 1973 we were completely ignorant of the chemicals we were working with. We never knew what we were working with. Would our opponents like to give up the new system where we now have union professionals examining the safety of the workplace jointly with management?

We also have joint training programs. We have an absolutely equal voice on the design of the programs, how much money to spend on the programs. We're talking about $150 million per year at GM, about a quarter of that at Ford, and a fifth of that at Chrysler. The committees jointly decide what programs are worthy of support and what are not. Would the critics do away with those joint programs?

And then we have substance abuse programs where joint committees determine how to handle workers afflicted with the terrible disease of alcoholism. I remember the days when those workers used to be discharged. It was practically revolutionary when the first decision came down in which the arbitrator had to decide the question of whether the grievant should be discharged or be treated as a person who is sick. Now we have joint programs.

We have joint employee assistance programs to deal with financial problems, family problems, any sort of problems workers may have, where assistance is available to them. Another program gives the union a joint voice as to the standard of quality. Obviously, if we can improve the quality of cars, that enhances the job security of the workers because we are then better able to compete in the international market place. We've been subjected to a lot of criticism on this program, which is hard to understand.

We're even beginning to address the problem of child care, a most pressing social problem. At the Chrysler plant in Huntsville, Alabama, a child care program has been initiated a quarter of a mile from the plant site. There are other similar child care programs at GM and Ford. In all of these programs the union has a joint voice. A new program has been established in Louisville, Kentucky, between the Ford Motor Company and the UAW, starting with handicapped people.

I would suggest that we have to call upon management to join with unions in areas that we can't control at the bargaining table. For example, companies ought to join with us to advocate that the government have a more forceful trade policy—one that better protects the jobs of American workers. I'm not talking about protectionism; I'm talking about fair trade. I could recite for the next two hours the lopsided, inequitable trade arrangement we have with Japan. I was on an advisory committee five years ago and listened to American businessmen recite a long litany of grievances they had with Japan because they couldn't market their products or even their services in Japan. Last year we had a $55 billion trade deficit with Japan. The U.S. Customs Service just recently decided to classify utility vehicles as trucks. Light trucks had a 25 percent tariff under that ruling. But then the Treasury Department ruled that the Customs Service was wrong and overturned that decision. That 25 percent tariff might have enabled the American manufacturer to raise the price, but that's not the point. At least we could have used that tariff as a bargaining chip to get Japan to remove some of its restrictions, to give us some relief on the products they discriminate against. We should have a tougher approach in dealing with other countries to bring about fair trade.

Another area we could cooperate with management on is to change the health delivery system in the United States. Costs are escalating wildly. When you buy an automobile, $700 of that price is the cost of health care for the auto workers and their families—a horrendous burden when you think about international trade and international competition.

We are spending almost 12 percent of our gross national product for health care in this nation. This year we will spend $2,000 for every man, woman, and child. And if you look around the world at expenditures for health care, you will find that Canada spends $1,200 (40 percent lower than we); Europe, $1,000 or $1,100; Japan, $750 or $800. In addition, look at the problems we have in America with 37 million people with no health insurance at all. And what kind of care do we get for that huge expenditure? Our infant mortality rate is about 11th in the free world; longevity for women, 9th; for men, 14th. Even with these massive expenditures, we have inadequate care for most of the population. I'm not complaining about the ability of doctors. We have the best, most talented doctors in the world, the best hospitals, the finest technology. It's the delivery system that's not working. I hope companies will join with unions to find a different and better way.

A couple of companies are coming out of the closet on this. Chrysler says we have to find a better way, some national scheme. Ford agrees that we have to have a national program. GM hasn't said anything yet. The Bethlehem Steel-United Steelworkers recent settlement seeks jointly to find a better health care system. The problem is that people don't have faith in our government to get things done right. They believe that our government can screw up a two-car funeral. But the point is that government does deliver services for the benefit of all the American people and does a good job in some areas. Take the Social Security system as an example.

In Germany they had national health insurance in Bismarck's time (about 1883). Every single democracy in the world has national health insurance except the United States. It would seem to me that companies could endorse such a government plan. Even a group of 400 physicians has backed a plan similar to what Canada has. We ought to sit down and try to figure out the best and most efficient way to deliver health care to all the American people and do it in a much more efficient way than the present system.

We know that competition won't work, can't work, because the health delivery system does not have the discipline of the marketplace. The consumer makes only one decision—to go to a doctor. Then the doctor decides what drugs are to be prescribed, what and how many laboratory tests are to be performed, if the patient should go into the hospital, and how long that hospital stay should be.

I would hope that we can get together with the companies and advocate a new system. The health delivery system is unmanageable and is not serving our population well. We could come together from different motivations. Management doesn't want to be strangled by the increasing costs of health care. They have to do it for financial reasons. We, on the other hand, want to change the system because we believe that every man, woman, and child in the United States is entitled to health care, not as a matter of privilege, but as a matter of right—not some constitutional right but a right to be enjoyed in a democratic, caring, compassionate society.

Theodore White wrote about an experience with President John F. Kennedy, who was reluctant to take on a few issues which the labor movement thought he should address. In 1963 the President apparently was reluctant to take on too many divisive issues since he had been elected by a razor-thin majority in 1960. He wanted to wait until 1964, when he could be reelected by a landslide (and he would have been so elected) and thus get a real mandate from the voters. But we decided to have a civil rights march in 1963 over his objections. That was when Martin Luther King gave his famous "I Have A Dream" speech. At that time White said Kennedy had a visitor in the Oval Office, and he said to the visitor: "Sometimes you look back at what you've done, and the only thing you ask yourself is what took you so long to do it."

(Mr. Fraser consented to answer questions from the audience.)

Question: Isn't there a danger that management will use the quality-of-work-life program to frustrate union organization?

Answer: I believe they can if they want to. The essence of the QWL program is democratization of the workplace. The GM southern strategy was to keep the UAW out of their southern plants. One of the ways they did it was to initiate QWL programs where elected representatives acted on behalf of the unorganized workers. Some UAW representatives were opposed to these programs for that reason. They said that you can't organize in those plants, and GM was doing it to prevent our organization.

And this points up the danger that is always present with these programs. They must not be confused with the grievance machinery. A union must be on guard that they don't get frozen out. That can happen. That's why the program must be jointly developed. The union can't just sit by and let the company organize the whole program. In a couple of cases I know of, when grievances could not be settled, the QWL committee took up the matter and they solved the whole thing. That, of course, undercuts the entire bargaining process, and the union has to guard against that. The union should exercise its voice in joint development of the program. They have to recognize the fine line between the grievance procedure and the QWL program.

Question: Do you think the forthcoming finalization of the agreement among European Economic Community nations is good or bad for the American union movement?

Answer: Europeans are also asking that question. In the United Kingdom they are looking forward to it. They anticipate a new view on a whole variety of social questions. But the German trade union movement is worried about the low wages in Portugal and Spain. We in the United States should be sitting down with management and discussing and planning for it now. We should have an agreement with the business community that competition should be based on technology, quality, ingenuity, management skills, engineering skills, market skills, and not on who can pay the lowest wages. If we travel down that road, you have seen the last of the middle class blue collar worker in America, and it will have a devastating effect on the economy. All of these things are in question, and I would hope that we would start discussing these issues now.

CHAPTER 3

ARBITRAL DISCRETION:
THE TESTS OF JUST CAUSE

I.

JOHN E. DUNSFORD*

Ten years ago at the Dearborn meeting of the Academy, a reckless program chairman invited two lawyers to play devil's advocates and tell the arbitrators what they were doing wrong in discipline and discharge cases. The results confirmed the truth of an old adage: Be careful what you ask for, you might get it. One of the speakers, William M. Saxton, went on a fishing expedition for prize specimens in the published opinions.[1] He came back with a good catch of "howlers":

1. For example, the arbitrator who found a company did not have just cause to discipline a grievant for using the "F" word to tell a supervisor what he could do with himself. The rationale was that the charge of profanity did not meet the definition of Webster's Third International Dictionary, Unabridged, since the four letter word does not violate sacred things.

2. Or the case in which no culpability was found of a grievant who, on being discovered sleeping, told the foreman, "I'll take care of you." When the foreman asked "Do you mean that as a threat?" grievant said, "You take it whichever way you want to." The arbitrator concluded the remark wasn't threatening because, after all, the choice was left to the foreman as to what the grievant meant.

3. Or another, one of my favorites, in which the arbitrator set aside a discharge of an employee who was found with company

---

*Past President, National Academy of Arbitrators; Chester A. Myers Professor of Law, Saint Louis University, St. Louis, Missouri.
[1]Saxton, *The Discipline and Discharge Case: Two Devil's Advocates on What Arbitrators Are Doing Wrong*, in Arbitration of Subcontracting and Wage Incentive Disputes, Proceedings of the 32nd Annual Meeting, National Academy of Arbitrators, eds. James L. Stern and Barbara D. Dennis (Washington: BNA Books, 1980), 63.

property in his lunch box at the end of a shift. The arbitrator found that the discharge was invalid for failure of the company to read the grievant his Miranda rights before ordering him to open the lunch box.

In all these cases the arbitrators were working under the conventional standard in collective bargaining agreements that requires "just cause" for a company to discipline. Their application of that standard was, to say the least, eccentric. Acknowledging the imprecision and elusiveness of the concept, the Dearborn speaker pointed out that this did not mean that the parties "committed the definition to the arbitrator's whim."[2] Far less was it intended as a springboard for the launching of the arbitrator's pet ideas for innovation in the workplace.

Despite the sardonic glee with which Saxton tackled his assignment (a compliment to his zeal as an advocate), the examples which he cited were generally thought to be aberrant, at least among experienced professional arbitrators. Members of the Academy defended themselves by repeating the remark of the Chicago politician: "Half the lies they are spreading about us are not even true." The speaker warned, however, that labor and management were reticent to choose new arbitrators because of a decline in confidence and "the fact that plain and commonly understood concepts such as just cause have been bent out of shape."[3] Perhaps the complaints of the devil's advocates were exaggerated, but the robust criticism was a sharp reminder of the potential for abuse in the spaciousness of the just cause standard.

It is commonplace in articles and books on labor arbitration to comment that the meaning of just cause is rarely defined in the contract. Standing as a major restriction on the freedom of management in imposing discipline on employees, the concept is variously expressed by a requirement that the company have cause, or proper cause, or sufficient cause, or just cause, the particular version seldom being thought significant in assessing the precise degree of restriction. The simplest definition of the term is tautological, namely, that the company must show that it had some cause for the discipline, and the cause relied on must be just. But this, admittedly, only restates the question if it does not beg it. For how does one determine what is properly a cause

---

[2]*Id.* at 64.
[3]*Id.* at 67.

for discipline in the industrial setting? And in that framework what are the attributes of justice?

Stated in this broad fashion, these questions apparently did not bother the early arbitrators. The concept of just cause appears to have emerged by spontaneous generation as soon as unions were in a position to negotiate for the security of the job. And arbitrators hit the ground running in their application of the concept, grappling with it in individual cases without any discernible need to discourse on its essential meaning. One looks in vain among the proceedings in the early years of the Academy to find a formal discussion of the phrase, though one may assume the members put their heads together in the corridor to swap stories about interesting cases they had heard. Occasionally, a thoughtful arbitrator would pause in the flow of an opinion to venture a general definition. One of those early comments was dropped by Harry Platt in a case in 1947, explaining how an arbitrator goes about deciding what is sufficient cause:

> To be sure, no standards exist to aid an arbitrator in finding a conclusive answer to such a question and, therefore, perhaps the best he can do is to decide what reasonable men, mindful of the habits and customs of industrial life and of the standards of justice and fair dealing prevalent in the community, ought to have done under similar circumstances and in that light to decide whether the conduct of the discharged employee was defensible and the disciplinary penalty just.[4]

Except for some tinkering to render it gender neutral, this definition by Platt may be as good as anything that has been offered in the intervening years.

One may speculate as to why the lack of a set of criteria to define just cause was not seen as a serious disadvantage by the early arbitrators. Was it because they were too intrigued with the challenge of breaking down each separate disciplinary problem into its component parts to worry about a deeper, more philosophical view? Or was it because, being practical men and women struggling to understand the individualized relationships within a shop, they intuited that the broad notion of just cause was defined only through many discrete judgments made in response to the exigencies of the situations before them?

This is not to ignore the fact that general principles and rules reflecting the preferred view on this or that facet of discipline

---

[4]*Riley Stoker Corp.*, 7 LA 764 (Platt, 1947).

began to emerge in arbitral decisions as time went on.[5] For example, the principle developed that an employee should obey an order from supervision and file his grievance later, subject to certain safety exceptions. The requirement of corrective discipline began to surface in the opinions, depending on the nature of the industrial offense for which discipline was imposed. Consistency in the application of discipline within a plant was recognized as a factor in evaluating its justness. These few examples are mentioned to illustrate the point that the idea of just cause began to translate into a set of rules and principles responsive to recurring problems.

Yet for some people the continuing open-endedness of the concept remains a frustration. Their instinct is to develop more exact criteria for a definition of just cause, a goal which is understandable. Theoretically at least, just cause is so expansive a notion that fears are inevitably aroused about an uncabined arbitral discretion. If considered in the abstract, the prospect of unprincipled decision making is highly unsettling both to the parties and their representatives, particularly lawyers who value few things more than predictability. Moreover, for the purpose of training newcomers who need an introduction to the elements that go to make up the idea of just cause, the hope of supplying a comprehensive and detailed definition of the phrase can be exciting. To put things in a proper perspective, however, one should recognize that fears regarding an unbridled freedom of the arbitrator in the discipline case can be exaggerated.

In the first place, and surprising to some, the issue of whether a given type of employee conduct is in nature objectionable in the industrial setting is seldom in dispute. When asked to recall cases in which they had to decide whether the very character of an act brought it within the legitimate boundaries of managerial discipline, most arbitrators will have trouble producing any examples. Work rules, either unilaterally promulgated by management or agreed to by the parties, tend to remove such questions from the table. And where work rules are missing, the parties are seldom at loggerheads over the basic obligations of an

---

[5]Some of the principles and standards developed by arbitrators are set forth in Seward, *Grievance Arbitration—The Old Frontier*, in Arbitration and the Expanding Role of Neutrals, Proceedings of the 23rd Annual Meeting, National Academy of Arbitrators, eds. Gerald G. Somers and Barbara D. Dennis (Washington: BNA Books, 1970), 153, 158. *See also* Robins, *Unfair Dismissal: Emerging Issues in the Use of Arbitration as a Dispute Resolution Alternative for the Nonunion Workforce*, 12 Fordham Urb. L.J. 437, 447–450 (particularly n. 48) (1984).

employee. Instead, the real disputes arise over whether those obligations have been breached.

Occasionally, to be sure, it will happen that the parties disagree regarding the activities which may represent cause for discipline. The subject of off-duty misconduct comes to mind as offering instances of this type. But these are the rare cases. Usually the dispute centers on such things as the factual determination of whether the grievants did the acts with which they are charged, the quantum of proof which is required, the significance of the failure to follow customary procedures, whether the punishment imposed is commensurate with the seriousness of the offense.

There are still other factors which serve to diminish the putative sweep of the arbitrator's power to expand the meaning of just cause. External law may impose limits to the application of discipline (for example, discharge for excessive garnishments on single indebtedness), and the parties are likely to advise the arbitrator of such matters. There may be past practices affecting the subject under review at hearing, or prior awards which the parties themselves expect to be honored if they are found to apply. These channel, and thus confine, the decision maker's thinking. In addition, and permeating the entire picture, the professional reputation of the arbitrator is at stake. To remain active in the process, she or he must meet the expectations of the parties in the decision to be rendered. The urgent need by the arbitrator to retain acceptability exerts a gravitational pull toward the exercise of judgment which is appropriate and conventional in the disciplinary setting.

Still, despite these built-in limitations on an arbitrator's conduct, the impulse persists in some quarters to translate the disciplinary concept into a set of tests or prescribed rules. This impulse can be detected in operation both internally within the profession of arbitration, and externally from the courts. What are the merits of proposals to systematize the criteria for just cause? Should there be tests established for defining the meaning of the term? Is the world of industrial discipline at loose ends?

The Seven Tests

Perhaps the most widely known attempt to reduce just cause to precise criteria is the checklist of seven tests devised by the late Carroll R. Daugherty, a member of this Academy and a professor of labor economics and labor relations at Northwestern University. The tests were first published by him in the early 1960s as an appendage to an arbitration opinion,[6] and were given their final formulation in another case in 1972.[7] The latter version is attached as an addendum to this paper.

My thesis with regard to these tests may be stated briefly. If taken as an introduction to an academic discussion of just cause in the classroom, or a schematic for organizing a textbook or commentary,[8] the seven tests may have some utility. But employed as agenda for resolving disputes in arbitration, the tests are in my judgment misleading in substance and distracting in application. Worse yet, they assume controversial positions with regard to the role of the arbitrator without frankly addressing the value judgments they embody.

In launching this broadside against the Daugherty tests as they are offered as a guide for deciding arbitration cases, I am in an embarrassing position. Daugherty was undeniably an established arbitrator, whose writings in industrial relations are substantial and respected. This estimable man had a career of distinction serving in the Roosevelt administration as the chief economist at the Bureau of Labor Statistics and at the Wage and Hour Administration. He also directed the Wage Stabilization Division of the National War Labor Board. His recent death makes my criticism the more unseemly as one recalls the proverb: "It doesn't take a very brave dog to bark at a dead lion." I trust my evaluation of the efficacy of the Seven Tests is received in the spirit in which it is offered, which is one of respectful though vigorous dissent.

The tests are presented in the form of seven questions, a negative answer to any one of which is normally supposed to indicate that just cause does not exist for the discipline. Daugherty recognized that his guidelines would not apply with precision in every case. However, by the time he refined them into their ultimate expression, he contemplated the possibility that occasionally a strong "yes" to one question might overwhelm a weak "no" to another, producing a decision in which both the company and the grievant would properly be taken to task for their deficiencies. From such refinements one is left undecided

---

[6]*Grief Bros. Cooperage Corp.*, 42 LA 555 (Daugherty, 1964).
[7]*Whirlpool Corp.*, 58 LA 421 (Daugherty, 1972).
[8]*See* Koven & Smith, Just Cause: The Seven Tests (San Francisco: Coloracre Publications, 1985).

whether to emphasize the flexibility of the guidelines or to assume that they can be administered rather rigidly if only the correct weight is assigned to each answer. This tension is never dissipated.

In the preface to his final expression of the tests, Daugherty cautions that it is impossible to develop a formula in which facts can be fed into a computer to produce a correct answer in a mechanical fashion. At the same time he proceeds to give instructions on those questions, by number, which can be omitted if the contract limits the scope of the arbitrator's inquiry, and emphasizes that without such restrictions in a given case it is not only proper but also necessary to consider the evidence on all seven questions and their accompanying notes.

In their substance many of the Seven Tests are unexceptional. They highlight such things as the obligation to give notice to employees of conduct which is forbidden; the need for work rules which are related to the orderly, efficient, and safe operation of the business; the requirement of evenhandedness in administering discipline; and the necessity for a proper proportionality between offense and penalty.

A jarring note is sounded, however, in connection with the subject of managerial investigation of an alleged offense prior to imposing discipline. In effect, through three of his seven questions, Daugherty lays it down that in order for just cause to be found for discipline the company must have conducted a fair and objective investigation prior to any discipline being imposed, through an official unconnected with the events in arbitration, where substantial and compelling evidence of guilt is obtained. It must be understood that in Daugherty's views these criteria are imposed by the arbitrator, separate and apart from any contractual requirements.

These requirements have often been uncritically repeated by both practitioners and arbitrators, in stating what just cause requires. While these tests concededly embody sound personnel policy in the administration of a disciplinary system and are admirable standards which many parties voluntarily follow, the proposition that an arbitral consensus dictates that their absence normally requires the invalidation of discipline is hard to justify either in practice or principle, at least in the private sector.

A good example of the tests in application is provided by the decision in *Grief Bros. Cooperage Corp.*,[9] a case of Daugherty's

---

[9]*Supra* note 6.

often cited for its embodiment of the Seven Tests. In that instance the grievant was a machine operator whose job required him to cap fiber drums with metal tops that he tapped on with a wooden mallet. Prior to the episode in dispute, the grievant had an unfavorable work record with several oral warnings and two suspensions. At the time in arbitration the foreman observed that two of the metal tops on the fiber drum had been damaged by unduly hard blows from the wooden mallet. The foreman also observed grievant damage a drum by kicking it. The foreman fired the employee on the spot and later, in an altercation in the office, manhandled him. Although Arbitrator Daugherty admitted that the poor work record of the employee otherwise supported discharge under the principles of progressive discipline, he reinstated the grievant because there was no pre-discharge investigation in accordance with his Seven Tests. His comment in support of this result reads as follows:

> [E]ven though the "no" answers to Questions 3, 4, and 5 might appear to have been made on technical grounds, said answers have great weight in any discipline case. Every accused employee in an industrial democracy has the right to "due process of law" and the right to be heard before discipline is administered. These rights are precious to all free men and are not lightly or hastily to be disregarded or denied. The Arbitrator is fully mindful of the Company's need for, equity in, and right to require careful, safe, efficient performance by its employees. But before the Company can discipline an employee for failure to meet said requirement, the Company must take the pains to establish such failure. Maybe X—was guilty as hell; maybe also there are many gangsters who go free because of legal technicalities. And this is doubtless unfortunate. But Company and government prosecutors must understand that the legal technicalities exist also to protect the innocent from unjust, unwarranted punishment. Society is willing to let the presumably guilty go free on technical grounds in order that free, innocent men can be secure from arbitrary, capricious action.[10]

Disregarding the dubious equation of industrial relations and the criminal law, it should first be emphasized that the present criticism is not directed at the right of Daugherty to interpret just cause to impose the investigatory requirements he describes in Questions 3, 4, and 5. His judgment is what the parties bargained for, and his judgment is what they got. Even in that connection, however, one should note the incongruity of the remedy provided by Daugherty in the *Grief* case: reinstatement

---

[10]*Id.* at 557.

without back pay. After declaring that it violates due process to discipline before a formal investigation and a prior hearing, the arbitrator permits de facto the imposition of a four month suspension.

But, to repeat, the argument here is not with Daugherty's exercise of judgment in that particular case but rather the clear suggestion that the tests which he follows are part of the "common law" of arbitration, that is, the product of the opinions of arbitrators generally. Even a cursory survey of the literature and published cases reveals that arbitrators differ radically on the issue of whether a failure to accord a complete and fair investigation and hearing prior to the arbitration requires an invalidation of discipline under the just cause standard.[11] In fact, a substantial number of reputable arbitrators approach such problems by measuring the significance of the claim of procedural deficiency (even those based on the terms of the contract, much less those derived from the so-called "common law" of arbitration) against the harm done to the interests of the grievant by the omission. It may be debatable what is the better view of the matter in applying the just cause concept. What is not debatable is that the Seven Tests misstate the posture of arbitral thinking.

The dedication of three of the seven tests for just cause to the subject of the method and manner of the company's pre-disciplinary investigation may seem odd, since these questions are not directed to the merits of a case but rather to the way in which the company handled it in the early stages. The mystery deepens as one examines the notes which Daugherty appended to these three questions. These notes are not always reported when the seven basic tests are quoted. But in them Daugherty explains that he thinks of the company investigation as the employee's "day in court," with the managerial person in charge of the investigation serving as a combination of judge and prosecutor. (This means, of course, that this person should not be a witness against the employee.) Further, since Daugherty conceives of the investigation as equivalent to the proceedings in a trial court, he also insists in one of his notes that the evidence

---

[11]*See, e.g.*, Hill, Jr., & Sinicropi, Remedies in Arbitration (Washington: BNA Books, 1981), 91–96. ("There is no uniform solution or preferred remedy when a procedural violation is found in a discipline or discharge case."); Hogler, *Employee Discipline and Due Process Rights: Is There an Appropriate Remedy?* 1982 Lab. L.J. 783; *Maui Pineapple Co.*, 86 LA 907 (Tsukiyama, 1986).

presented to the company investigator must be "weighty and substantial."[12]

Inasmuch as the company investigation serves the purpose of giving an employee his or her day in court, what is the function of the arbitrator in the Daugherty world view? He is quite specific in his answer to that question, in his comments introducing the Seven Tests in their final formulation:

> It should be understood that, under the statement of issue as to whether an employer had just cause for discipline . . . it is the employer and not the disciplined employee who is "on trial" before the arbitrator. The arbitrator's hearing is an appeals proceeding designed to learn . . . whether the employer, as sort of trial court, had conducted, before making his decision, a full and fair inquiry into the employee's alleged "crime"; whether from the inquiry said trial court had obtained substantial evidence of the employee's guilt . . . . In short, an arbitrator "tries" the employer to discover whether the latter's own "trial" and treatment of the employee was proper. The arbitrator rarely has the means for conducting, at a time long after the alleged offense was committed, a brand new trial of the employee.[13]

With the full picture of the Daugherty design of the arbitral process before us, it becomes quite clear why he concludes that a "no" answer to any of the questions posed by his Seven Tests normally requires setting aside the discipline. Since the arbitrator is sitting as an appellate court, he merely has to decide if the "trial court," that is, management, has followed the proper procedures. That explains, too, why the standard for reviewing the discipline is whether it contained (quoting Daugherty) "one or more elements of arbitrary, capricious, unreasonable or discriminatory action to such an extent that said decision constituted an abuse of managerial discretion warranting the arbitrator to substitute his judgment for that of the employer."[14]

What on its face, then, purports to be a set of conventional tests for applying the just cause standard, actually masks a distinctive view of the arbitral function quite different from that experienced by most of the members of this Academy. In the

---

[12]In the earlier formulation in *Grief Bros.*, *supra* note 6, Daugherty specifically states that the evidence required before the company "judge" need not be "preponderant, conclusive or 'beyond reasonable doubt.'" In the final formulation in *Whirlpool*, *supra* note 7, the same note drops "preponderant" but retains "conclusive or 'beyond a reasonable doubt.'" Does this suggest the "substantial" evidence should approach the standard of preponderance?

[13]*Supra* note 7 at p. 427.

[14]*Id.*

context of the Seven Tests, the arbitrator is not expected to be a fact finder but instead simply reviews what management has already determined to be the facts. Since arbitrators are one step removed from the level at which the operational decisions about discipline are concluded, they can only review what management has done to determine that it has not abused its discretion. Finally, arbitrators cannot substitute their judgment for that of management, since such an intrusion would disrupt the structured arrangement between the "trial" court and the appellate body.

These views, I venture to say, will strike most arbitrators in the private sector as peculiar and misbegotten. They know that an important and often excruciatingly difficult part of the arbitral function is to determine the facts. Furthermore, in reviewing managerial judgments they do not usually feel limited merely to deciding whether there has been an abuse of discretion. It comes as a surprise, then, to learn that the Department of Education and Training of the American Arbitration Association (AAA) includes the Seven Tests in its Discipline Workshop Manual for the education of new advocates and arbitrators. While it is true that a full statement of Daugherty's philosophy of arbitration is not included in the AAA Manual, the tests as reported there still convey the following propositions:

1. If there is a "no" answer to any of the seven questions, normally there is no cause for discipline.

2. Arbitrators are entitled to substitute their judgment for management's only if there is an abuse of managerial discretion.

3. A full and fair investigation must normally be made before a disciplinary decision is made, since the subsequent use of the grievance procedure will not suffice to give the employee his "day in court."

4. At the investigation the "judge" for the company must obtain substantial evidence that the employee is guilty.

These propositions are offered to the neophyte as a reliable guide for deciding if management had just cause for its action. Every one of them, I submit, is highly controversial.

It is also remarkable that the arbitrator training handbook of the Section of Labor and Employment Law of the American Bar Association reproduces as a "model" or "instructional aid" one of Daugherty's opinions with the Seven Tests and accompanying notes attached.[15] In the version of the tests used in that particu-

---

[15]Barreca, Miller & Zimny, Labor Arbitrator Development: A Handbook (Washington: BNA Books, 1983), 408.

lar case, Daugherty discusses as a hypothetical case a long-term employee with an unblemished record who is discharged for drunkenness on the job. The question is asked: "Should the company be held arbitrary and unreasonable if it decided to discharge such an employee?" His answer is, in part, as follows:

> [L]eniency is the prerogative of the employer rather than of the arbitrator; and the latter is not supposed to substitute his judgment in this area for that of the company unless there is compelling evidence that the company abused its discretion. This is the rule, even though an arbitrator, if he had been the original "trial judge," might have imposed a lesser penalty. Actually, the arbitrator may be said in an important sense to act as an appellate tribunal whose function is to discover whether the decision of the trial tribunal (the employer) was within the bounds of reasonableness above set forth . . . .[16]

Few people will quarrel with the assertion that "leniency is the prerogative of the employer rather than of the arbitrator." But it may be doubted that the comments of Daugherty in this context adequately address the underlying considerations involved in determining whether management has just cause for discharge as opposed to some lesser form of discipline. Indeed, reading remarks such as these, one wonders that the Seven Tests have been called "the most practical and incisive criteria for employee discipline and discharge."[17]

One explanation for the uncritical acceptance of the Seven Tests is that few people bother to read the full explanation by Daugherty of what his tests are supposed to accomplish. Nor does anyone take the time to investigate the assertion that the tests are merely the compilation of what arbitrators through the years have developed as a "common law." That is certainly inaccurate with respect to the subjects of Questions 3, 4, and 5.

Perhaps the greatest reason that the tests have been blindly endorsed is that most people do not appreciate the professional background out of which Daugherty developed them. Indeed, if one limits them to the environment in which they were conceived and nurtured, the tests make eminent good sense. As explained in an article by Donald S. McPherson tracing the development of the Seven Tests,[18] the inspiration came out of

---

[16]*Id.* at 418.

[17]Arbitration Times, Spring 1988, at 2 (newspaper of the American Arbitration Association).

[18]McPherson, *The Evolving Concept of Just Cause: Carroll R. Daugherty and the Requirement of Disciplinary Due Process,* 38 Lab. L.J. 387 (1987).

Daugherty's experience as a referee on the National Railroad Adjustment Board. The tests were a product of his deep concern about the due process rights of employees working on the railroad, which he may also have believed were rooted in constitutional requirements applicable to the railroad industry.

As a referee Daugherty did not hear witnesses testify about the events surrounding the discipline. The grievant did not appear before him. Instead, he heard representatives of the parties argue over the meaning of facts uncovered earlier by the investigation of management and presented to a division of the Adjustment Board. The nature of his work consisted of reviewing, as an appellate court would, what others had done in imposing discipline. With such a limited function, the importance of an insistence upon procedural safeguards, such as a full investigation, becomes obvious. Yet it is interesting to note that, even before the Third Division of the National Railroad Adjustment Board in 1958 when Daugherty for the first time set forth the substance of his tests in deciding a case, a dissenting opinion by the railroad employer members sharply criticized his setting aside a discharge on a narrow technical point. The dissenting members of the Division objected that "the conduct of hearings and appeals in disciplinary proceedings does not require adherence to all the attributes of hearings and appeals of criminal cases, nor of civil liberty cases, in the Courts."[19]

Whatever their virtues in the railroad industry, the undiscriminating transfer of these tests to the private sector, where hearings before an arbitrator are de novo and an almost infinite variety of grievance arrangements are found, is inappropriate. Designed for an arbitration system different from the one in which they are now employed, the tests generate a vague confusion about the meaning of due process further compounded by the pretense that they simply reflect prevailing practice.

There is another criticism of the Seven Tests which, in the final analysis, may be the most serious of all. At least in the manner in which Daugherty employed them, they not only produce an opinion in format which is as convoluted as a Rube Goldberg invention but also threaten to distort the process by

---

[19]National Railroad Adjustment Board, Third Division, Vol. 81, Award No. 8431, at 174, 178 (Daugherty, 1958).

superimposing artificial problems of the arbitrator's own making upon the real issues which are separating the parties.

The classic form of a Daugherty opinion is a short statement of the facts, followed by a plunge into a discussion seriatim of the seven numbered questions, either assuming the reader knows the questions or will consult an attached copy of them (with comments) at the foot of the opinion. Though Daugherty maintained (erroneously, I believe) that the tests are products of the "common law" development of the definition of just cause by other arbitrators, the inner structure of his opinions actually has more of the flavor of a civil law approach. The pattern of the common law is to decide only that which is unavoidable to resolve a dispute, moving inductively from one case to another, with principles evolving as circumstances require. In contrast, the Daugherty format carries with it a complex of problems from outside the relationship, and then seeks to resolve them with the principles contained in the statement of the Seven Tests.

Thus, the appendix setting forth the Seven Tests in a Daugherty opinion serves as a kind of code against which the decision maker measures the events revealed by the case. A reader must move from the numbered answers in the opinion to the numbered questions of the appendix. The sensation is similar to assembling a packaged bicycle by following the instruction sheet. In form, the disjointed opinion has little cohesion.

Putting aside the aesthetics of the matter, the striking danger for arbitrators attempting to follow this format is that they may neglect to focus on the issues of central concern to the parties in the hot pursuit of questions which were not raised. The premise of the Daugherty tests seems to be that an arbitrator knows better than the parties what is troubling them (or should be troubling them) and is going to resolve those problems whether the parties want it or not.

On another occasion I have expressed my reservations about allowing the full logic of the adversary system to dominate arbitration.[20] That does not mean we should neglect its virtues. If there is one thing which an adversary system does superbly, it is to identify and particularize the issue or issues dividing the

---

[20]Dunsford, *The Presidential Address: The Adversary System in Arbitration*, in Arbitration 1985: Law and Practice, Proceedings of the 38th Annual Meeting, National Academy of Arbitrators, ed. Walter J. Gershenfeld (Washington: BNA Books, 1986), 1.

parties. The advantages of such an achievement are that the true interests of those involved in the case are illuminated, the dispute is reduced to its narrowest and sharpest dimensions, and the energies of everyone concerned can be concentrated on a proper resolution.

After all, the disputants know better than anyone else what constitutes their disagreement. (They may not always be able to articulate their differences effectively, but with assistance and patience they will normally be led to be able to convey them.) When an arbitrator comes to a hearing with a predetermined list of questions to be answered, the basic purpose of the hearing is defeated. The hearing is not designed to answer questions which the arbitrator thinks ought to be answered; the hearing is held to allow the arbitrator to hear the questions which the parties want answered. To the degree that arbitrators become absorbed in satisfying the needs of some prefabricated tests, they run the risk of not paying sufficient attention to the issues that truly matter to the parties.

The Limitations of Tests

My apprehensions regarding the use of tests such as Daugherty's are not fueled by any conviction that such an approach necessarily favors one side over another. It is difficult to judge whether management or labor would benefit more from the use of the tests. Daugherty stated that one of his objects was to protect innocent employees from arbitrary and discriminatory acts of management, and of course his Seven Tests build an obstacle course for supervisors and personnel managers on which they may trip and stumble. On the other hand, the heavy deference which Daugherty pays to managerial judgment in his tests frequently would be prejudicial to the interests of grievants.

The difficulty with the use of tests is not that they inevitably threaten impartiality. Rather, the difficulty is that a process whose strength and uniqueness lies in the personal responsiveness of the decision maker to the daily problems of flesh and blood human beings in the shop may be transformed into an academic exercise, as tests and rules imported from extraneous sources begin to dominate the discretion and judgment of the arbitrator.

Whenever it is proposed that tests or criteria ought to be developed to define just cause, the following question should be asked: What is the purpose of such an enterprise? If the object is to mechanize the process of decision making for arbitrators, or to achieve efficiency and uniformity for the parties at the cost of overlooking the subtleties and contingencies of particular cases, great care must be exercised to avoid a debilitation of the process. If, on the other hand, the object is simply to deepen our understanding of the central concept around which so many decisions turn, that is a different matter. Obviously there is much to be said for a continuing effort to master the elements that make up the just cause standard.

One of the most ambitious attempts at creating a theory of just cause is the product of two members of this Academy, Roger Abrams and Dennis R. Nolan.[21] They propose a fundamental understanding of the employment relationship as follows:

> Just cause . . . embodies the idea that the employee is entitled to continued employment, provided he attends work regularly, obeys work rules, performs at some reasonable level of quality and quantity, and refrains from interfering with his employer's business by his activities on or off the job.[22]

These basic elements of the definition are supplemented by a consideration of the distinctive interests of management and union implicated in the various applications to which the just cause concept may be put. For example, the authors maintain that for just cause to be present, management must have one of three legitimate objects in mind: (1) rehabilitation of an employee; (2) deterrence of similar conduct, or (3) protection of profitability, which is taken in a broad sense to refer to the employer's efficient operation of its business. On the other side, the authors locate the union's interests in the assurance of fairness to the employee in the disciplinary situation, which in effect means industrial due process, equal protection, and individualized treatment. In the theory as proposed, these varying interests of the two parties are considered reconcilable and congruent, offering to the arbitrator a basis upon which to "make sound judgments about the probable expectations of the parties."[23]

While the theorizing of Abrams and Nolan is instructive and insightful, the authors themselves are quick to admit that "there

---

[21]Abrams & Nolan, *Toward a Theory of "Just Cause" in Employee Discipline Cases*, 1985 Duke L.J. 594.
[22]*Id.* at 601.
[23]*Id.* at 600–601.

will never be a simple definition of 'just cause' nor even a consensus on its application to specific cases."[24] More importantly, they emphasize that the concept cannot be applied to a dispute without the exercise of arbitral judgment.

That is, of course, always the rub: the recognition of that unvarnished element of discretionary judgment that the arbitrator must often bring to bear in the particular case, when the rules from whatever source do not relieve the sharp and nagging uncertainty that surrounds a critical factor in a dispute. In order to perform the job honestly and effectively, the arbitrator is forced to go into uncharted terrain where rules do not reach. The problem may call for a difficult factual determination based on the credibility of witnesses, or a ruling regarding the fairness of procedures, or a choice between conflicting interpretations of contract language, or the assessment of the severity of a disciplinary penalty. In such circumstances it is conceivable that an arbitrator may wander off the reservation and render judgments that appear arbitrary and rootless. Indeed, the reason that tests or sets of criteria are sought is the hope of preventing these mistakes.

Yet here we encounter the dilemma. One of the reasons the parties originally choose a broad concept like just cause as the measure of limitation on managerial freedom to discipline is the desire to remain flexible enough to encompass the multitude of unforeseen situations that come up in industrial relations. They want to allow room for the decision maker to exercise discretion in response to the exact circumstances present in the case. But to the extent that a set of prescribed tests are devised to regulate the application of the just cause concept, the values represented by the opportunity to exercise close judgment begin to fade.

The parties are put to a choice. They can minimize the risk of unacceptable decisions by agreeing to strip the arbitrator of the judgment and discretion that almost invariably accompany the use of the just cause concept. From time to time management may opt to follow such a path, perhaps suggesting that the union agree to a provision like the following:

> In discipline cases, the arbitrator shall be confined to a determination of whether the employee committed the misconduct for which the discipline was imposed; the arbitrator in no event shall have the

---

[24]*Id.*

authority to inquire into the appropriateness or degree of discipline imposed.[25]

The alternative is to take the chance of a poor decision in order to keep the process open to the value judgments that may prove necessary fairly to resolve closely contested cases. For the most part, it appears that the parties have been willing to leave the elucidation of what just cause means in a given situation to the judgment of the particular arbitrator they have chosen. On that subject, however, another voice is increasingly heard in the land to restrict the limits of arbitral discretion by still another set of tests.

Restrictive Judicial Tests

These other criteria for defining just cause are the product of a source external to the process itself, that is, the lower federal courts which undertake to review the disciplinary decisions of arbitrators. The tests announced in some of the judicial opinions are ominous signs as far as the finality of the award is concerned, since they are little more than the substitution of a court's interpretation of the contract for that of the arbitrator. The two *Warren* decisions issued by the First Circuit,[26] on which certiorari was denied, are recent examples of this judicial disposition to second-guess the arbitrator on the meaning and scope of the just cause clause.

In *Warren*, employees were discharged for violating a rule on possession, use, or sale of drugs on company premises. The contract provided that the company had the sole right to discharge for proper cause. Under the title "Causes of Discharge" work rules negotiated by both parties read, in part, as follows:

. . .

Violation of prescribed rules are cause for disciplinary action of varying degrees of severity.
Violations of the following rules are considered causes for discharge.

---

[25]Phillips, *Their Own Brand of Industrial Justice: Arbitrators' Excesses in Discharge Cases*, 10 Emp. Rel. L.J. 48, 56 (1984).
[26]*S.D. Warren Co. v. Paperworkers Local 1069*, 846 F.2d 827, 128 LRRM 2432 (1st Cir. 1988) (Warren II); *S.D. Warren Co. v. Paperworkers Local 1069*, 845 F.2d 3, 128 LRRM 2175 (1st Cir. 1988) (Warren I), *on remand from*, 126 LRRM 3360 (1987), *vacating* 815 F.2d 178, 125 LRRM 2086 (1st Cir. 1987), *rev'g* 632 F.Supp. 463, 122 LRRM 2186 (D. Me. 1986), *cert. denied*, 129 LRRM 3072 (1988).

a) Possession, use or sale on Mill property of intoxicants, marijuana, narcotics or other drugs. . . .

At the arbitration hearings the company was able to establish that the accused employees had violated the work rule. Did that end the matter, as the company argued? The arbitrators who heard the two cases recognized that a question of contract construction was before them regarding whether the "proper cause" provision controlled the interpretation and application of the rule, or whether the negotiated rule represented the embodiment of an agreement by the parties that every instance of drug possession, use, or sale on the premises gave management the right to terminate an employee without regard to the circumstances. Each arbitrator concluded that the contract was ambiguous but ultimately held that the parties intended that the validity of a discharge under the rule would remain subject to the conventional just cause analysis. On review of the record, each arbitrator set aside the discharge in favor of a suspension. When the awards were contested in court, the First Circuit in two separate opinions announced that the arbitrators had exceeded their contractual authority.

The reason the arbitrators had exceeded their authority, according to the First Circuit, is that the contract was so plain in meaning that only one interpretation was possible. The arbitrators had not read the contract properly. Of course, given the standards for judicial review reaffirmed in *Misco*,[27] it is not at all clear why the awards should have been set aside even on the assumption that the arbitrators were wrong in their interpretation. *Misco* states that "a court should not reject an award on the ground that the arbitrator misread the contract."[28] Moreover, as Reginald Alleyne has pointed out,[29] if the courts are so eager to apply the plain-meaning rule in reviewing the awards of arbitrators, they might consider what that rule means when applied to the words in the contract which say the award shall be "final and binding." For present purposes the point to emphasize is that if the *Warren* cases accurately state the law, a new test has been devised to limit the judgment of the arbitrator in just cause cases.

---

[27]*Paperworkers v. Misco*, 484 U.S. 29, 126 LRRM 3113 (1987).
[28]*Id.*, 126 LRRM at 3117.
[29]"Law and Arbitration" column, *The Chronicle*, newspaper of National Academy of Arbitrators (October 1988), at 3.

How shall we state the new test? One formulation might be as follows: When the just cause provision is accompanied by negotiated rules listing certain offenses as grounds for discharge, the contract as a matter of law must be interpreted to give management the freedom to decide on the severity of the penalty in the event of violation. Representatives of unions, no doubt, will be surprised to learn that by accepting proposed work rules they have conceded not only that involvement with drugs is generally a serious enough act to merit discharge but also that the circumstances surrounding an event are totally irrelevant and in every case management is free to determine unilaterally what the discipline shall be. Furthermore, the acceptance of this test produces the following anomaly. If arbitrators in *Warren*-type cases seek to perform their function, which is to bring informed judgment to bear on the meaning of the contract, they will provide grounds for the invalidation of their awards. Arbitrators may think the parties intended the just cause concept to monitor the application of work rules, but that is no longer of any moment. Only if arbitrators give the contract an interpretation which fits the anticipated opinion of the court will they be considered as adequately discharging their duty. Arbitrators, in effect, are asked to guess what a judge would say about the meaning of the contract, even though the parties in choosing arbitrators bargained for their judgment and not that of a court. Thus, while professing to follow the *Enterprise*[30] and *Misco* standards, the First Circuit has turned them inside out.

Courts have not hesitated to enunciate other tests as well to determine when arbitral discretion should be revoked in applying the just cause standard or its equivalent. Thus, it is said that an award will not be enforced if it is without rational support or unfounded in reason and fact; or if it is erroneously based on a crucial assumption that is not a fact.[31] If one were so inclined, these judicial criteria could be examined in the light of the facts of the cases in which they were announced in order to develop more rules of law for the diligent arbitrator to follow in discipline cases.

---

[30]*Steelworkers v. Enterprise Wheel & Car Corp.*, 363 U.S. 593, 46 LRRM 2423 (1960).
[31]*E.g., Posadas de P.R. Assocs. v. Asociacion de Empleados de Casino de P.R.*, 821 F.2d 60, 63, 125 LRRM 3137 (1st Cir. 1987); *Mistletoe Express Serv. v. Motor Expressmen's Union*, 566 F.2d 692, 694, 96 LRRM 3320 (10th Cir. 1977); *Bettencourt v. Boston Edison Co.*, 560 F.2d 1045, 1050, 96 LRRM 2208 (1st Cir. 1977); *Amanda Bent Bolt Co. v. Automobile Workers Local 1549*, 451 F.2d 1277, 1280, 79 LRRM 2023 (6th Cir. 1971).

All these court-inspired tests seem to be based on the general premise that arbitrators in making their decisions do not have the latitude to be wrong, at least not so wrong as to boggle the judicial mind. One judge has commented that where just cause is concerned, a court should not uphold the reinstatement of an employee who has committed an offense which a court would conclude no rational employer would ever excuse.[32] (The offense which the judge had in mind was theft.) Perhaps the most endearing formulation (although not in a just cause case) is the one which describes the unenforceable award as "based on palpably faulty reasoning to the point that no judge could conceivably have reached the same result."[33] The author of that statement seems not to have entertained the possibility that such a point cannot be imagined.

These judicial attempts to define the limits of arbitral discretion in discipline cases often bear a tone of frustration, perhaps understandable in view of the periodic arbitration award which turns out, in the words of Bernard D. Meltzer, to be just plain "goofy."[34] At the same time, they endorse a scope of review which seems incompatible with the admonition of the Supreme Court that when arbitrators are even arguably interpreting and applying the contract, a court is not to substitute its judgment. Perhaps in some decisions the court is unwilling to credit the claims of arbitrators that they are trying to interpret the contract. If so, the grounds of reversal should be these arbitrators have shown an infidelity to their obligation, a charge that is not satisfactorily established merely by showing that the reading of the contract appears erroneous or even irrational to a judge.

On the other hand, the source of the confusion over the proper authority of arbitrators in discipline cases may go deeper, both for reviewing courts and arbitrators themselves. Recently Judge Stephen R. Reinhardt described for us two views

---

[32]*E.I. du Pont de Nemours & Co. v. Grasselli Employees Independent Ass'n of E. Chicago*, 790 F.2d 611, 620, 122 LRRM 2217 (7th Cir. 1986) (J. Easterbrook, concurring), *cert. denied*, 123 LRRM 2592 (1986).

[33]*Safeway Stores v. Bakery & Confectionary Workers Local 111*, 390 F.2d 79, 82, 67 LRRM 2646 (5th Cir. 1968). This was aptly described as the "Lowest common denominator of federal judge" approach by Gottesman, *Judicial Review: As the Parties See It*, in Labor Arbitration at the Quarter-Century Mark, Proceedings of the 25th Annual Meeting, National Academy of Arbitrators, eds. Barbara D. Dennis and Gerald G. Somers (Washington: BNA Books, 1973), 183, 185.

[34]Meltzer, *After the Arbitration Award: The Public Policy Defense*, in Arbitration 1987: The Academy at Forty, Proceedings of the 40th Annual Meeting, National Academy of Arbitrators, ed. Gladys W. Gruenberg (Washington: BNA Books, 1988), 39, 40.

of the arbitral process, one labelled the "formal" view emphasizing the contractual nature of the relationship between the parties, the other the "expertise" view stressing the problem-solving nature of industrial decision making.[35] Does this dichotomy, which Judge Reinhardt employed in analyzing the ways in which courts review the awards of arbitrators, also reflect the competing ways in which arbitrators see themselves? Is a claim being made under the banner of "expertise" that arbitrators have authority to shape the contract in any way that they deem best? It is one thing to talk about the discretionary judgment of arbitrators, and contrast this with tests or rules to govern their decision making. But what precisely do we mean by discretion, and in what areas may arbitrators legitimately employ their own judgment? These are questions of interest not only in considering the scope of judicial review, but also in setting norms for those within the profession to assure its integrity.

In the *Enterprise* case, Justice William O. Douglas noted that an arbitrator "does not sit to dispense his own brand of industrial justice. . . . his award is legitimate only so long as it draws its essence from the collective bargaining agreement."[36] In a paradoxical retort to that statement, Edgar A. Jones, Jr., has pointed out that actually that is all an arbitrator does dispense, "his own brand of industrial justice."[37] In particular reference to the disciplinary case where just cause is the standard, Jones added: "Where lies the 'essence' from which to deduce what is, and what is not, 'just cause' for the employer's disciplinary response?"[38]

It is hardly to be doubted that in uttering his pronouncement Justice Douglas understood that there are elements of discretion and judgment exercised by every kind of decision maker including arbitrators. At the same time, Jones presumably does not believe that arbitrators are free to follow their own personal whims in deciding cases. The statements are reconcilable, however, by recognizing that the only discretion which arbitrators may properly exercise is derived from the necessities of the functions they perform in interpreting and applying the collec-

[35]*Id.* at 25.

[36]*Supra* note 30 at 599.

[37]Jones, Jr., *His Own Brand of Industrial Justice: The Stalking Horse of Judicial Review of Labor Arbitration*, 30 U.C.L.A. L. Rev. 881 (1983).

[38]*Id.* at 885.

tive bargaining agreement. The discretion is not plenary but is commensurate with the arbitral role.

Instead of looking for tests to make the performance of that function easier, our efforts might better be devoted to mapping out in greater detail the areas in which judgment and discretion are properly claimable by arbitrators, and the limits beyond which they ought not to go.

As one of the masters of this profession, Gabriel Alexander, said many years ago:

> One cannot ignore the necessity of resolving disputes on the basis of judgment, or the elements of personality that affect human judgment. Although seldom invested with specific authority to exercise "discretion," arbitrators could not reach or express their judgments without exercising their will.[39]

That is a comment which ought to be studied by courts faced with the temptation to second guess the awards of arbitrators. But on the same occasion, Alexander added a cautionary note that has a sobering relevance for arbitrators: "Justice demands that such exercise [of discretion] not be wholly unrestrained."[40]

Addendum

The Seven Tests of Carroll R. Daugherty for Learning Whether Employer Had Just Cause for Disciplining an Employee, as reproduced in Whirlpool Corp., 58 LA 421 (1972)

Few if any union-management agreements contain a definition of "just cause." Nevertheless, over the years the opinions of arbitrators in innumerable discipline cases have developed a sort of "common law" definition thereof. This definition consists of a set of guidelines or criteria that are to be applied to the facts of any one case, and said criteria are set forth below in the form of seven Questions, with accompanying Notes of explanation.

A "no" answer to any one or more of said Questions normally signifies that just and proper cause did not exist. In other words, such "no" means that the employer's disciplinary decision contained one or more elements of arbitrary, capricious, unreasonable, or discriminatory action to such an extent that said decision constituted an abuse

---

[39]Marshall, *Comment, Discretion in Arbitration*, Arbitration and the Public Interest, Proceedings of the 24th Annual Meeting, National Academy of Arbitrators, eds. Gerald G. Somers and Barbara D. Dennis (Washington: BNA Books, 1971), 84, 88.
[40]*Id.*

of managerial discretion warranting the arbitrator to substitute his judgment for that of the employer.

The answers to the Questions in any particular case are to be found in the evidence presented to the arbitrator at the hearing thereon. Frequently, of course, the facts are such that the guidelines cannot be applied with precision. Moreover, occasionally, in some particular case an arbitrator may find one or more "no" answers so weak and the other, "yes" answers so strong that he may properly, without any "political" or spineless intent to "split the difference" between the opposing positions of the parties, find that the correct decision is to "chastise" both the company and the disciplined employee by decreasing but not nullifying the degree of discipline imposed by the company—e.g., by reinstating a discharged employee without back pay.

It should be understood that, under the statement of issue as to whether an employer had just cause for discipline in a case of this sort before an arbitrator, it is the employer and not the disciplined employee who is "on trial" before the arbitrator. The arbitrator's hearing is an appeals proceeding designed to learn whether the employer in the first instance had forewarned the employee against the sort of conduct for which discipline was considered; whether the forewarning was reasonable; whether the employer, as a sort of trial court, had conducted, before making his decision, a full and fair inquiry into the employee's alleged "crime"; whether from the inquiry said trial court had obtained substantial evidence of the employee's guilt; whether the employer, in reaching his verdict and in deciding on the degree of discipline to be imposed, had acted in an even-handed, nondiscriminatory manner; and whether the degree of discipline imposed by the employer was reasonably related to the seriousness of the proven offense and to the employee's previous record. In short, an arbitrator "tries" the employer to discover whether the latter's own "trial" and treatment of the employee was proper. The arbitrator rarely has the means for conducting, at a time long after the alleged offense was committed, a brand new trial of the employee.

It should be clearly understood also that the criteria set forth below are to be applied to the employer's conduct in making his disciplinary decision *before* same has been processed through the grievance procedure to arbitration. Any question as to whether the employer has properly fulfilled the contractual requirements of said procedure is entirely separate from the question of whether he fulfilled the "common law" requirements of just cause before the discipline was "grieved."

Sometimes, although very rarely, a union-management agreement contains a provision limiting the scope of the arbitrator's inquiry into the question of just cause. For example, one such provision seen by this arbitrator says that "the only question the arbitrator is to determine shall be whether the employee is or is not guilty of the act or acts resulting in his discharge." Under the latter contractual statement an arbitrator might well have to confine his attention to Question No. 5 below—or at most to Questions Nos. 3, 4, and 5. But absent any such restriction in an agreement, a consideration of the evidence on all seven Questions (and their accompanying Notes) is not only proper but necessary.

The above-mentioned Questions and Notes do not represent an effort to compress all the facts in a discharge case into a "formula." Labor and human relations circumstances vary widely from case to case, and no formula can be developed whereunder the facts can be fed into a "computer" that spews out the inevitably correct answer on a sheet of paper. There is no substitute for sound human judgment. The Questions and Notes do represent an effort to minimize an arbitrator's consideration of irrelevant facts and his possible human tendency to let himself be blown by the variable winds of sentiment on to an uncharted and unchartable sea of "equity."

The Questions

1. Did the company give to the employee forewarning or fore-knowledge of the possible or probable disciplinary consequences of the employee's conduct?

Note 1: Said forewarning or foreknowledge may properly have been given orally by management or in writing through the medium of typed sheets or booklets of shop rules and of penalties for violation thereof.

Note 2: There must have been actual oral or written communication of the rules and penalties to the employee.

Note 3: A finding of lack of such communication does not in all cases require a "no" answer to Question No. 1. This is because certain offenses such as insubordination, coming to work intoxicated, drinking intoxicating beverages on the job, or theft of the property of the company or of fellow employees are so serious that any employee in the industrial society may properly be expected to know already that such conduct is offensive and heavily punishable.

Note 4: Absent any contractual prohibition or restriction, the company has the right unilaterally to promulgate reasonable rules and give reasonable orders; and same need not have been negotiated with the union.

2. Was the company's rule or managerial [sic] reasonably related to (a) the orderly, efficient, and safe operation of the company's business and (b) the performance that the company might properly expect of the employee?

Note 1: Because considerable thought and judgment have usually been given to the development and promulgation of written company rules, the rules must almost always be held reasonable in terms of the employer's business needs and usually in terms of the employee's performance capacities. But managerial orders often given on the spur of the moment, may be another matter. They may be reasonable in terms of the company's business needs, at least in the short run, but unreasonable in terms of the employee's capacity to obey. Example: A foreman orders an employee to operate a high-speed band saw known to be unsafe and dangerous.

Note 2: If an employee believes that a company rule or order is unreasonable, he must nevertheless obey same (in which case he may file a grievance thereover) unless he sincerely feels that to obey the rule or order would seriously and immediately jeopardize his personal safety and/or integrity. Given a firm finding to the latter effect, the employee may properly be said to have had justification for his disobedience.

3. Did the company, *before* administering discipline to an employee, make an effort to discover whether the employee did in fact violate or disobey a rule or order of management?

Note 1: This Question (and No. 4) constitutes the employee's "day in court" principle. An employee has the right to know with reasonable precision the offense with which he is being charged and to defend his behavior.

Note 2: The company's investigation must normally be made *before* its disciplinary decision is made. If the company fails to do so, its failure may not normally be excused on the ground that the employee will get his day in court through the grievance procedure after the exaction of discipline. By that time there has usually been too much hardening of positions. In a very real sense the company is obligated to conduct itself like a trial court.

Note 3: There may of course be circumstances under which management must react immediately to the employee's behavior. In such cases the normally proper action is to suspend the employee pending investigation, with the understanding that (a) the final disciplinary decision will be made after the investigation and (b) if the employee is found innocent after the investigation, he will be restored to his job with full pay for time lost.

4. Was the company's investigation conducted fairly and objectively?

Note 1: At said investigation the management official may be both "prosecutor" and "judge," but he may not also be a witness against the employee.

Note 2: It is essential for some higher, detached management official to assume and conscientiously perform the judicial role, giving the commonly accepted meaning to that term in his attitude and conduct.

Note 3: In some disputes between an employee and a management person there are not witnesses to an incident other than the two immediate participants. In such cases it is particularly important that the management "judge" question the management participant rigorously and thoroughly just as an actual third party would.

Note 4: The company's investigation should include an inquiry into possible justification for the employee's alleged rule violation.

Note 5: At his hearing the management "judge" should actively search out witnesses and evidence, not just passively take what participants or "volunteer" witnesses tell him.

5. At the investigation did the company "judge" obtain substantial and compelling evidence or proof that the employee was guilty as charged?

Note 1: It is not required that the evidence be fully conclusive or "beyond all reasonable doubt." But the evidence must be truly weighty and substantial and not flimsy or superficial.

Note 2: When the testimony of opposing witnesses at the arbitration appeals hearing is irreconcilably in conflict, an arbitrator seldom has any means for resolving the contradictions. His task is then to determine whether the management "judge" originally had reasonable grounds for believing the evidence presented to him by his own people instead of that given by the accused employee and his witnesses. Such grounds may include a decision as to which side had the weightier reasons for falsification.

6. Has the company applied its rules, orders, and penalties even-handedly and without discrimination to all employees?

Note 1: A "no" answer to this question requires a finding of discrimination and warrants negation or modification of the discipline imposed.

Note 2: If the company has been lax in enforcing its rules and orders and decides henceforth to apply them rigorously, the company may avoid a finding of discrimination by telling all employees beforehand of its intent to enforce hereafter all rules as written.

Note 3: For an arbitral finding of discrimination against a particular grievant to be justified, he and other employees found guilty of the same offense must have been in reasonably comparable circumstances.

Note 4: The comparability standard considers three main items—the degree of seriousness in the offense, the nature of the employees' employment records, and the kind of offense. (a) Many industrial offenses, e.g., in-plant drinking and insubordination, are found in varying degree. Thus, taking a single nip of gin from some other employee's bottle inside the plant is not so serious an offense as bringing in the bottle and repeatedly tippling from it in the locker room. Again, making a small, snide remark to and against a foreman is considerably less offensive than cussing him out with foul language, followed by a fist in the face. (b) Even if two or more employees have been found guilty of identical degrees of a particular offense, the employer may properly impose different degrees of discipline on them, provided their records have been significantly different. The man having a poor record in terms of previous discipline for a given offense may rightly, i.e., without true discrimination, be given a considerably heavier punishment than the man whose record has been relatively unblemished in respect to the same kind of violation. (c) The words "same kind of violation," just above, have importance. It is difficult to find discrimination between two employees found guilty of totally different sorts (not degrees) of offenses. For example, poor work performance or failure to call in absences have little comparability with insubordination or theft.

7. Was the degree of discipline administered by the company in a particular case reasonably related to (a) the seriousness of the employee's proven offense and (b) the record of the employee in his service with the company?

Note 1: A trivial proven offense as such does not merit harsh discipline unless the employee has properly been found guilty of the same or other offenses a number of times in the past. (There is no rule as to what number of previous offenses constitutes a "good," and "fair," or a "bad" record. Reasonable judgment thereon must be used.)

Note 2: An employee's record of previous offenses may never be used to discover whether he was guilty of the immediate or latest one. The only proper use of his record is to help determine the severity of discipline once he has properly been found guilty of the immediate offense.

Note 3: Given the same proven offense for two or more employees, their respective records provide the only proper basis for "discriminating" among them in the administration of discipline for said offense. Thus, if employee A's record is significantly better than those of employees B, C, and D, the company may properly give A a lighter punishment than it gives the others for the same offense; and this does not constitute true discrimination.

Note 4: Suppose that the record of the arbitration hearing establishes firm "Yes" answers to all the first six questions. Suppose further that the proven offense of the accused employee was a very serious one, such as drunkenness on the job; but the employee's record had been previously unblemished over a long, continuous period of employment with the company. Should the company be held arbitrary and unreasonable if it decided to discharge such an employee? The answer depends of course on all the circumstances. But, as one of the country's oldest arbitration agencies, the National Railroad Adjustment Board, has pointed out repeatedly in innumerable decisions on discharge cases, leniency is the prerogative of the employer rather than of the arbitrator; and the latter is not supposed to substitute his judgment in this area for that of the company unless there is compelling evidence that the company abused its discretion. This is the rule, even though the arbitrator, if he had been the original "trial judge," might have imposed a lesser penalty. In general, the penalty of dismissal for a really serious first offense does not in itself warrant a finding of company unreasonableness.

II. A UNION VIEWPOINT

DONALD W. COHEN*

Friends, arbitrators, advocates, lend me your ears; I come to bury the Daugherty Doctrine, not to praise it. The evil that doctrines do lives after them; the good is oft interred with their bones; so be it with the Daugherty Doctrine. The noble Dunsford hath told you the Doctrine was overreaching: if it were so, it

---

*Director, Asher, Gittler, Greenfield, Cohen & D'Alba, Ltd., Chicago, Illinois.

was a grievous fault; and grievously hath the Doctrine answered it. Here, under the leave of Dunsford and the rest, for Dunsford is an honorable man; so are they all, all honorable men, come I to speak in the Doctrine's funeral. It was my friend, faithful and just to me: but Dunsford said it was overreaching; and Dunsford is an honorable man. The Doctrine brought many standards home to arbitration, whose ransoms did the general coffers fill: did this in the Doctrine seem ambitious? When that the grievants have cried, the Doctrine hath wept: overreaching should be made of sterner stuff: yet Dunsford says the Doctrine is over-reaching; and Dunsford is an honorable man. I speak not to disprove what Dunsford spoke, but here I am to speak what I do know. You all did love the Doctrine once, not without just cause: What just cause withholds you then to mourn for it? O judgment, thou are fled to brutish beasts, and men have lost their reason! Bear with me; mark you the name of Jacobellis, for it is one which has great impact upon the concept of just cause, one to which I will return at a later time.

Come I now to comment upon the observations of the learned Bruce Miller.[1] Miller it was, on the other side of the coin than that reflected by the witty Will Saxton, to whom Dunsford adverts. Miller it was, who said the questions posed by Daugherty provided a model of due process for disciplinary and discharge cases. Miller it was, who observed that "the employer has substantial psychological momentum before the case gets to arbitration because the arbitrator is called upon to reverse a company action, a fait accompli. An arbitrator must consciously neutralize that momentum by insisting scrupulously that the employer carry his burden."

Now and then comes there an arbitrator who ventures to define just cause. Such was Hyman Parker.[2] Parker ventured that:

> In general, the "just cause" which will justify a discharge should be in connection with the work, and should reflect a willful disregard of the employer's interests. Thus, any conduct, action or inaction by an employee which arises out of, or is directly connected with the work, and which is inconsistent with an employee's obligations to his employer under his contract of hire, or union contract, might very well be determined to be "just cause."

---

[1]Miller, *The Discipline and Discharge Case*, in Decisional Thinking of Arbitrators and Judges, Proceedings of the 33rd Annual Meeting, National Academy of Arbitrators, eds. James L. Stern and Barbara D. Dennis (Washington: BNA Books, 1980).
[2]*Employing Lithographers Ass'n of Detroit (Madison Co.)*, 21 LA 671, 673 (Parker, 1953).

Parker was on the right track to the extent that just cause is connected to an employee's impact upon the job, but to define the employee's actions as being just cause is ungrammatical at best. Clearly it is the employer's action which is at issue when we seek to define the phrase. Arbitrator Sam Harris came much closer when he said:[3]

> Without attempting precisely to define "cause," it is the arbitrator's view that the true test under a contract of the type involved here is whether a reasonable man, taking into account all relevant circumstances, would find sufficient justification in the conduct of the employee to warrant discharge.

I like that; I like that a lot. Really, what is the Doctrine but an advisory opinion saying that, while you have to feel it in your bones, here are certain standards that can assist you in coming to your final decision? To a large degree then, I belive we find that disciplinary matters fall into the twilight zone of "uncabined arbitral discretion." "Uncabined," how I adore that term! It gives me a feel of the great outdoors, of not being circumscribed and, to a degree, the arbitrator must have that discretion. Thus, if Dunsford is correct, if the Doctrine does lock in an arbitrator to merely affirming or reversing *in toto* an employer's decision, then should not that portion be buried?

I do not dispute that the parties are free to place such restrictions as they may deem appropriate. However, one such restraint, which I advise against, is that the arbitrator has no discretion; that a finding that certain events have occurred strips the arbitrator of all further authority. If the parties specifically negotiate such language (and typically this is found with regard to participation in a wildcat strike), so be it.

If the constraint does not appear, however, remember that the arbitrator is not an appellate review court but is a judge in the first instance. The employer is not the prosecutor and judge but rather the police and prosecutor. The function of the judge is one which has been bargained by the parties. When the Supreme Court speaks of arbitrators being learned in the law of the shop, it implies the doing of equity. This is what keeps the process functioning, and this is what must never be forgotten. If the noble Dunsford's pronouncements on company rules are to be accepted, we will see a rapid diminution in the importance and

---

[3]*RCA Communications*, 29 LA 567, 571 (Harris, 1957).

use of the arbitral process. What need, when the rules have such finality? I would suggest, however, that there is always the essence of the underlying collective bargaining agreement which must be taken into consideration.

Consider the rationale of Arbitrator Sabo[4] when he observed:

> The word "cause" has been interpreted as meaning a "fair and legitimate reason" and not just any "reason." Some Arbitrators have equated "cause" with "Just Cause" or with "reasonable" and "sufficient" justification. In the final analysis, the concept of Just Cause had its start in Collective Bargaining Agreements negotiated by Labor and Management and has evolved over many years and untold Arbitrations to the point where today it is a highly developed theory of reasoning based on standards which must be precisely met by an Employer to sustain a Disciplinary Penalty up to and including Discharge by an Arbitrator.

Roberts' Dictionary of Industrial Relations has an apt description of just cause.[5] The *Dictionary* explains: The term is commonly used in agreement provisions to safeguard workers from disciplinary action which is unjust, arbitrary, capricious or which lacks some reasonable foundation for its support. Disciplinary action may also be held to be lacking 'just cause' if the penalties bear no reasonable relationship to the degree of the alleged offense." The definition goes on to give specific examples and concludes with the Daugherty Doctrine.

Let us now trace the genesis of just cause. In the 1800s we saw the courts create the concept of employment at will. Thus, an employee could be fired for any reason or no reason. Collective bargaining agreements weren't even a twinkle in their father's eye, and employees were continuously at risk. During the early 1900s unions became more active and pressures began to build. The concept of workers' compensation arose. This was an effective medium to eliminate the need to define just cause in cases of industrial accidents. The next step was to define what was not just cause. The prime example was the Wagner Act. Now we had legislation which prohibited termination of employees on account of their protected, concerted activities. If an employee was fired for joining with fellow employees in a job-related action, this was a termination without just cause.

---

[4]*Rohr Indus.*, 78 LA 978, 981 (Sabo, 1982).
[5]Roberts, Roberts' Dictionary of Industrial Relations, 3d ed. (Washington: BNA Books, 1986), 331.

In the 60s there was born Title VII. Now we knew that it was not just cause to terminate an employee because of race, color, creed, or sex and, eventually, physical impairment. The statutes were designed to deal with those egregious acts of misconduct by an employer which were easily definable. They could not and should not be directed, however, to the gray areas which comprise the vast majority of managerial decisions. This portion in the unionized sector has been ceded to the arbitrators. They were confronted with the task of creating the parameters within which the disciplinary function could be tolerated by management and labor.

It is critical at this juncture that we understand the difference between a collective bargaining agreement and an arm's-length business transaction. With the latter each party takes its best position and is entitled to enforce it absolutely. Whatever blood is spilled is merely a byproduct of that format. Collective bargaining agreements, on the other hand, are plastic, movable, to accommodate the needs of the parties. They must live with each other.

The essence of collective bargaining is that employees not only have rights under the contract but also have rights in their jobs as such. Thus, an employee who has stood the test of time, who has served the employer for a number of years, has expectations beyond that of an employee with, say, less than a year or less than three years. The arbitrator must have the flexibility to take into account these job rights. An employee of six months who has attendance problems sends up a red flag. The arbitrator may have scant choice but to follow the company line. An employee with 20 years encountering attendance problems presents a different situation. There the arbitrator must and does have the flexibility to accommodate the job rights which have accrued.

Let me venture an observation from the viewpoint of labor as to what constitutes just cause, keeping in mind the ancient homily that once an arbitrator's nose is in the tent, we are going to be confronted with the entire beast. I would suggest that just cause encompasses both the procedural aspects of the case (i.e., something along the lines of the Daugherty standards) and the substantive aspects of the case (to wit, did the complained-of action constitute a basis for the discipline meted out?). They are: (1) Did the company observe procedural niceties? (2) Did the blighter do the dirty deed? (3) Is the offense of a grade warranting the discipline administered? Let this be known as the *Jacobellis* Doctrine!

Ah, yes, I almost forgot Jacobellis, the noblest citizen of them all. Actually, Mr. Jacobellis is only a vehicle for my plea for arbitral discretion. You see, he was the operator of a movie theatre in Ohio at a time when a film entitled *The Lovers* was being shown. For the curious among you, the flick depicted an unhappy marriage and the wife falling in love with a young archaeologist. They consummated that love in an explicit albeit fragmentary and fleeting love scene. Mr. Jacobellis was subsequently confronted with the unappetizing prospect of serving time on account of the showing of this movie, eventually prompting Justice Stewart to utter the immortal words which we oft quote without knowing the citation; said he, commenting upon hard-core just cause (or was it pornography?):

> I shall not today attempt further to define the kinds of material I understand to be embraced within that shorthand description; and perhaps I could never succeed in intelligibly doing so. But I know it when I see it, and the motion picture involved in this is not that.[6]

Heeding Justice Stewart, let the arbitrators among us look into their own hearts, for there the meaning of just cause will they find.

III. A MANAGEMENT VIEWPOINT

ROBERT J. MIGNIN*

Over the past years, few issues have received greater attention from academics, arbitrators, and practitioners than establishing a proper definition for "just cause" in the labor arbitration context. The question can be summarized by asking what, if any, discretion should labor arbitrators exercise in evaluating whether a particular employer had "just cause" to discipline an employee.

Having reviewed numerous arbitration cases and various published works on the subject, I can only conclude that there is even less consensus now there was 20 or 30 years ago as to the definition of just cause or the amount of discretion that can be

---

[6]*Jacobellis v. Ohio*, 378 U.S. 184 (1964).
*Seyfarth, Shaw, Fairweather & Geraldson, Chicago, Illinois.

exercised by an arbitrator in reviewing disciplinary decisions of management. Most arbitrators who attempt to define just cause reach a conclusion very similar to that expressed by Justice Potter Stewart in the now famous Supreme Court case involving pornography and obscenity. In his concurrence, Justice Stewart declined to attempt a precise definition of obscenity but stated, "I know it when I see it."[1]

A majority of arbitrators are equally unsure about a precise definition or test for just cause. As a result, they often simply rely on the concept of an "arbitrator's discretion" to rationalize and explain those decisions which overturn management's judgment. Some arbitrators have gone so far as to impose their own brand of industrial justice and workplace morality under the mistaken belief that they are empowered to do what is fair and right and to follow "the standards of justice and fair dealing prevalent within the community."[2]

What is just cause? How do you define it? How do you balance the right of an employer to manage and operate its business with the interest of unions or employees in receiving fair treatment? How broad is an arbitrator's discretion? According to John Dunsford, the seven tests established by Arbitrator Daugherty may be too restrictive in defining just cause because they place the arbitrator in a narrow reviewing role which limits exercise of decision-making authority. Dunsford also feels that recent decisions by appellate courts further restrict an arbitrator's discretion by requiring the arbitrator to adhere to the specific terms of a contract and negotiated work rules. Dunsford's thesis seems to be that just cause is a very broad concept that gives to arbitrators broad authority not only to exercise their independent judgment but also to exercise their discretion in an attempt to render awards that will not only satisfy all of the parties and meet expectations but bring about industrial peace and stability and also treat employees fairly. Those are very ambitious and admirable objectives!

I am compelled to strongly disagree, however, with the fundamental premise of Dunsford's comments. Indeed, I submit that the unbridled discretion sometimes exercised by arbitrators in discipline cases has tarnished management and labor relations by making the parties more suspicious and distrustful of each

---

[1]*Jacobellis v. Ohio*, 378 U.S. 184, 197 (1964).
[2]*Riley Stoker Corp.*, 7 LA 764 (Platt, 1947).

other as a result of awards which are compromising and inconsistent or plainly lacking in common sense. Furthermore, by continuously substituting their business judgment for that of management, arbitrators often render awards that lessen productivity, quality, and profitability and, in the end, negatively affect an employer's ability to compete and efficiently provide services.

The mistaken belief that a just cause clause somehow grants broad discretion is central to the decision-making process of most arbitrators and is certainly central to the analyses of many commentators. I submit that any analysis of just cause that is premised on the assumption that arbitrators have the discretion to substitute their judgment for that of management is wrong. An arbitrator has no discretion in reviewing management's discipline of employees. Contrary to the comments of Dunsford, the decision maker is management, not the arbitrator. It is the employer, not the arbitrator, who exercises discretion when deciding in the first instance whether an employee should be disciplined. It is the employer, not the arbitrator, who exercises discretion to determine what degree of discipline should be imposed. The arbitrator simply serves as a neutral third party who reviews an employer's exercise of discretion. An arbitrator, therefore, in reviewing the discipline of an employee, should only be analyzing whether the employer had good faith or legitimate business reasons to discipline an employee.

When they exercise their own discretion to overturn management's discipline of employees, arbitrators are applying their own universal standards of decency, justice, and fair treatment. They are imposing their own view of industrial justice in the workplace. Indeed, the greater the exercise of discretion, the more an arbitrator reaches a compromise decision in an attempt to appease the interests of all the parties. It is commonplace for arbitrators to overturn disciplinary penalties on the basis that the penalty did not meet a common standard of fairness or justice.

What's wrong with this approach? From a global, philosophical, moral, or even ethical approach, there may be nothing wrong with an arbitrator's attempts to insert a community standard of justice in formulating a test for just cause. The problem, however, is that universal standards of fairness, decency, and justice are defined by the personal views, experiences, and philosophy of arbitrators as well as their own perception of industrial and community values and morals. By imposing these universal standards in a particular workplace, arbitrators are usurping the function of management and, in fact, are often disregarding problems unique to that particular workplace. By imposing broad community standards, arbitrators ignore competitive issues unique to a particular employer such as productivity, quality, service, and profitability.

Arbitrators must never forget to recognize that every employer is unique. Employers differ not only because of the type of industry and size but because of their particular operating philosophies, their own views of workplace ethics and morality, and their own business plans that outline strategies for becoming more competitive, profitable, efficient, service oriented, and quality conscious. The unrestricted right of employers to respond uniquely and creatively to the pressures of business, no matter how large or small the operation, is a right that is basic to the philosophy upon which our free market system is founded.

Of greatest concern, especially in the private sector, is the fact that those arbitrators who exercise broad discretion in discipline cases often disregard the employer's particular business plan and its need to survive and prosper in an ever-changing and very competitive world. We all recognize the tremendous upheaval that has taken place over the past 10 years in the labor environment and business climate in our country. All employers, public and private, large and small, service and manufacturing, have been and are continuing to be faced with significant demands for increasing productivity, reducing costs, improving quality, and increasing profitability. Now more than ever before, employers are concerned about issues such as—cost control and cost containment; reductions in force; quality circles; profit sharing; group incentives; economic education of employees; communication and employee involvement; guest and customer relations; just-in-time inventory control; participative management; training for new skills and new jobs; raising capital for investment in tools and machinery; combining, consolidating, and eliminating jobs; mergers, acquisitions and realignment of work forces; early retirement of employees; and Japanese method of management.

I have heard these issues and concerns raised, especially in cases involving outsourcing or contracting out, layoff, plant shutdown, transfer of work, job consolidation or merger, acquisition or takeovers, as well as job biddings and recall disputes. It is equally important for arbitrators to recognize, however, that the same issues of profitability, productivity, quality, and service, as well as cost reduction and cost containment, are also the basis for an employer's decision to discipline or discharge an employee. These issues are more than just "buzzwords"; they are real issues and concerns that are confronting management in all sectors on a daily basis.

A few examples of disciplinary situations that simply cannot be considered under any type of universal standard of fairness and justice are set forth for illustrative purposes. The types of cases discussed below can be considered only in view of a particular employer's work environment and the particular employer's unique values, business judgment, and operating philosophy.

1. For most employers, *the theft of employer or employee property* is commonly accepted as cause for some sort of discipline. In a warehouse operation or in a health care setting, theft of any item, such as nuts and bolts or drugs or medication, even though the item may cost only pennies or nickels, may be cause for immediate termination—no questions asked! On the other hand, in a large factory, theft of a nail or pieces of scrap, or in an office environment, theft of time by not working or theft of employer property (such as note paper, paper clips, pens, and pencils), may not be of such magnitude as to require immediate termination but certainly would require progressive disciplinary penalties. Who is to decide what is fair or just?

2. *Use or abuse of drugs and alcohol* is another controversial issue which can be decided only on a case-by-case basis in view of the particular standards of the particular employer. There simply is no universal definition of fairness or justice that can be applied in these cases. Many health care employers, for example, have either a religious orientation or certainly a mission to heal and help the sick. These employers are sometimes much more willing to look at drug and alcohol problems with more compassion and treat these employees as handicapped and give them greater opportunities for rehabilitation. Certain other employers, however, especially in industries where employees are handling hazardous materials or using dangerous machinery or driving company vehicles or are engaged in public transportation, are less tolerant of drug or alcohol problems and are more willing to impose immediate termination for drug or alcohol use. The right answer is what the particular employer decides, based on

its business needs, not what an arbitrator may feel is right or fair or just.

3. *An employee's poor attitude, use of bad language, slow work, or generally uncooperative nature* also may be a cause for discipline. In the hospitality/service industry, where guest and customer relations are an important issue, employee attitude towards the job, demeanor and appearance, and the relationship with co-workers, customers, guests, and supervisors, is an extremely important and essential requirement for the job. In the manufacturing and industrial setting, however, employee attitude, ability to communicate, or overall demeanor is sometimes less important than technical skills and ability. Again, the employer makes the decision, not the arbitrator.

4. *Absenteeism and tardiness* is another important issue for employers. Employers with greater ability to transfer and substitute employees may have a more lenient absenteeism policy. Other employers may operate in a job market where it is hard to hire new employees. Still other employers who operate very lean and highly productive operations need the full efforts of every employee and can be less tolerant of absenteeism. Who is to say what is a proper policy or whether one or two occurrences will result in discipline or discharge? Isn't that up to the employer who must take into account the local labor market and the costs involved in discharging or hiring and training new employees? These are not decisions which are subject to an arbitrator's discretion.

5. *Off-the-premises misconduct.* Arbitrators carefully scrutinize any type of discipline for off-the-premises misconduct, whether for theft, driving while under the influence, use of drugs, sale of drugs, or other matters of moral turpitude. More and more, however, employers, especially in the hospitality and service industries where public image is important, are examining the impact of such employee behavior in the workplace, on co-workers, and on the employer's reputation. Who is to say what is a legitimate business interest for the employer to consider?

6. *Work performance and quality of work* are issues of increased importance in the workplace. As employers are forced to become more competitive and to redesign and redefine jobs, many employees (especially older, long-service employees who no longer have the technical skills to adapt to changes in the workplace), may be faced with discipline or termination. Is it fair in the interests of productivity and competition to penalize an

employee because of economic pressures and forces brought to bear in the workplace beyond the employee's control? Who is to say what is fair or just? Certainly not the arbitrator!

These are just a few examples of situations that I have seen over the past years where arbitrators have issued awards substituting their judgment for that of management. For every decision made by a particular employer, I have seen another employer with a different solution and a different approach to a business problem. What is significant about each of these situations is that they raise issues that are unique to particular employers, and can only be evaluated by those employers in the overall view of the competitive work environment.

American employers, both private and public, are on the threshold of even greater challenges and demands in the future years. The increased competition that we saw in the 1980s—the demand for greater productivity and quality, the demand for greater profitability, the cutbacks in government funding, the increased concern for health and safety of employees in the workplace, the increase in government regulation of the workplace, the pressure to increase service to customers and the public—all of these pressures are going to require greater *flexibility and creativity* by management not only to manage their operations correctly and efficiently but also to evaluate and reevaluate their employees. Each employer is different and this difference must be recognized by arbitrators. How management will involve its employees and how management will react to employees who do not want to become part of the new organizations are decisions that are uniquely vested in management.

Summary

The concept of an arbitrator's discretion in disciplinary cases has become a fundamental but unsound premise that has been passed from one commentator to another and from one arbitrator to another. It is a premise that is incorrect. In discipline cases I submit that it is not proper to examine or even discuss arbitral discretion because, in fact, arbitrators simply *do not have* any discretion.

There is no question that the just cause concept imposes some limitations upon management. Indeed, without these contract clauses, employers could terminate or discipline any employee at any time and for any reason without either notice or cause. The fact that this concept imposes limitations on management's exercise of discretion does not, however, mean that this transfers to an arbitrator the right to exercise discretion and become a self-appointed decision maker. On the contrary, when management gives up the right to discipline employees "at will," it does not intend (and I cannot find any support for a contrary contention) to turn over to a third party the right to review de novo the appropriateness of a particular disciplinary penalty.

Employers who accept just cause clauses are simply agreeing that in disciplining employees they must have some legitimate or good-faith business reason for their actions. This is not a particularly difficult concept—nor is it a hard burden for an employer to meet. The arbitrator's role is very limited. The arbitrator is not the decision maker. The decision has already been made. The arbitrator is simply reviewing the facts to see whether the employer had a reason or "cause" to discipline an employee based upon what the employer has determined is inappropriate or unacceptable employee conduct in the workplace.

What is just cause? I submit that you cannot define just cause because just cause is not so much a universal standard as it is a procedure or process of review. In determining whether an employer has just cause to discipline an employee, an arbitrator needs only to look at the evidence offered by the employer as to the business reason for disciplining an employee. In determining whether an employer was acting in good faith or for good business reasons or both, an arbitrator will consider the contract, notice to the employee, work rules, the investigation, prior warnings, or past practice. All these factors may be taken into consideration to determine whether there was a good-faith business reason for disciplining an employee.

Assuming that management did have a good-faith business reason for disciplining an employee, the next question is whether the penalty was appropriate. Here the issues of just cause and due process are often confused. If a grievant admits having engaged in the particular misconduct, or if the proof is clear, there is very little judgment that an arbitrator needs to exercise in rendering a decision. If there is a dispute as to whether the grievant committed the misconduct or the degree of guilt, it is frequently necessary to analyze circumstantial evidence and the credibility of witnesses. Here the employer's investigative process may help an arbitrator evaluate the employer's decision-making process. Was the grievant confronted with the misconduct? What was said by the grievant? Was there an investigation? What did witnesses say? Who was talked to? Was the grievant given a chance to answer the charges? Who was involved in the decision-making process? Why did the company not believe the grievant? If the investigation shows that the grievant engaged in misconduct for which the company had a good-faith business reason to impose discipline, then the employer's disciplinary decision should be upheld. If the employer's investigation fails to show that the grievant engaged in the misconduct charged, then the employer's disciplinary decision should be overturned.

Significantly, the determination of an appropriate penalty is a decision *uniquely vested* in the employer. Once arbitrators determine that an employer has cause to discipline, I submit that they may not substitute their judgment about the appropriate disciplinary penalty unless it is established that the employer acted arbitrarily, capriciously, or discriminatorily. Under this approach, no matter how unfair the discipline may seem to the arbitrators, no matter how sympathetic arbitrators may be for the older, or the long-service, or even the distracted or impaired employee, the penalty may not be disturbed even if the arbitrators would have done something different had they made the decision. It is important to recognize in all circumstances that management is in the best position to evaluate the needs of its own business and its own operations and the appropriateness of a particular penalty.

I am not suggesting that there should be no limitations on management in disciplining employees. I am suggesting, however, that whatever public policy or public interest is furthered by allowing arbitrators to exercise discretion in discipline cases is outweighed by the overall national interest of allowing employers to be competitive, productive, efficient, and to create a safe and healthful workplace. All of these are issues uniquely within the realm of management to evaluate. How a particular employer chooses to compete—to control costs and to educate, train and assimilate its employees—are decisions for management, and not an outside third party such as a labor arbitrator.

What is a proper test for determining just cause? Should arbitrators exercise discretion in discipline cases? I submit that there are no universal standards and that the discipline of employees is an issue that must be uniquely confronted by every employer in today's competitive environment. Employers must be able to evaluate discipline in light of their own particular business needs and demands. This is the essence of competition. Issues of competition, productivity, quality, service, and even profitability should outweigh any interest or desire of an arbitrator to impose universal standards of fairness or justice. Yet this is exactly what has been done under the rationalization that arbitrators have discretion in discipline cases. Just cause, I submit, does not give arbitrators that type of discretion.

CHAPTER 4

ARBITRAL IMPLICATIONS: HEARING THE SOUNDS OF SILENCE

I.

RICHARD MITTENTHAL*
RICHARD I. BLOCH**

This Academy has heard scholarly and excellent dissertations on contract interpretation functions that involve the "rules" of parsing words, clauses, and codicils. This paper focuses on what we believe is an equally significant function, interpreting and applying the contract silences. When the promise is written, arbitrators are "readers of the contract"[1] and find the bargain with the use of standard interpretive tools. On the other hand, when the promise is implied, arbitrators must find the bargain by assessing the import of the agreement, its unwritten assumptions and purposes.

Arbitral decisions are always expressed in terms of the relevant facts and applicable contract language. That is as it should be. But the more difficult cases involve matters that fall within a gap in the contract language, matters that raise an issue on which the contract appears to be silent. What is the arbitrator to do? There are two possibilities. One may rule that the problem is not covered by the contract and dismiss the grievance. Or one may rule that the problem is governed by certain obligations that may be reasonably implied from the contract and then determine whether those implied obligations have been satisfied.

An important caveat is in order. As a general matter one starts from the premise that parties to a contract say what they mean

*Past President, National Academy of Arbitrators, Birmingham, Michigan.
**Member, National Academy of Arbitrators, Washington, D.C.
[1]See St. Antoine, *Judicial Review of Labor Arbitration Awards: A Second Look at Enterprise Wheel and Its Progeny*, in Arbitration—1977, Proceedings of the 30th Annual Meeting, National Academy of Arbitrators, eds. Barbara D. Dennis and Gerald G. Somers (Washington, BNA Books, 1977), 29.

and that, when they wish to incorporate a set of promises in the contract, they do so. Surely arbitrators have no business filling in blanks with assumptions of their own creation from whatever source derived. We are not suggesting that silence on a subject is in all cases to be construed as somehow invoking ghosts of bargains past or inviting unexpected forays into uncharted and previously unexplored territories. Nor do we propose a new approach to contract interpretation. To the contrary, implications, as will be noted, are standard stuff in the process of contract reading. The contribution here, we hope, is to identify a common thread among arbitration decisions in the context of topics that are so basic to the employment relationship that, in a very real sense, it "goes without saying" that they impact the contract.

Implications[2] arise from existing but unstated realities of the world in which the contracting parties live and the circumstances that surround the making of their bargain. These realities, these "facts of life," have little or nothing to do with what is actually said at the bargaining table. It is this world of implications that puts arbitrators to the sternest test.

Implications are not new. They have been a basis for arbitral decisions for years. Although well aware of these awards, most parties have done little to prevent arbitrators from drawing these implications. A few contracts (General Electric and the IUE is one such example)[3] expressly prohibit the use of implications, but the absence of any such prohibition in the vast majority of contracts[4] suggests that most managements and unions are not likely to be surprised when we rely on an implied obligation in justifying our decisions.[5]

---

[2]A semantic observation is in order. A contract *implies*; an arbitrator *infers* that the contract implies. But the prospect of discussing the "process of inferring implications" was so vexatious and potentially disconcerting to writer and reader alike that we have opted for some literary license and will generally refer simply to the process of implication, trusting that this disclaimer will dispel any inference of antisemantic tendencies.

[3]Article XV, Section 4(a)(iii) states: "This Agreement sets out expressly all the restrictions and obligations assumed by the respective parties, and *no implied restrictions or obligations inhere in this Agreement or were assumed by the parties in entering into this Agreement.*"

[4]Unions would probably resist such a prohibition because of the potential breadth of the commitment, because of the difficulty of identifying how much was actually being surrendered. Managements would probably not pursue this kind of issue to impasse because it appears to be largely a theoretical point and because it would be difficult to quantify what the prohibition would mean in actual operation of a facility.

[5]One might protest that implications, whatever the theory behind them, are an arbitral "addition" to the contract and that any such "addition" is inappropriate. But arbitrators are in a real sense always "adding" to the contract. When they are confronted by a vague or general contract term such as the meaning of "just cause," their rulings "add" new life to

When, and in what manner, does the arbitrator recognize these implications? Implication issues arise in a wide range of disputes—past practice, contracting out, trade and craft jurisdiction, external law, and so on. Arbitral awards deal with these subjects separately. A particular rationale is developed for handling each of these very different areas. Yet, close study reveals some remarkable similarities in the manner in which these cases are resolved.

Our theory begins with a basic proposition, namely, that arbitration is a conservative institution in accordance with the clear mandate of the parties. Arbitrators are not trail blazers or innovators. They are not employed to make the plant a better place to work. Their job is to protect the principles and values, good or bad, established by the collective bargaining contract. Their overriding concern is to *preserve the parties' bargain*, not to change it. Most contracts expressly restrict the arbitrator to matters of "interpretation or application" and prohibit any "addition to or modification of" contract terms. Such limitations on arbitral authority are the parties' way of saying they want the arbitrator to give them what they bargained for, no more and no less. The parties would never have embraced arbitration if they had doubted the primacy of their contract or if they had doubted that arbitrators as a class would faithfully adhere to the terms of that contract.

But what exactly is the parties' bargain? When contract language is clear and unambiguous and plainly governs the matter in question, there is no problem. The arbitrator can then state the parties' bargain, their mutual intent, with a high degree of confidence. The difficulty arises when the contract is ambiguous. Many devices are available to help resolve ambiguity. Those devices should be familiar to anyone experienced in the arbitration process. Perhaps the most difficult problem arises when the contract is silent on the matter in question. In such circumstances can it fairly be said that the parties had no bargain at all? The answer depends on what implications, if any, the arbitrator is willing to draw from some specific contract clause or from the

---

these words. When they are confronted by ambiguous contract language, their rulings confirm one of the competing interpretations and thus "add" a definitiveness that was previously lacking. Similarly, when they are confronted by contractual silence, their willingness to find an implied obligation also "adds" to the contract. As long as that "addition" draws its essence from some express contract provision or from the underlying purposes of the contract, it remains a legitimate form of contract interpretation.

contract as a whole. Contract promises do exist and may be discovered by means other than strict interpretation of words and in circumstances where, in fact, there has been no specific assent by the parties.

In the world of commercial contracts, the process of implication is a common procedure. Corbin,[6] for example, devotes 80 pages to the concept in an exhaustive treatment of its variations and themes. We believe that this process of implication is nowhere more important than in the discrete and specialized world of labor relations, because this remarkable document we call the labor contract is something markedly different from a standard commercial agreement. In this special context, implication as an interpretive tool requires a thinking process mandated by a series of unwritten bargaining realities that pervade the labor agreement.

Our theme can best be illustrated through a number of examples.

Employee Conduct

Some implications emerge naturally from the contract and are widely accepted by both labor and management. For instance, suppose that an employee is ordered to perform a task, refuses on the ground that the assignment is a contract violation, and is disciplined. Assume that there is no health or safety question and that the assignment was indeed, as the employee claimed, a violation. Should the discipline be affirmed?

Most arbitrators would say "yes," arguing that the employee's proper course was to perform the assignment and then file a grievance. This "work now, grieve later" principle, however, is not found in the typical contract. It is an implication drawn from the existence of the grievance procedure and the need for an orderly method of settling disagreements. If employees were free to refuse to comply with assignments whenever they had good reason to believe an assignment violated the contract, the workplace would be subject to random, unnecessary interruptions. The grievance procedure, not the workplace floor, is the proper arena for resolving disputes. By accepting this implication, the arbitrator channels all disagreements into the grievance

---

[6]Corbin, Contracts (St. Paul, Minnesota: West Publishing Co., 1952), Ch. 25, Secs. 561–572 A.

procedure and thus preserves the parties' bargain. That surely is what the parties must have contemplated.

"Work now, grieve later" typically involves a single employee, but this same principle, in a somewhat different form, has been magnified to embrace an entire bargaining unit in the U.S. Supreme Court's decision in *Lucas Flour*.[7] There the Court held that a no-strike pledge will be implied from the parties' adoption of a grievance and arbitration procedure. The basis for this implication is clear. The existence of a contractual grievance procedure necessarily means that the union must seek vindication of employee rights through the grievance procedure rather than a work stoppage.[8]

Management Rights

Suppose that management has always used four employees on a piece of equipment and reduces this crew to two. Assume that the reduction does not impose an excessive workload on the remaining employees. Assume also that the contract includes neither a "management rights" clause nor any language with respect to manning levels. The union complains that management, by chipping away at the jobs available to its members, is undermining both the integrity of the bargaining unit and the vitality of the recognition clause. They contend that if the employer wished to exercise this kind of staffing flexibility, it should have bargained for a "management rights" clause.

Most arbitrators would reject this type of complaint. The critical element is the absence of any contract provision that freezes manning levels. True, in our example, there is no "management rights" clause, but arbitrators are prepared to assume that the employer has all rights other than those it has contracted away. That assumption, commonly called the "reserved rights" theory, is so fundamental to bargaining relationships that it is seldom challenged. The parties themselves surely recognize at the bargaining table that the employer will continue to run the enterprise as it sees fit apart from those obligations, express or

---

[7]*Teamsters Local 174 v. Lucas Flour Co.*, 369 U.S. 95, 49 LRRM 2717 (1962).
[8]This assumes, of course, that the employee right in dispute is one which is indeed subject to the grievance and arbitration machinery.

implied, that arise from the contract. The silence of the contract will not bar a change in manning levels in these circumstances.[9]

The "reserved rights" concept is in a sense the equivalent of a broadly stated management rights clause. Arbitrators embrace this concept or infer such a clause, notwithstanding the silence of the contract. Given the realities we have already mentioned, this result preserves the parties' bargain. To rule that management may do only that which the contract says it may do would make the management rights clause the centerpiece of the contract and a battleground for determining the meaning of contractual silence. From what we know of the history of labor contracts, such a ruling would represent a major alteration of the parties' bargain.

Indeed, the management rights clause becomes irrelevant, once the arbitrator accepts the "reserved rights" theory. The issue in each case then is simply whether a management action has violated some contract provision. If it has, the presence of a "management rights" clause is meaningless. If it has not, the presence of a "management rights" clause is also meaningless. In short, there is no need for arbitrators to refer to "management rights" in resolving the typical grievance dispute.

* * *

Thus far, we have addressed implications that further management's interests. "Work now, grieve later" guarantees order. "Reserved rights" guarantees a large measure of managerial flexibility by placing the burden on the union to point to some contract obligation, express or implied, that prohibits a particu-

---

[9]This is one of the more visible, and important, distinctions between the labor agreement and the standard commercial contract. One normally assumes that the parties to a commercial contract will bargain any and all of the rights and obligations that are to control their dealings; there is no pre-existing package of rights that is somehow retained by one of the parties and superimposed on the relationship. But in the labor context the expectation that management will continue to manage, except to the extent rights have been contracted away, is so basic that it is routinely read in by the arbitrator as a reflection of the bargaining realities.

Comparing the interpretive techniques is instructive. Note that a court reading the labor agreement as a commercial document would probably resolve the staffing issue the same way. But the analysis would differ. A court might conclude that, to the extent the parties wished to provide a set manning level, it was incumbent upon them to say so. In the absence of any such language, no restriction will have been created by the parties—the slate remains blank. An arbitrator, on the other hand, would recognize a continuing affirmative right on the part of management to continue to exercise the prerogatives it has always had. This right has not been created by arbitral fiat. It is one that survives because the parties recognize it, impliedly, as a basis of the bargain.

lar management action. There exists also a competing and powerful set of implications that arise from the very existence of the contractual relationship and that serve to restrict management rights. These implications, like most contract provisions, act to limit managerial discretion and thus further union interests. In all cases, however, implications are reflections of recognized bargaining realities and operate to preserve the basis of the parties' bargain.

Past Practice

Suppose that employees have enjoyed for many years a paid 15-minute wash-up period at the end of their shift, that this practice developed with full knowledge of the parties' top representatives, and that the subject of wash-up time is nowhere mentioned in the contract. There is also no "maintenance of conditions" (or "local working conditions") clause in the contract, that is, no provision that would make long-established practices a binding condition of employment. Suppose further that management decides to discontinue this practice because of business losses and thereafter requires an additional 15 minutes of work on each shift with employees washing up on their own time. The union claims the practice of a paid wash-up period has become a binding condition of employment that cannot be unilaterally terminated during the life of the contract. The employer replies that the contract says nothing about wash-up time or "past practice" and that hence there is no obligation to continue the paid wash-up period.

Most arbitrators, we believe, would accept the union's position in this hypothetical dispute. The rationale is that the contract includes not only its written provisions but also the joint understandings and mutually agreed-to practices that have existed over the years.[10] Because the contract is executed in the context of these understandings and practices, the negotiators must be presumed to have been fully aware of them and to have relied upon them in arriving at an agreement. Hence, if such a practice is not repudiated during negotiations, it may fairly be said that the contract was entered into on the assumption that the practice would continue in force. In this way a practice may by implica-

---

[10]This conclusion might not be possible where the arbitration clause is extremely narrow and specifically rejects the concept of implied obligations.

tion become an integral part of the contract.[11] "Its binding quality is due . . . not to the fact that it is past practice but rather to the [mutual] agreement in which it is based."[12] Arbitrators accept the implication in these circumstances because it appears to preserve the parties' bargain.

Other practices, crew size or work schedules, for example, will ordinarily be treated differently. Here the practice is typically not the result of mutual agreement at all. To quote from Harry Shulman:

> [Such practices] may be mere happenstance, that is, methods that developed without design or deliberation. Or they may be choices by Management in the exercise of managerial discretion as to convenient methods at the time. In such cases there is no thought of obligation or commitment for the future. Such practices are merely present ways, not prescribed ways, of doing things. The relevant item of significance is not the nature of the particular method but the managerial freedom with respect to it. Being the product of managerial determination in its permitted discretion such practices are, in the absence of contractual provisions to the contrary, subject to change in the same discretion. . . .[13]

Arbitrators reject the implication in these circumstances because it would enlarge the parties' bargain.

However, if mutuality is the distinguishing test between enforceable and nonenforceable practices and if, as seems evident, mutuality can sometimes be inferred from a longstanding course of conduct, how are arbitrators to decide? The answer may well depend upon the nature of the practice. Arbitrators are more likely to infer mutuality and enforce a practice with respect to real employee benefits like a paid lunch period because this practice can realistically be viewed as part of the parties' bargain. On the other hand, one is far less likely to infer mutuality and enforce a practice that infringes on some basic management function, such as establishing a work schedule.

The point is that collective bargaining reality, at least the arbitrator's perception of that reality, plays a large role in determining the outcome of these practice disputes.

Contracting Out

Suppose that the bargaining unit includes a large number of janitors, that they have been responsible for in-plant cleaning

---

[11]See Mittenthal, *Past Practice and the Administration of Collective Bargaining Agreements*, 59 Mich. L. Rev. 1017, 1030–1040 (1961).
[12]*Ford Motor Co.*, 19 LA 237, 241–242 (Shulman, 1952).
[13]*Id.*

for many years, that management nevertheless engages a contractor to perform all such work in order to reduce its cleaning cost, and that the janitorial employees are then laid off. Assume too that the agreement nowhere mentions the subject of contracting out. The union argues that the recognition, wage, and seniority clauses together forbid the use of a contractor in this situation. The employer replies that the agreement is silent on contracting out, hence it is free to make these arrangements with a cleaning contractor regardless of the impact on bargaining unit employees.

Most arbitrators, we suspect, would accept the union's position. They recognize that management has a broad right to contract out work. However, they stress that this right is not unlimited and is subject to certain restrictions that can reasonably be implied from specific provisions of the agreement or perhaps from the agreement as a whole.

That implication has been expressed in many ways. Some arbitrators say management cannot contract out if its action would frustrate the basic purposes of the agreement; others state that management cannot contract out in such a way as to arbitrarily or unreasonably reduce the scope of the bargaining unit; still others assert that contracting out is improper if it ignores management's implied obligation of good faith and fair dealing. The common theme of these decisions is that there are implied limitations on management's right to engage contractors.[14]

This implication has been accepted by arbitrators and courts alike. Consider the above hypothetical example again. If management is free to ignore its negotiated wage promises to janitors merely because it finds a contractor who will do the janitorial work for lower wages, it will have effectively frustrated the basic purposes of the agreement. By prohibiting such contracting out, arbitrators are in a real sense preserving the parties' bargain. It is that bargain, the web of promises the parties made to one another, that prompts the implication. Those promises sometimes reach beyond the words that contain them. They surely are

---

[14]In this connection *see* Sinicropi, *Revisiting an Old Battleground: The Subcontracting Dispute*, in Arbitration of Subcontracting and Wage Incentive Disputes, Proceedings of the 32nd Annual Meeting, National Academy of Arbitrators, eds. James L. Stern and Barbara D. Dennis (Washington: BNA Books, 1980), 125; and Crawford, *The Arbitration of Disputes Over Subcontracting*, in Challenges to Arbitration, Proceedings of the 13th Annual Meeting, National Academy of Arbitrators, ed. Jean T. McKelvey (Washington: BNA Books, 1960), 451.

capable of preventing management from using labor cost savings alone as a means of escaping the burdens of the agreement.

The real problem in these cases is not so much the propriety of the implication as its application. It is one thing to say as a general principle that the agreement implies certain limitations on management's right to engage a contractor. It is quite another to apply this implication to the facts of a given case, that is, to determine whether the use of a particular contractor under a particular set of circumstances is actually improper. In matters of application the notion of preserving the parties' bargain is of little help.

Arbitrators focus instead on reasonableness and examine the competing interests, the employer's wish for flexibility versus the union's wish for stability. The relevant considerations include the impact of contracting out on the bargaining unit, the practices within the plant, the ability or availability of unit employees, the need for special equipment or skills, the existence of time constraints, the occurrence of some peak condition. Thus there are circumstances in which bargaining unit work may properly be assigned to nonunit people. To quote from one of Syl Garrett's most quotable awards:

> The group of jobs which constitute a bargaining unit is not static and cannot be. Certain expansions, contractions, and modifications of the total number of jobs within the defined bargaining unit are normal, expectable and essential to proper conduct of the enterprise.[15]

All these factors are weighed, no doubt on a scale calibrated with the arbitrator's value judgments, and a decision is made. The element of arbitral discretion here is enormous.

Trade and Craft Duties

Suppose that a contract has established various trade and craft jobs and an apprenticeship program. Suppose further that each of these jobs is described and classified in terms of the full range of duties a craft incumbent may be called upon to perform. One of the pipefitter's duties, for example, is the installation of conduit, and pipefitters have performed this task for years. In the interest of efficiency the employer decides to have simple installation of small pieces of conduit done by production

---

[15]*United States Steel*, Case N-159, II Basic Steel Arb. 777, 779 (1951).

employees. Assume that the matter of work assignments is nowhere mentioned in the contract apart from a general statement that management "shall direct the work force." The union grieves, protesting this reassignment of conduit installation.

Many arbitrators would be sympathetic to such a grievance. The special nature of craft jobs and the special system designed to describe, classify, and pay for craft work cannot be ignored. Consider those contracts that create craft jobs along with apprenticeship programs, wage schedules for apprentices on the road to journeyman status, craft seniority for journeymen in the event of layoff or promotion, and separate seniority units for each craft. These contracts often incorporate job evaluation manuals that provide for separate and distinct treatment of crafts. Given these circumstances, arbitrators have said that management has an implied obligation not to transfer established craft duties to a noncraft job. That implication stems not so much from interpretation and application of express contract terms as from recognition of an entire system that the parties have embraced to promote and protect craft status. To permit craft duties to be dispersed and paid for at a rate other than that agreed upon for the relevant craft job would plainly undermine the craft system. The implication thus appears to preserve the parties' bargain, the parties' negotiated craft arrangements. This issue has arisen primarily in such basic industries as steel and automobiles.

One significant proviso should be noted. Just as the parties change their contracts in response to new economic circumstances, arbitral willingness to find a particular implication may also change because of new contractual circumstances. For instance, in recent years some employers have successfully prevailed upon unions to revise craft systems. Multicraft jobs have been created, and minor craft work has been reassigned to production employees. As craft systems are modified, the basis for the implication prohibiting reassignment of craft work diminishes. If the parties no longer honor traditional craft boundaries, how can the arbitrator do so? Here again, the point is that implications derive from arbitral perceptions of the parties' bargain. Our perceptions must necessarily change as the reality of the bargain changes.

Transfer of Bargaining Unit Work

Suppose that a stock clerk is in the midst of regular job duties but, due to an unexpected surge in orders, is falling behind in the work. Management seeks to get the system back on track by assigning a supervisor to assist for several hours. The contract neither defines the scope of bargaining unit work nor expressly prohibits supervisors from performing unit work. The union grieves, claiming that supervision may not be assigned this work.

Many arbitrators would sustain this grievance. They would cite the recognition and wage clauses, and infer from these provisions that management may not ordinarily use supervisors to perform bargaining unit work. Like the contracting out restrictions, this implication is a means of preventing actions that frustrate the basic purposes of the agreement. If unit work could be transferred from unit employees to supervisors at will and without good reason, the concept of a bargaining unit would have little meaning. Therefore, the implication serves to preserve the parties' bargain, but it surely would be tempered by the notions of reasonableness discussed earlier. An arbitrator would hardly apply the implication, for example, where the supervisor performed the work on a *de minimis* basis, or for the purpose of training another unit worker.

External Law

Thus far we have examined a variety of situations in which the willingness to recognize contract implications has supplemented the written terms. There are also implications that, while relatively common in standard commercial agreements, are rejected in the labor arena.

Suppose that the employer for good business reasons advances the starting time of the day shift from 9:00 a.m. to 7:00 a.m. without prior discussion with the union. Suppose further that the contract includes a management clause granting the employer "sole jurisdiction over all matters concerning the management of the plant subject only to the terms of the agreement." No other provision of the agreement in any way concerns shift starting time, nor had the parties discussed this subject during contract negotiations. The employer had never before found it necessary to change a shift starting time. The union grieves, urging that the employer's unilateral action was a violation of both the recognition clause and Section 8(a)(5) of the National Labor Relations Act, and that statutory rights and duties should be considered part of the contract.

Most arbitrators would flatly reject the union's statutory claim. The prevailing view, particularly in the private sector, is that laws are not part of the contract and that arbitration is not a forum for enforcing statutory rights. That view has been forcefully expressed at Academy meetings by Bernard Meltzer, Dick Mittenthal, Ted St. Antoine, Ted Jones, Michael Sovern, Dave Feller, and others.[16] The theoretical and policy arguments for this position need not be repeated here.

The implication that applicable law is incorporated in the contract would be warranted where there is a real or tacit understanding to that effect. Perhaps such an understanding exists in a few bargaining relationships, but they are the rare exception not the rule. It is doubtful that there is any general understanding among employers and unions on this matter. Negotiators are concerned with wages, hours, working conditions, and fringe benefits. They seldom traffic in such abstract notions as the role of law under the contract. Even if this subject were raised, it is highly improbable that the parties would agree that applicable law is incorporated in their contract. They would instinctively shy away from any such open-ended and uncertain commitment. Instead, their reaction would be to relegate public law issues to the administrative and judicial arenas, leaving to their own knowledge and expertise the private contractual matters. Significantly, that is also the response of the NLRB. The *Collyer*[17] case and its progeny reflect the Board's willingness to refer cases

---

[16]Meltzer, *Ruminations About Ideology, Law and Labor Arbitration*, in The Arbitrator, the NLRB, and the Courts, Proceedings of the 20th Annual Meeting, National Academy of Arbitrators, ed. Dallas L. Jones (Washington: BNA Books, 1967), 1; Meltzer, *The Role of Law in Arbitration: Rejoinder*, in Developments in American and Foreign Arbitration, Proceedings of the 21st Annual Meeting, National Academy of Arbitrators, ed. Charles M. Rehmus (Washington: BNA Books, 1968), 58; Howlett, *The Arbitrator, the NLRB, and the Courts*, in The Arbitrator, the NLRB, and the Courts, *supra* at 67; Howlett, *The Role of Law in Arbitration: A Reprise*, in Developments in American and Foreign Arbitration, *supra* at 64; Mittenthal, *The Role of Law in Arbitration*, in Developments in American and Foreign Arbitration, *supra* at 42; Sovern, *When Should Arbitrators Follow Federal Law?* in Arbitration and the Expanding Role of Neutrals, Proceedings of the 23rd Annual Meeting, National Academy of Arbitrators, eds. Barbara D. Dennis and Gerald G. Somers (Washington: BNA Books, 1970), 29; St. Antoine, *Discussion* in Developments in American and Foreign Arbitration, *supra* at 75; Platt, *The Relationship Between Arbitration and Title VII of the Civil Rights Act of 1964*, 3 Ga. L. Rev. 398 (1969); Jones, *The Role of Arbitration in State and National Labor Policy*, in Arbitration and the Public Interest, Proceedings of the 24th Annual Meeting, National Academy of Arbitrators, eds. Barbara D. Dennis and Gerald G. Somers (Washington: BNA Books, 1971), 42; Morris, *Comment*, in Arbitration and the Public Interest, *supra* at 65; Feller, *The Coming End of Arbitration's Golden Age*, in Arbitration 1976, Proceedings of the 29th Annual Meeting, National Academy of Arbitrators, eds. Barbara D. Dennis and Gerald G. Somers (Washington: BNA Books, 1976), 97, 109–112.
The minority view, expressed by Howlett, has gained few adherents.
[17]*Collyer Insulated Wire*, 192 NLRB 837, 77 LRRM 1931 (1971).

to arbitrators in the expectation not that arbitration will treat NLRA questions, but that contract issues are best resolved internally and that allied legal issues may be mooted.

These are the collective bargaining realities that help to explain why arbitrators reject external law implications. By doing so, they preserve the parties' bargain or, more appropriately, refuse to enlarge that bargain.

Remedies: Payment of Interest

Implication also plays a major role in the fashioning of remedies. Most contracts simply express rights and duties. They say nothing about how a contract violation is to be corrected. Nevertheless arbitrators have held, with judicial blessing, that the authority to decide a violation has occurred necessarily includes the authority to remedy the violation. If contract rights could not be vindicated through an arbitrator's remedial order, the award would often be little more than a recommendation. The parties would routinely go to the courts for enforcement of contract rights, and there would be little point to the arbitration process. The remedy power is implied to preserve the parties' bargain, to make the arbitration process meaningful. All of this is well-accepted today.

Suppose that the arbitrator finds an employee has been discharged without just cause and orders reinstatement with back pay. Such an order is commonplace even where these remedies are nowhere mentioned in the contract. Suppose further that the union requests interest on the back pay due, that management objects, and that the contract says nothing about interest or about how a back-pay award is to be constructed.[18] How should the arbitrator respond?

A forceful argument can be built for the union's claim. The purpose of back pay is to make the injured employees whole, and they cannot truly be made whole unless interest is paid on monies they have been improperly denied. This view has a strong equitable appeal and is supported by NLRB and court decisions in labor-management cases. However, for the most part, arbitrators reject any interest payment. They do so because

---

[18]Where the contract spells out what is to be included in back pay (e.g., loss of earnings) or excluded (e.g., unemployment compensation, outside earnings) but nowhere mentions interest, it can be persuasively argued that these express provisions alone should govern and that no interest should be paid.

they know that interest claims have for years generally been rejected in arbitration, that labor and management are fully aware of this history, and that nevertheless the parties have not changed their contract to provide for interest. The parties' silence on this question seems to constitute acceptance of the customary "make whole" remedy. The arbitral instinct once again is to preserve the parties' bargain, not to expand it.[19] Thus, even where reason and fairness seem to call for a larger remedy, arbitrators limit themselves to the parties' apparent expectations.

Conclusion

It is beyond dispute that arbitrators may, in performing their interpretive function, find implied obligations that are nowhere mentioned in the contract. That implication process has been supported by the courts. Justice William O. Douglas, speaking for the U.S. Supreme Court in *Warrior & Gulf*, explained:

> The collective bargaining agreement states the rights and duties of the parties. It is more than a contract; it is a generalized code to govern a myriad of cases which the draftsmen cannot wholly antici- pate. . . . The collective agreement covers the whole employment relationship. It calls into being a new common law. . . . *The labor arbitrator's source of law is not confined to the express provisions of the contract, as the industrial common law—the practices of the industry and the shop—is equally a part of the collective bargaining agreement although not expressed in it.* The labor arbitrator is usually chosen because of the parties' confidence in his knowledge of the common law of the shop and their trust in his personal judgment to bring to bear considera- tions which are not expressed in the contract as criteria for judg- ment. . . . (emphasis added)[20]

The crucial question is no longer whether arbitrators possess the authority to find implications but rather how they are to exercise that authority wisely. Arbitrators approach different implication problems through the use of different rationales. In past practice cases, they ask whether the practice is supported by mutual agreement; in contracting-out cases, they ask whether

---

[19]This same instinctual reaction no doubt accounts for arbitral unwillingness to award costs or attorney's fees.

[20]*Steelworkers v. Warrior & Gulf Navigation Co.*, 363 U.S. 574, 578–582, 46 LRRM 2416 (1960).

the use of the contractor served to frustrate the basic purposes of the collective agreement. They look for some rule of contract interpretation; they search the published awards to find precedents on which to rely; they note with favor court-imposed implications in commercial contracts. While all of this is useful, it is not enough.

There is a common thread that ties these very different implications together. Specifically, arbitrators embrace those implications that help to *preserve the parties' bargain* and reject those that alter or enlarge it. This is a more broadly based criterion for evaluating the validity of a proposed implication. It serves to change the focus of the inquiry from a juggling of rules of construction and arbitration precedents to, what is far more important, a sympathetic consideration of collective bargaining reality. That reality best informs the arbitrator as to how far the implication process may reach in a given case.

One might ask, of course, how can arbitrators grasp the collective bargaining reality of parties with whom they have had only a fleeting acquaintance. Consider, however, the background of a well-seasoned arbitrator who has decided hundreds, if not thousands, of cases. He or she certainly should have developed a true appreciation of the purpose of various contract clauses, the problems they address, the reasonable expectations of those who negotiate those provisions, and the practical impact of accepting or rejecting a given implication. Arbitrators should have developed, in short, an appreciation of what collective bargaining is all about. This knowledge is critical. It provides an indispensable sense of reality through which arbitrators determine when an implication may be appropriate and where this implication should begin and end. It also provides the filter through which the facts of a given case are viewed.

Syl Garrett expressed a similar thought at the Academy's 1985 Annual Meeting:

> The dominant fact is that—even if we elect to characterize it as a "contract" for convenience—a collective bargaining agreement almost always is the product of a unique negotiating context. For one to seek to interpret such a document without full awareness of its unique nature—and particularly the context of the specific relationship—is nothing short of naive. In retrospect it may be inferred that Harry Shulman preferred to characterize the collective bargaining agreement as a "code" (rather than a contract) in order to avoid

ensnaring the interpretive process in rules developed for "ordinary" contract interpretation.[21]

Some examples may help to illustrate the point. Arbitrators know that all practices are not equal. Reality tells them that a work-scheduling practice is not ordinarily so basic a condition of employment as to warrant saying it constitutes an enforceable practice. Arbitrators know that contracting out takes many forms. Reality tells them that the use of a contractor to do bargaining unit work during an occasional period of peak demand is not ordinarily an improper exercise of management's powers. Arbitrators know that contract and law are different spheres. Reality tells them that the overwhelming majority of parties have no intention of incorporating the National Labor Relations Act into their contract.

It is true, of course, that not every arbitrator has the same sense of reality, but that proves only that arbitrators possess an extraordinary range of discretion in the implication cases. It is precisely because of this broad discretion that it is important to think more deeply about implications. This paper suggests an analytical tool, a starting point for consideration of the proposed implication. Specifically, will the implication preserve or alter the parties' bargain? The answer to that question will not necessarily resolve the matter but it should help to lead the arbitrator to a better understanding of the problem. We believe that this concept of preserving the bargain is at the very heart of the implication process even though it may seldom be expressed in awards.[22]

Some years ago Ted St. Antoine used a felicitous phrase to describe the arbitrator's function. He spoke of us as "contract readers."[23] We believe that this description is accurate where, as is usually the case, there are contract terms to be interpreted. However, where the contract is silent on the matter in dispute,

---

[21]*See* Garrett, *Contract Interpretation, the Interpretive Process: Myths and Reality*, Arbitration 1985: Law and Practice, Proceedings of the 38th Annual Meeting, National Academy of Arbitrators, ed. Walter J. Gershenfeld (Washingtion: BNA Books, 1985), 121, 143.

[22]Corbin suggests the importance of adjudicators acknowledging, to themselves at least, the true basis for their rulings:

It would probably be advantageous if, when finding a promise by "implication" the Court would ask itself whether it finds the promise by actual interpretation—that is, by searching for the meaning given to the words of the contract by one or both of the parties or is putting into promissory language its finding that the party to the contract ought now to act as if he had made such a promise even though nobody actually thought of it or used the words that expressed it. *Contracts*, Ch. 25, Sec. 561.

[23]*See supra* note 1.

arbitrators are more than "contract readers." They then become "bargain readers" who must construe this silence from the standpoint of the purposes of the contract and collective bargaining reality.

If it is true that an understanding of bargaining reality is essential to a wise exercise of discretion in implication cases, then arbitrators should possess some collective bargaining background. This sense of reality ordinarily flows from experience alone. One cannot gain the necessary exposure through books or lectures. It is not enough to read Sumner Slichter, James Healy, and Robert Livernash, *The Impact of Collective Bargaining on Management*[24] or other first-rate texts. Hence, those interested in a career as an arbitrator should be encouraged first to learn about collective bargaining—what managements and unions seek, why they have such goals, and how they go about achieving them. When training programs are structured, they should place no less emphasis on bargaining reality than on legal analysis.

It is true that there is no such thing as a single bargaining reality. Each bargaining relationship has its own distinct reality born of countless pressures, fears, expectations, and dreams. Out of this remarkable mix, contracts are created.

We are speaking of interpreting the contract in a way that avoids wooden adherence to contract "rules" and doctrines as the first resort to understanding the basis of the bargain. They are, instead, the last resort. A better result, a "better brand of justice" in Corbin's words, is achieved by an approach that accommodates both reading the words and listening to the bargain, and in so doing, recognizes that the execution of the contract cannot be fully understood without a true feeling for the profound unarticulated forces surrounding its conception.

II. A Union Viewpoint

Barry A. Macey*

Richard Mittenthal and Richard Bloch have written an excellent paper, and it is a privilege and a pleasure to be asked to comment on it.

---

[24]Slichter, Healy & Livernash, The Impact of Collective Bargaining on Management (Washington: Brookings Inst., 1960).
*Segal & Macey, Indianapolis, Indiana.

Let me begin by saying that I agree with probably 80 percent of what they have written. Specifically, I agree with the general principle that arbitrators properly find specific obligations that are implied by the existence of more general contractual provisions, by the contract as a whole, and/or by the existence of the bargaining relationship itself. Not only is it proper for them to find these implied obligations, it is necessary that they do so if they are to fulfill their function within our industrial system. As anyone who has spent time in the area of labor relations recognizes, a collective bargaining agreement is general by nature and cannot be expected to contain specific agreements concerning the myriad problems and situations that will arise during its existence. For the agreement to have the life and vitality that the parties intended, arbitrators must resolve many of the problems that arise by seeking and finding implied contractual obligations.

Mittenthal and Bloch contend that in finding these implications (an exercise they refer to as "hearing the sounds of silence"), arbitrators are guided by their concern "to preserve the parties' bargain, not to change it." I agree with the authors that this concern, which is clearly an appropriate one, undoubtedly guides the process of "implication finding" in many cases. However, there is, in my view and in the view of most other union representatives, another guiding force which the authors do not acknowledge that is not so benevolent. This other guiding force, which remains unarticulated in most arbitral decisions, is the view of arbitrators that they should not interfere with the manner in which management has chosen to run its business by "second-guessing" management operational decisions. If this guiding principle were to be expressed as a commandment, that commandment would state: "Thou shalt not meddle in the employer's operation of its business unless the contract clearly requires it."

I share the view of most union representatives that it is much more difficult for a union to win a contract interpretation case than it is to win a discipline case. I believe that the difference in result in the two types of cases is that deciding any but the clearest of contract cases against the employer is viewed by most arbitrators as interference with management's operational prerogative, a result not permitted by the "thou shalt not meddle" commandment. This exaggerated concern with management prerogative is a principle "found" by arbitrators interpreting the

sounds of silence. However, it cannot be defended as an attempt
to preserve the parties' bargain.

In my view this exaggerated concern with management operational prerogative has nothing to do with what the parties said,
intended, or agreed to at the bargaining table. It is inconsistent
with the respective rights of the parties in the bargaining context
from which the agreement arose. The source of this preoccupation with managerial prerogative is, I submit, the view of
arbitrators as to what the appropriate roles of the parties in our
capitalist, market economy should be. While arbitral decisions
shaped by this view reflect the belief that our economy operates
better when management alone operates the business, those
decisions cannot be said to have their basis in arbitrators' concern with preserving the parties' bargain.

Let me illustrate my point by using the examples of implied
obligations that the authors develop in their paper. I believe that
four of the examples discussed by the authors do, in fact, reflect
arbitral decision making in which the implied obligations that
arbitrators find are legitimately explainable as attempts to preserve the parties' bargain. Those four are what the authors refer
to as (1) employee conduct, (2) trade and craft duties, (3) contracting out, and (4) transfer of bargaining unit work.

Three of these examples, however, are explainable not as
implications found to preserve the parties' bargain but as reflections of arbitrators' "thou shalt not meddle" attitude. These
three examples are what the authors call (1) management rights,
(2) past practice, and (3) external law.

Implications That Preserve the Parties' Bargain

Employee Conduct

The authors correctly identify the "obey and grieve" principle
that virtually all arbitrators follow as an implication arising from
the provision of the contract which establishes the grievance
procedure. Most contracts do not expressly state that if employees are given a work order which they believe violates the contract, they must obey the order and then protest it through the
grievance procedure. The contract is silent with respect to this
obligation.

Nevertheless, the contract does contain a grievance procedure
that establishes a system for resolving disputes involving alle-

gations that the employer has violated the contract. When arbitrators interpret the contract as requiring employees to obey and grieve, they are concluding that the presence of the grievance procedure implies that it is the exclusive method of resolving alleged contractual violations and that other methods of resolving disputes, such as arguments on the shop floor, are not permitted. Arbitrators conclude that general contract language concerning dispute resolution implies the specific employee obligation to follow work orders that violate the contract and to remedy the violation through the grievance procedure. Because the parties have agreed to a grievance procedure as the method for resolving disputes, arbitrators' reliance on the "obey and grieve" rule serves to preserve the parties' bargain because it assures that disputes are submitted to the procedure rather than being fought out on the shop floor.

Trade And Craft Duties

The authors contend in their discussion of trade and craft duties that where the agreement contains provisions establishing various trade and craft job classifications and an apprenticeship program, arbitrators are inclined to sustain grievances which protest the assignment of trade and craft work to production employees rather than to employees in the established trade and craft classifications. The analysis that leads to that arbitral conclusion is nearly identical to the analysis that gave rise to the "obey and grieve" rule. In the trade and craft case, as in the obey and grieve case, the parties have agreed to a certain system. In the trade and craft case the system is that employees performing trade and craft work will hold certain job classifications, earn the amounts stated for those classifications in the contract, and undergo certain training requirements to attain their positions.

However, as in the obey and grieve situation, the contract does not explicitly make the system to which the parties have expressly agreed the *exclusive* system by which trade and craft work is to be done. Thus, where the question in the obey and grieve case is whether the grievance procedure is the exclusive method for resolving disputes, the question in the trade and craft case is whether the trade and craft system established in the agreement is the exclusive means for performing trade and craft work. The affirmative answer that arbitrators give in both cases serves to preserve the parties' bargain by protecting the system to which the parties have agreed from being undermined by nonsystem alternatives: arguments on the shop floor in the former case, and production workers performing trade and craft work in the latter.

Contracting Out

The implied obligations that prohibit certain types of sub-contracting have their roots in the same type of analysis. The collective bargaining agreement as a whole represents a system or arrangement under which the bargaining unit work will be performed. At the bargaining table the parties accept the work that is currently being performed as a given, and they simply negotiate the terms under which it will continue to be performed. Even in the absence of specific language prohibiting subcontracting, arbitrators find an implied restriction on subcontracting because the entire collective bargaining agreement is premised on the performance of bargaining unit work by bargaining unit employees. If substantial bargaining unit work is assigned to subcontractors, all of the contractual provisions specifying the terms under which the subcontracted work is to be performed lose their meaning. Accordingly, when concluding that the contract contains implied restrictions on subcontracting, arbitrators often describe their decisions as prohibiting management action which frustrates the purposes of the collective bargaining agreement or which undermines the agreement as a whole. However expressed, the concern is with preserving the bargain that was struck at the table. As in the obey and grieve and trade and craft cases, the parties have negotiated a system. Although the agreement does not explicitly state that nonsystem alternatives are prohibited, arbitrators find implied obligations preventing the parties from engaging in nonsystem alternatives because nonsystem alternatives threaten to undermine the system that was negotiated. The authors correctly attribute this type of implication finding to arbitrators' concern with preserving the bargain, not changing it.

Transfer of Bargaining Unit Work

The analysis here is identical. The system negotiated by the parties is premised on the concept of bargaining unit work. As the authors note, "If unit work could be transferred from unit employees to supervisors at will and without good reason, the concept of a bargaining unit would have little meaning." Thus, in finding an implied obligation that prohibits management from assigning bargaining unit work to supervisors, arbitrators preserve the system by prohibiting nonsystem alternatives.

Implications That Have Nothing to Do With the Parties' Bargain

In the examples of implications discussed thus far, the specific obligations which arbitrators find to be implied are not explicitly stated in the agreement; however, the agreement does contain provisions such as the grievance procedure, recognition clause, or classification system, to which the implied obligations are closely tied. These contractual provisions imply that the parties are obliged to confine their actions to the systems created in the agreement and not to engage in nonsystem alternatives that, although not explicitly prohibited, nevertheless tend to undermine the systems to which the parties have agreed. For this reason the finding of these implications, as the authors demonstrate, serves to preserve the parties' bargain.

In the three following examples which the authors discuss, the conclusions cannot be so explained. In these cases there is no contractual language to which the supposed implication can be tied. In these cases it is my contention that, rather than finding implications which serve to preserve the bargain, arbitrators fashion a guiding principle which reflects their own reluctance to interfere with management operational decisions, but which has nothing to do with what the parties intended, said, or agreed to.

Management Rights

In the management rights example in their paper, the authors correctly state that most arbitrators would permit an employer to reduce a work crew on a piece of equipment from four to two employees even in the absence of a management rights clause. The reason for this, which the authors correctly identify, is that "arbitrators are prepared to assume that management has all rights other than those it has contracted away."

The key word here is "assume." Arbitrators assume that management has reserved all rights; they do not, as the authors incorrectly state on the next page, infer that conclusion. The process of inference involves drawing a conclusion from something else which, in this case, is the contract. Assuming something, on the other hand, means to take something for granted without any proof.[1] The difference between the two processes is significant because it reveals how differently an inferred conclusion and an assumed conclusion are related to the contract. To say that arbitrators infer something from the contract is to acknowledge that the conclusion is tied to the contract. On the other hand, to say that arbitrators assume something is to acknowledge that there is no analytical connection between the arbitrators' conclusion and the contract they are asked to interpret.

Moreover, this is not just a question of unfortunate word choice. In their section on the issue of management rights, the authors are unable to point to any contractual provisions which imply the existence of reserved management rights. In fact, they do not mention the contract as the basis of the conclusion that management has reserved all rights. They link that conclusion instead to "bargaining realities," stating that the reserved rights theory "is routinely read in by the arbitrator as a reflection of bargaining realities."

Since there is no reasoned connection between the arbitral conclusion and the contract, it is extremely difficult to understand how the arbitrators' acceptance of the reserved rights theory can preserve the bargain. How can the bargain not be related to the contract? What is much easier to see is that this theory is consistent with the "thou shalt not meddle" commandment. Guided by this theory, arbitrators consistently deny grievances protesting management operational decisions unless the contract specifically prohibits the action that management has taken. The result is consistent but unrelated to the parties' bargain.

Not only is the reserved rights theory unrelated to the substance of the contract, it is also inconsistent with the legal rights of the parties in the collective bargaining relationship that gives rise to the agreement. To say that the employer reserves all rights not given up in the agreement is to assume that the employer enters collective bargaining negotiations with all rights of control. Under this theory the employer relinquishes some of

---

[1]*See* Webster's New Twentieth Century Dictionary (unabridged), 2nd edition (Springfield, Mass.: G. & C. Merriam Co.).

those rights in contract provisions to which it agrees but retains all rights not relinquished.

The fallacy on which this theory is premised is that the employer enters negotiations with all rights of control. In fact, once the union is certified, the employer must submit all decisions involving wages, hours, and working conditions to the collective bargaining process. If it makes any changes in these items without bargaining with the union, it commits an unfair labor practice. Thus, if the reserved rights theory served merely to secure the rights that the employer actually possessed and did not give up in the collective bargaining agreement, as it purports to do, it would "reserve" for the employer the right to make changes in wages, hours, or working conditions not specified in the agreement only through bargaining with the union.

This, of course, is not what arbitrators mean when they speak of the reserved rights theory. They mean that they are willing to accord management all rights not fixed in the contract. This means that, even in the absence of contract language, they are willing to assume that the union has waived the right to bargain over wages, hours, and working conditions.

Past Practice

In past practice cases the same result is achieved by employing the distinction between past practices dealing with benefits and with operational decisions. The authors correctly note that arbitrators generally sustain a union's past practice grievance concerning a paid wash-up period but deny a similar grievance concerning crew size. They write:

> Arbitrators are more likely to infer mutuality and enforce a practice with respect to real employee benefits like a paid lunch period, because this practice can realistically be viewed as part of the parties' bargain. On the other hand, one is far less likely to infer mutuality and enforce a practice that infringes on some basic management function, such as establishing a work schedule.

Once again the "thou shalt not meddle" commandment is silently operating in the background, guiding the result.

External Law

The authors correctly observe that most arbitrators refuse to interpret collective bargaining agreements as incorporating applicable law. Their contention, however, that arbitrators are guided to this result by their concern for preserving the parties' bargain is not persuasive.

The external law most likely at issue is Section 8(a)(5) of the National Labor Relations Act, which requires the employer to bargain in good faith over wages, hours, and other terms and conditions of employment. In the example that the authors discuss, the employer unilaterally (i.e., without bargaining) changed the starting time of the day shift from 9:00 a.m. to 7:00 a.m. This unilateral change in hours is clearly a violation of Section 8(a)(5), but, as the authors correctly note, most arbitrators, relying on a generally worded management rights clause, would deny a grievance protesting the change. Although the authors do not say so, most arbitrators would reject the grievance even in the absence of a management rights clause because of their fondness for the reserved rights theory.

The authors do not support their claim that refusing to read the law into the contract serves to preserve the parties' bargain by anything other than generalized speculation concerning what is probably on the minds of the negotiators. Since the authors' contention is that the result preserves the bargain, the better place to look for intent is the contract itself. What provision in the contract implies that the parties did not intend to incorporate applicable law? There is no such provision. In fact, the one contract provision that is most relevant to this issue—the recognition clause—strongly suggests just the opposite. The standard recognition clause states that the employer "recognizes the union as the exclusive representative for the purposes of collective bargaining." Surely, this language just as forcefully implies the incorporation of the law governing the duty to bargain as the mere existence of the grievance procedure implies that employees must "obey and grieve."

In contending that negotiators do not intend to incorporate applicable law, the authors write, "Negotiators are concerned with wages, hours, working conditions, and fringe benefits. They seldom traffic in such abstract notions as the role of law under the contract." If negotiators are motivated only by "bread and butter" concerns, why is the recognition clause in the agreement at all? It does not establish wages, hours, or fringe benefits. All it does is establish the legal basis of the relationship, a basis that includes the employer's duty to bargain.

Arbitrators do not hear the duty to bargain resounding throughout the recognition clause because they are listening too intently to the ringing of their own preoccupation with management operational prerogative, not because they are concerned with preserving the parties' bargain. Were they to acknowledge a continuing duty to bargain throughout the term of the agreement, they would have to abandon the theory of reserved management rights, and more management action would become subject to union challenge because the union could successfully challenge any management action concerning wages, hours, and working conditions that was undertaken unilaterally.

Conclusion

The authors have set themselves the difficult task of discovering a single theme to explain the approach arbitrators take to cases where there is no explicit contract language covering the dispute. Their conclusion that arbitrators, in finding contractual implications, are guided by a concern for preserving the parties' bargain is an insightful one which is accurate in many cases. However, the authors ignore an equally compelling concern of arbitrators, reflected in many contract interpretation decisions, that has nothing to do with preserving the parties' bargain. That concern is best described as an unwillingness to interfere with management operational decisions. The concern is founded neither in the contract nor, to the extent that there is a difference, in the parties' bargain. It is founded in the world view of arbitrators that the economy operates best when management makes the operational decisions.

The "thou shalt not meddle" commandment is not defensible as a contractual implication. Because it does not draw its essence from the contract, it is an improper principle to apply in arbitral decision making. This is particularly true because its antithesis, the contractual duty to bargain, which is rejected by most arbitrators, is fairly implied by the recognition clause of the collective bargaining agreement.

Purely as an observation I would note that the "thou shalt not meddle" viewpoint may be facing a challenge with the growth of employee involvement in operational decisions throughout the country. The old view that things work better when management manages and the workers work is giving ground to the new philosophy that employees are more productive when they are permitted to take initiative and participate in operational decisions.

Although significant change in the presuppositions that arbitrators bring to the cases they are called upon to decide cannot be expected in the near future, arbitrators listening to contractual silence should ask themselves whether they are preserving the parties' bargain or indulging their own predilections.

III. A MANAGEMENT VIEWPOINT

SUSAN B. TABLER*

Introduction

As a spokesperson for management on the subject, I find the substance of the Mittenthal/Bloch paper puzzling and troublesome. Although the paper distinguishes the collective bargaining process from negotiations in commercial transactions, it overlooks the most fundamental differences. In a commercial transaction each side has something the other wants—the "quid pro quo" aspect—and each side is vying with competition to get the contract. Labor negotiations would be like that if each union had in tow a work force possessing the requisite skills and, in competition with other unions offering comparable services, it offered the desired services at a certain price on specified terms. Then the employer could choose the best deal—as in a commercial transaction.

Instead, in labor negotiations the situation is quite different. Neither side to the transaction is vying with a competitor, and there is essentially no quid pro quo. Management comes to the bargaining table with all the apples, and bargaining is a process wherein the union asks for more apples in return for the employees' continuing to do what they are supposed to do—work. Under this view of collective bargaining, it is obvious that management does not need arbitrators to bestow "reserved rights" upon it. Reserved rights are not an "implication from silence" to be tossed, like a bone, to employers by arbitrators. It is not even something that requires the union's recognition as a basis of the bargain. It is simply a reality, a fact of life in our capitalistic society—a right stemming from controlling the purse strings.

---

*Ice, Miller, Donadio & Ryan, Indianapolis, Indiana.

Similarly, the doctrine of "work now, grieve later" is not an "implication" of the grievance procedure. To management it is simply a question of the right to discipline employees for "needless interruptions" of work. In the absence of a grievance procedure, management clearly possesses the right to discipline in this situation. The right to discipline is a fundamental right, one of the so-called "reserved rights" referenced above; in addition, it is often an expressed right in the contract. Management's acceptance of a grievance procedure implies no erosion of the inherent right to discipline, and thus the notion that arbitrators infer the "work now, grieve later" doctrine as a gift to management is nonsense.

Since these two items (i.e., "reserved rights" and "work now, grieve later") are the only significant "implication bones" thrown to management in the paper,[1] the paper substantiates what should be obvious: 99 percent of arbitral "implications" favor the union. "Implication" is a guise for giving the union what it did not—or could not—get at the bargaining table. Whenever the union emerges from an arbitration hearing feeling that it has somehow "snookered" the company (and this happens frequently when arbitrators infer a "bargain" unstated in the agreement), the question must be asked: Could that really have been the parties' bargain to begin with?

To the extent that the lead paper is intended as a road map to guide arbitral conduct, it is misdirected. From management's perspective it is not the role of arbitrators to infer promises or impose presumptions of their own concoction. Arbitral implications are unfair to management, and they (1) undermine the arbitration process, (2) undermine the negotiation process, and (3) ultimately hurt the employees.

Effect of Arbitral Implication on the Arbitration Process

Arbitral implication undermines the integrity of the arbitration process and the confidence of management in that process. First and foremost, there is the problem of inconsistent results.

---

[1]The only other promanagement recognition in the paper stems from the *rejection* of an implication: the remedial implication of interest on back-pay awards. This "gift" to management is also phony: arbitration awards have been vacated too many times for "fashioning remedy" implications to allow arbitrators to give in to unions on such points anymore. *See, e.g., S.D. Warren Co. v. Paperworkers Local 1609*, 815 F.2d 178, 125 LRRM 2086 (1st Cir. 1987); *Firemen & Oilers Local 935 B v. Nestle Co.*, 630 F.2d 474, 105 LRRM 2715 (6th Cir. 1980).

"Preserving the bargain" by implication means that the arbitrator *divines* the bargain—based, as the authors put it, on "profound unarticulated forces surrounding [the bargain's] conception." It is not surprising that this sounds like reading entrails: it is "voodoo arbitration." The "voodoo" aspect is illustrated by the following sentence from the paper (with extraneous verbiage removed): "Contract promises do exist . . . where . . . there has been no specific assent by the parties." Think about it: Does this statement make sense?

At a minimum, arbitral implication reduces the arbitration process to one that is highly subjective, impressionistic, and discretionary on the part of the arbitrator. The "bargaining reality" touted in the paper is simply an individual arbitrator's own background of experience. This phenomenon is admitted in the paper: the authors state that "collective bargaining reality—*at least the arbitrator's perception of that reality*—plays a large role in determining the outcome of these practice disputes" (emphasis added). Later the authors admit that the factors underlying implication are weighed on a scale "calibrated with the arbitrator's value judgments."[2]

In a world where implication governs, the outcome of a case is dependent upon a particular arbitrator's understanding as to "what is right" and what the parties should have known, should have understood, and should have taken into account. Accordingly, the results of arbitration are rendered varied and unpredictable when each arbitrator brings to the case (1) a different sense of what his or her license is to add to contracts, and (2) different kinds and degrees of experience from which to divine the bargain.

If this were not bad enough, a further negative effect of the implication doctrine upon the arbitration process is its inherent destruction of a union's incentive to winnow out cases that should not be arbitrated. With arbitration reduced to a crap shoot, unions are encouraged to take all cases to arbitration "to see what we can get the arbitrator to imply." The effect of such latitude (if not whimsy) on the part of arbitrators is to both overburden and demean the process.

---

[2]It is as if even the parol evidence of the parties themselves as to what they intended—as questionable as such evidence is—is insufficient. Instead, the arbitrator's "parol evidence" of what the parties *should* have known, assumed, and intended is accorded superior evidentiary weight.

Effect of Arbitral Implication on the Negotiation Process

Implication destroys the need for bargaining. The premise of the paper with respect to negotiations is false. It assumes that bargaining relationships are static, ad hoc, and transitory. They are not, and this constitutes another significant distinction between labor contracts and commercial contracts.[3] Collective bargaining agreements do not last forever without change. The parties renegotiate the contract at intervals (typically three years or less), and they frequently bargain informally in between. In the labor world the bargaining relationship is dynamic, ongoing. It is designed to allow change to meet the changing realities confronting the parties. If something is not in the collective bargaining agreement that arguably should be, it will soon be subject to the negotiating process. This is exactly where the matter should be resolved, not in some *pectorem deum* by an arbitrator who believes that he or she knows what the parties really intended but failed to express. Accordingly, arbitrators should not assume that the union has "missed the last bus to town" because the current contract does not state all the union wishes it did.

A second negative effect of implication on the negotiation process is the disincentive it poses for a party to make proposals at the bargaining table. The parties are already wary of making proposals for fear that failure to obtain them will result in an estoppel against their later claim of right because of such failure in negotiations. This reluctance to make proposals is exacerbated with the dynamic of implication added to the arbitration process. Why fight an uphill battle at the table when there is hope that an arbitrator will later come to the party's rescue with a helpful "implication"? In this way implication turns the negotiation process into a black comedy of deliberate nonassertion of intentions.

---

[3]This factor distinguishes arbitral implications from an analagous "implication" I find troublesome intellectually (however laudable one might find the result). I refer to the U.S. Supreme Court's inference of the right of privacy from the "penumbra" of the Bill of Rights, as if it were something the Founding Fathers must have intended but inadvertently overlooked. At least the Supreme Court had the excuse that the Founding Fathers were not around to reconsider the issue when it arose in the 20th century. Conversely, in labor contracts there is no need to postulate as to what the parties would have decided had they addressed a particular issue. They are still around to address it, and to resolve it as they see fit.

In addition, implication causes confusion as to whose burden it is, anyway, to bring an item to the table. The paper posits a dichotomy between practices which give rise to implication (those which are the result of "[mutual] agreement") and practices which do *not* give rise to implication (those which are the result of "mere happenstance"). Does that mean that it is management's burden to negotiate a change in a practice which is a "result of mutual agreement," and that it is the union's burden to negotiate the continuation of a practice that is the "result of happenstance"? And who is to say which kind of practice it was in the first place?

Finally, implication destroys the incentive of the parties to solve their own problems. The parties are better equipped to define their own "bargaining reality" than is an arbitrator. It is the parties who know best what bargain they have created, not the arbitrator. In sum, the doctrine of arbitral implication is simply arbitral "Father Knows Best" arrogance. It assumes that the two parties are incapable (1) of negotiating what they want, (2) of fully expressing what they agree to, and (3) of managing their relationship on any long-term basis. This is *not* the fact.[4] It is merely a miscomprehension of industrial reality, a manifestation of the kind of ivory-tower thinking that comes of unfamiliarity with the realities of the collective bargaining process. If there is any message to be derived from the lead paper, it is that arbitrators should possess "some kind of collective bargaining background."

The Effect of Arbitral Implication on Employees

The term "implication" sounds so innocuous and innocent that it is inconceivable that it could have an adverse effect on employees. But, in fact, by raising uncertainty about what the deal is between the employer and the employees (if it is something more than it says on paper), implication has the potential of undermining the job security of the workers.

---

[4]The paper's allusion to recent changes in the craft system is implicit recognition of the vitality of the negotiating process. Unfortunately, the authors overlook the give-and-take of the process by attributing the change in the craft system to the fact that "some employers have successfully prevailed upon unions to revise craft systems." Although in many instances management may have initiated the discussions on this issue, the fact is that the parties *negotiated* these changes, and that is the way it is supposed to work.

In these days of diminishing continuity in the bargaining representatives of the parties, it is nearly impossible to know what the bargain was understood to be each time the contract was renegotiated. To do so, one must ask what were the realities of the industrial world (legally, sociologically, economically) at the time each provision was negotiated, and each time thereafter it was renegotiated. What were the practices in effect *each time* the contract was negotiated;[5] what were the understandings, awarenesses, and sophistication levels of the bargaining representatives *each time* the contract was negotiated? The implication doctrine seems to be predicated on a merger of universal and particular realities at myriad points in time.

The uncertainty interjected by the implication doctrine as to the scope of the bargain has practical consequences. If the bargain is more than is written (and the boundaries of the unwritten are unknown and left to the vagaries of outsiders), no successor employer will want to assume that contract. In these days of mergers, acquisitions, and foreign takeovers, this is a real consideration. The buyer of an enterprise has a right to know what the bargain is. To avoid being saddled with the baggage of past practices, past understandings, and other ephemeral conditions, the buyer has only a couple of realistic options. First, the buyer can insist on an absolute, iron-clad zipper clause as a condition of the deal. The effect of this option on the employees is that they will doubtless lose more "unstated" rights than they might have otherwise. Alternatively, the buyer may try to avoid successorship by revamping the work force, bringing in its own employees, and/or closing facilities with collective bargaining agreements. The effect here is obvious: the employees covered by the contract will be out of work. Either way the employees are hurt in this situation because the new managers cannot trust the bargain enough to accept it.

---

[5]For example, with respect to the 15-minute wash-up period cited in the paper, it might very well have been the understanding between the parties' representatives at the time the practice was instituted that it was a "gift" from the company—something management did not have to give and was under no particular pressure to give, but something that was unilaterally accorded out of good will or because, at the time, it seemed civilized, convenient, or perhaps desirable to supervisors. Whatever the reason, the understanding between the parties was that management would continue to be "good guys" about the wash-up period as long as it could afford this luxury, but that the wash-up period would have to go if belt tightening required it. That is generally the understanding about any economic gift (Christmas turkeys are another example) that is not locked in through express language of the contract.

Conclusion

Management's reaction to the notion of arbitral implication is perhaps best summed up in an analogy posed by one of my partners. He asks:

> How would you feel if, as you lie in the recovery room following a scheduled removal of a wart on your chin, your surgeon smugly advises you that he has also performed an unanticipated and unrequested nose job on you because he knew from his vast surgical experience, his "surgical reality," that most persons of your age and circumstances really wanted rhinoplasty and, if they had thought about it, would have *consented* to such a surgical procedure and, in any event, will be *happier* because of having had such surgery?

In the same way management is the unwitting victim of arbitral reshaping of the contract through implication.

More lyrically, I would sum up management's assessment of "the sounds of silence" as follows: it is the "sound of one hand clapping," and that hand is the union's.

Response—

Richard Mittenthal and Richard Bloch

Regrettably, while Susan Tabler received an advance copy of our paper, we did not receive hers and thus we were unable to read it. Having heard her presentation, however, one might conclude that the disability was mutual. In the name of a dramatic, even melodramatic, presentation, Tabler has ignored the premise of our paper, contenting herself instead with the fabrication of a straw man that she has, one must concede, quite effectively demolished. She speaks of the "arbitral arrogance" of reading into silence provisions that do not exist and indulging in precisely the type of forays into unauthorized territory that we specifically acknowledge and disclaim at the very outset of our paper.

We do not suggest that arbitrators may somehow create rights, from silence or anywhere else, that do not exist. Rather, we are talking about the notion of recognizing, as the parties recognize, underpinnings of the labor relationship that are so well accepted as to be beyond dispute by both parties. Their existence, as we note in the paper, "goes without saying." The entire process of implication is so basic a premise of contract interpretation that we found occasional pause in writing this paper, due to our concern that the topic simply might be too unremarkable. As Mark Twain observed with respect to Columbus' discovery of America: "Discovering America was not such a remarkable thing. It would have been far more remarkable to have *missed* it." Our contribution, we hope, is not to suggest or promote this implication process, that is a given, but rather to identify it as an important thread running through a wide variety of arbitral responses to a broad spectrum of labor relations contract problems.

Listening to Tabler (exhorting that management holds "all the apples," while simultaneously complaining over its inability to truly bargain for the labor force of its choice), one may conclude that her objections go not to arbitral implications but, more profoundly, to arbitral intervention at all, and to 50 years of experience under the National Labor Relations Act. Oscar Wilde's words well reflect Tabler's apparent view of employee relations: "If this is the way the Queen treats her prisoners, she doesn't deserve to have any."

CHAPTER 5

BUILDING THE EVIDENCE RECORD:
THE BOUNDS OF "ARBITRAL ADVOCACY"

I.

JOSEPH F. GENTILE*

Building the evidence record during a labor-management arbitration hearing is not uncharted water to those present. On the contrary, to many of you the hearing procedures are well mapped, they proceed along predictable lines, and in most instances the actual hearings are usually routine. Issues are framed, opening statements presented, witnesses examined and cross-examined, documents submitted, closing arguments made, and the evidence record ultimately closed.[1]

Much has been published about this process and a good many of the authors are present today. Opinions have been expressed on just about every imaginable angle, nuance, and perspective of the arbitration hearing. The Academy has experienced the "golden years,"[2] passed the "crossroads,"[3] adapted to the transitions,[4] weathered ethical storms, debated the usage of external law, and is now staring down creeping legalisms.[5] To use an appealing metaphor, like fine wine, labor-management arbitration has been swirled, smelled, tasted, retasted, compared, chemically profiled, and historically traced from grape seedling to the tasting room.

What more need be said? Certainly not another discussion of the mechanics! However, continuing the theme of this year's

---

*Member, National Academy of Arbitrators, Los Angeles, California.
[1]Waltz & Kaplan, *"The Record": What It Means and How It Is "Made"*, in Evidence: Making the Record (Mineola, N.Y.: Foundation Press, 1982).
[2]Feller, *The Impact of External Law Upon Labor Arbitration*, in The Future of Labor Arbitration in America (New York: American Arbitration Ass'n, 1976), 83–112.
[3]Edwards, *Labor Arbitration at the Crossroads: The "Common Law of the Shop" v. External Law*, 32 Arb. J. 65 (1977).
[4]Gross, *The Labor Arbitrator's Role*, 25 Arb. J. 221 (1970).
[5]Nolan & Abrams, *The Future of Labor Arbitration*, 37 Lab. L.J. 438 (1986).

Annual Meeting, the exercise of arbitral discretion is and will continue to be a very real challenge.

The purpose of this paper is to provoke thought, to be critical but not judgmental, and to open discussion as to the exercise of arbitral discretion in the context of building the evidence record. Subsumed in this discussion will be references to the arbitrator's approach, demeanor, temperament, and "style" during the hearing; however, the emphasis will be on the arbitrator's involvement. The intent is to stimulate interest in mapping the common boundaries which circumscribe the arbitrator's conduct in controlling the hearing and in building the evidence record.

Exercise of Arbitral Discretion

In reviewing the substantial body of commentary regarding the arbitration hearing, the concept of arbitral discretion was identified, but in most instances this identification was in general terms. More specifically, the comments relate to the exercise of this discretion. The subject was directly or impliedly intertwined in every aspect of the hearing process. There were further comments, though few in number, regarding the bounds of arbitral discretion as exercised during the building of the evidence record. Unfortunately these comments were all too brief and generally conclusionary. Arbitrators could do just about as they pleased unless expressly prohibited by the agreement, the framed issue, or other general guidelines which often call for arbitral interpretation. Even then, however, arbitrators may do things during the hearing in the name of "equity" or "justice" as an extension of arbitral discretion. One author characterized this as "the 'license to do good' school."[6] Boundaries exist, but where?

There were no suggestions by the commentators that the exercise of arbitral discretion be unbridled. On the contrary, it is clear that the exercise of arbitral discretion should be neither unlimited nor exercised with impunity. Arbitrators exceeding their authority and abusing discretion are grounds for possible

---

[6]Davey, *Situation Ethics and the Arbitrator's Role,* in Arbitration of Interest Disputes, Proceedings of the 26th Annual Meeting, National Academy of Arbitrators, eds. Barbara D. Dennis and Gerald G. Somers (Washington: BNA Books, 1973), 162, 224.

vacature of the award in most jurisdictions. Thus, boundaries do exist, but they are not easily identified and defined.

Arbitrators are guided procedurally by the broad rules which govern the particular case and are then given wide latitude to interpret the application of those rules. As will be noted later, the Code of Professional Responsibility provides ethical instructions in this regard; however, these instructions are often subject to individualized "situation ethic" interpretation and applications.[7] One can rationalize almost any conduct if one determines to do so.

The exercise of arbitral discretion is the product of experiential development influenced by the growth and expansion of arbitration as an adjudicative dispute resolution forum. This is highlighted by the transition of arbitration in many instances from simple problem-solving procedure to a more defined, adversarial model.[8]

When questions are raised by advocates, arbitrators, or knowledgeable observers regarding the propriety of a particular approach or style for the control and flow of the evidence record or the propriety of an arbitrator's intervention during an advocate's presentation, the simple, straightforward answer, if it is not an ethical concern, appears to be: "Oh, that is a matter of arbitral discretion." Thus, the inquiry is considered answered, but is it?

In my readings I did not find anyone who disagreed with the proposition that the arbitrator enjoys considerable discretion and latitude with respect to the conduct of the hearing, both as to its control and the making of evidentiary rulings as witnesses are called, documents introduced, and procedural arguments made. What was left unsaid were details as to the "bounds." What are the boundaries for the exercise of arbitral discretion during the building of the evidence record?

Surveying the Boundaries of Arbitral Discretion

Advocates inquire, and understandably so, as to these boundaries, since there surely must be defined limits. Advocates query, if the arbitrator has this broadly accepted discretion, there must be boundaries to ascertain when the exercise of that discretion

---

[7]*Id.*
[8]Dunsford, *The Role and Function of the Labor Arbitrator,* 30 St. Louis U.L.J. 109 (1985).

crosses the line into the area of possible abuse and thus misconduct. Without some mapped directions it is difficult even to identify gross departure. Such a departure could constitute what the U.S. Supreme Court has recently called "affirmative misconduct" and thus trigger a vacature action.[9]

Vacature actions in various jurisdictions have produced volumes of decisional law regarding the exercise of arbitral authority or discretion and its abuses; however, most of these recent decisions turn more on the actual decision or award and pre or post arbitral "misconduct" rather than the actual exercise of arbitral discretion during the building of the evidence record. Not allowing relevant evidence into the record and making comments which manifest a predisposition on the disputed issues may constitute "affirmative misconduct." However, "in those cases which held that the arbitrators had exceeded the bounds of their authority, the courts consistently note the strong public policy favoring arbitration and the need to support this alternative dispute-resolution forum."[10]

It is somewhat paradoxical that advocates ask for the identification and establishment of more clearly defined boundaries for the exercise of arbitral discretion. Why? Because the advocates have within their power the ability to limit this exercise either through the collective bargaining agreement, which establishes the arbitration procedures with their built-in arbitral limitations or through a submission agreement, which frames the issues in dispute. These two sources can and often do circumscribe or map the boundaries for the exercise of arbitral discretion. A host of court decisions have reminded arbitrators of these two sources, when reviewing whether arbitrators have abused their discretion in particular cases.[11] However, it is interesting to note that most of these cases support the conclusion that great deference must be accorded the arbitrator's interpretation of the submission agreement.[12]

Over the years advocates have not been bashful about drafting new limitations into the arbitration provisions of their agree-

---

[9]*Paperworkers v. Misco*, 484 U.S. 29, 126 LRRM 3113, 3118 (1987).

[10]*Conduct of Hearings: The Arbitrator's Authority*, 5 Lawyers' Arb. Letter, (1981).

[11]*Delta Lines v. Teamsters*, 55 Cal.App.3d 960, 966, 136 Cal. Rptr. 345 (1972); *County of Santa Clara v. Service Employees Local 715*, 159 Cal. Rptr. 352, 357 (1979); *Newspaper Guild Local 35 (Washington-Baltimore) v. Washington Post Co.*, 442 F.2d 1234, 1236, 76 LRRM 2274 (D.C. Cir. 1971).

[12]*Mobil Oil Corp. v. Oil Workers Local 8-831*, 679 F.2d 299, 302, n.1, 110 LRRM 2620 (3d Cir. 1982).

ments. The usual limitation that the arbitrator may not "add to, subtract from, amend, or modify the agreement" has been expanded by the addition of such qualifying terms as "or nullify, ignore, establish new terms and conditions and shall be expressly limited to a decision upon the question of alleged violation of an express term of the agreement." A classic limitation was found which stated:

> The arbitrator shall not render any decision or award, or fail to render any decision or award, merely because in his/her opinion such decision or award is fair or equitable.

There are additional reference points which provide some general insight as to boundary locations, such as the Code of Professional Responsibility, the Voluntary Labor Arbitration Rules of the American Arbitration Association, the regulations of the Federal Mediation and Conciliation Service, the state arbitration statutes, decisional law, and other particularized requirements imposed by special panels. These are broad guidelines, and arbitrators are granted considerable latitude in interpreting and applying them. Thus, it is understandable that arbitrators disagree as to what constitutes a "full, fair, and impartial hearing."

Arbitral Discretion's Rubicon and the Debate

Advocates have expressed strong opinions when they perceive that an arbitrator has crossed discretion's Rubicon. Some have characterized this as overreaching, while others have been less kind and described it as "activism." Still others have been quite nasty and have described arbitrators as overt advocates—advocates in the sense that arbitrators by their conduct during hearings, reasonably appear to be pleading the cause of one party to the dispute or providing too much guidance as to what theory to develop, what witnesses to call, or what questions to ask. In precise terms, the arbitrator "tried or defended the case for either party."

In the view of many advocates, the arbitrator who moves in the direction of advocacy has ceased to be the neutral trier of fact called to resolve the matter at the terminal step of the grievance procedure, and has demonstrated partiality at a minimum or at the maximum has usurped the role of a participating advocate.

Thus, the genesis of the internally inconsistent term "arbitral advocacy." One advocate's appraisal of an arbitrator's conduct was polemical when he called an arbitrator a "self-appointed, arbitral advocate."

The arbitral rejoinder to these characterizations is generally a pious "pursuit of truth": "I must get to the truth of the matter," or in more forceful terms: "You abdicated your responsibilities as an advocate, the facts were not forthcoming, or the record was becoming too clouded or confused." Thus, the arbitrator would continue, "The circumstances required it . . . . I had to intervene to protect the grievant, protect other employees' interests, maintain the completeness of the evidence record, clarify the issues, preserve the integrity of the procedure and arbitration as an institution," or some other similar reason persuasive to the particular arbitrator. Even the statement to render "justice under the contract" as an "educator-facilitator," as some authors have suggested, has been put forward as a recent approach to support increased arbitral activism and intervention during the hearing.[13]

Justice Louis Brandeis once commented, "A judge rarely performs his functions adequately unless the case before him is adequately presented."[14] An arbitrator's view of "adequately" is one of the areas of arbitral discretion that will be debated for some time to come.

Parallel Tracks: The "Involvement Continuum" and the "Style Continuum"

In building the evidence record, the exercise of arbitral discretion is strongly felt in two areas: the arbitrator's involvement and the arbitrator's philosophy or style. Intertwined in both areas is the arbitrator's demeanor or temperament. For analysis purposes these areas can be described as resting or running on two parallel tracks or existing on two continua.

The first is the involvement continuum. At one end is a passive, seemingly detached arbitrator dutifully and quietly taking notes, and at the other end in a "full-court press" is an arbitrator who has been previously characterized as an arbitral advocate.

---

[13]See Sacks & Kurlantzick, Missing Witnesses, Missing Testimony and Missing Theories (Stoneham, Ma.: Butterworth Legal Pubs., 1988), 10–20.
[14]Brandeis, Living Law, 10 Ill. L. Rev. 461, 470 (1916).

Between these two extremes rest varying degrees of what can be called arbitral activism or intervention.

The second track is the style continuum. At one end is an arbitrator who follows the philosophy of laissez-faire as to the receipt of evidence and hearing formalities, usually allowing everything into the evidence record (the "kitchen sink" approach), and at the other is an arbitrator who should be wearing a robe because of the legalistic approach and judicial-like formality.[15]

An arbitrator's placement on either continuum rests with his or her philosophy of how arbitral discretion should be exercised. This includes the arbitrator's understanding of the boundaries and the interpretation and application of the guidelines directly or impliedly in place for any given hearing. There is diversity among arbitrators in these areas and this is healthy for the process. However, this diversity should not be used as a shield from inquiry as to the bounds of arbitral discretion.

The Involvement Continuum

Experience has taught me that the traditional arbitration hearing requires some degree of arbitral activism. Procedural and evidentiary rulings, such as relevancy, must be made. Activism per se should not be tagged as improper arbitral conduct during the hearing. "Activism," however, must be tempered and exercised with prudence, fidelity, and integrity.

What arbitrators may want to do is not always what they should do! Justice Harlan Stone once stated in the context of judicial restraint, "The only check upon our own exercise of power is our own sense of self-restraint."[16] Thus, the term "prudent activism" as used in this paper incorporates as its touchstone the concept of self-restraint. Application of this concept keeps in check movement toward an abuse of discretion in the form of arbitral advocacy.

An arbitrator is concerned with the quality of the evidence record, for it is from this record that the decision and award will be issued. When required, "prudent activism" must be exercised to make certain issues are joined, rulings on evidentiary matters

---

[15]Raffaele, *Lawyers in Labor Arbitration*, 37 Arb. J. 14, 17 (1982).
[16]*United States v. Butler*, 297 U.S. 1, 78 (1936).

are decisively made, and leadership is provided to ensure the orderly building of a complete and clear evidence record. In one sense the arbitrator is there to see that the "quality assurance" of the hearing's product, the evidence record, is maintained.

Arbitral activism may move toward the arbitral advocacy extreme on the continuum when the parties mutually request such a move or when the circumstances dictate to the arbitrator that such movement must be accomplished to maintain the quality of the evidence record. Justice Oliver Wendell Holmes said, "The character of every act depends upon the circumstances in which it is done."[17] This is certainly apropos as to the exercise of "prudent activism."

The structure and diversity of arbitration hearing procedures may also dictate movement on the involvement continuum. From experience the exercise of arbitral discretion may vary, and properly so, in these contrasting record building situations: expedited versus traditional, rights versus interest matters, ad hoc versus permanent umpireships, and public versus private sector cases. Continued survival as an arbitrator in these many situations requires adaptation to the changing hearing circumstances—a type of Darwinian approach.

Some degree of arbitral intervention or activism is triggered when the arbitrator perceives an inability of the advocates to build a quality evidence record. This takes us back to Justice Brandeis' comment about performing "adequately." The arbitrator must determine the appropriate degree of "prudent activism" necessary to build a complete evidence record short of arbitral advocacy.

Advocates may position the arbitrator on the involvement continuum at one location, while the arbitrator may draw the line in a different location. Each may have sufficient justification for the location. The greater the distance between the locations, the greater the possibility of friction and spirited confrontations between advocates and arbitrators as to their respective roles.

Parenthetically, movement on the style continuum may produce similar reactions when the advocates anticipate a hearing that will follow the laissez-faire approach only to find an arbitrator with a judicial-like style.

---

[17]*Schenck v. United States*, 249 U.S. 47, 52, 63 L.Ed 470, 473, (1919).

Roles of Advocates and Arbitrators

Within the traditional arbitration setting,[18] the advocate and the arbitrator have roles to play and functions to perform in building the evidence record. This division of responsibility has been acknowledged in the "how-to" literature for many years.[19] It is a joint involvement with shared responsibilities. As one author put it, a "cooperative endeavor."[20]

The responsibility of preparing, presenting, and proving the facts in a case rests with the advocate, and the responsibility of "trying a case" or finding facts and drawing inferences from the facts rests with the arbitrator. The arbitrator as the "trier of fact, fact finder or decision maker," tests and candles the facts as presented by the advocates with care, reason, and trained scrutiny. The advocates bring the facts to the arbitration table through testimony, writings, or material objects and, like an artist, use this evidence to paint for the arbitrator the fact portrait. As part of their responsibility, arbitrators must make credibility determinations, separating truth from fiction without the benefit of a divining rod, regardless of some arbitral claims, and must make judgments as to the probative value of the presented evidence.[21]

The arbitrator must also provide a hearing environment that allows for a full, impartial, and fair hearing for the parties and the aggrieved. The extent of any "right" of the aggrieved employee, independent of the exclusive bargaining representative in the traditional bilateral grievance/arbitration procedure, has been and will continue to be discussed and debated.[22] Regardless of where one stands on this subject, the arbitrator's role must be to assure a clear and complete evidence record.

---

[18]In this paper the "traditional arbitration setting" means an arbitration hearing as the terminal step of the grievance procedure in a collective bargaining agreement when a neutral, third party is brought in to resolve the dispute.

[19]*Labor Management Arbitration,* Bulletin No. 013 (Asian-American Free Labor Inst., 1977).

[20]Garrett, *The Role of Lawyers in Arbitration,* in Arbitration and Public Policy, Proceedings of the 14th Annual Meeting, National Academy of Arbitrators, ed. Spencer D. Pollard (Washington: BNA Books, 1961), 102, 106.

[21]*Supra* note 8.

[22]Aaron, *The Role of the Arbitrator in Ensuring a Fair Hearing,* in Arbitration 1982: Conduct of the Hearing, Proceedings of the 35th Annual Meeting, National Academy of Arbitrators, eds. James L. Stern and Barbara D. Dennis (Washington: BNA Books, 1982), 30, 38.

It is easy to understand why some advocates take a strong position on arbitral advocacy when the analogy to painting a portrait is used. An arbitral advocate takes the brushes, palette, and canvas from the advocate and uses them to paint over what the advocate has painted. The advocate looks at the finished product only to find it impressionistic rather than the intended abstract. This conduct by the arbitrator is clearly an abuse of discretion, though it may be motivated by good intentions.

The arbitrator must determine the appropriate balance between these considerations and the traditional role of the arbitrator as a trier of fact. Wherever arbitrators place themselves on the involvement continuum and style continuum, they must have full, fair, and impartial hearings that produce clear and complete factual portraits. It is hoped that, in the final analysis, neither advocate can state with evidence-record support that two advocates presented one side's case—one being the arbitrator at the end of the hearing table.

The demeanor and temperament are important. Arbitrators not only must be impartial but also must conduct themselves with reference to the parties, witnesses, and representatives so that all concerned clearly receive the impression of impartiality. This holds true during the actual hearing and during the informal periods before and after the hearing.[23]

In discussing the roles of the participants, particularly those of judge and attorney, in a criminal matter, Scott Turow in his fine novel, *Presumed Innocent*, made this statement, often heard in the hallways of the criminal courts: "There are two defense lawyers in the courtroom, and the one who's hard to beat is wearing a robe."[24] This is something to think about as we consider arbitral discretion.

Establishing Boundaries for Arbitral Discretion

As already indicated, there exist certain general guidelines for the exercise of arbitral discretion, in addition to the terms of the agreement and the submission agreement. It is instructive at this point briefly to review and to place in focus the better known and

---

[23]Adapted from Harris, Robinson, Warnlof & Brandt, Practicing California Judicial Arbitration, §4.13 [CEB, 1983 w/ '89 Supp.].
[24]Turow, Presumed Innocent (New York: Farrar, Straus & Giroux, 1987), 55.

established boundary markers. Three principal markers are as follows:

(1) The Code of Professional Responsibility. The Code directs the arbitrator to "conscientiously endeavor to understand and observe, to the extent consistent with professional responsibility, the significant principles governing each arbitration system in which he or she serves." The pivotal section of the Code as to the conduct of the hearing is Section 5.

In essence, Section 5.1 states that the arbitrator "provide a fair and adequate hearing" and, in accomplishing this responsibility, assure that both "parties have sufficient opportunity to present their respective evidence and argument." Section 5.1.a reaffirms that the arbitrator "conform to the various types of hearing procedures desired by the parties," and Section 5.1.e states that the arbitrator "not intrude into a party's presentation so as to prevent that party from putting forward its case fairly and adequately." Section 5.1.b enumerates a number of discretionary functions the arbitrator "may" perform during the building of the evidence record. These discretionary functions may upset an advocate if fully exercised; however, they are in place. I would suggest that it is reasonable to draw from these sections of the Code the concept of "prudent activism" as previously discussed.

2) Rules of the Federal Mediation and Conciliation Service. Section 1404.14 of these rules follows the general approach of the Code and directs in mandatory terms that the arbitrator "shall" conduct the hearing "in conformity with the contractual obligations of the parties." To this end, "[t]he conduct of the arbitration proceeding is under the arbitrator's jurisdiction and control, and the arbitrator's decision is to be based upon the evidence and testimony presented at the hearing or otherwise incorporated in the record of the proceeding."

(3) Voluntary Labor Arbitration Rules of the American Arbitration Association. These rules detail the scope of arbitral conduct. Given the level of sophistication of this audience, and the apparent ability of the group to recite these rules as liturgy, let me note only two: Rule 26 and Rule 28.

Rule 26 mandates that the arbitrator "afford [a] full and equal opportunity to all parties for the presentation of relevant proofs." Rule 28 directs that the "arbitrator shall be the judge of the relevance and materiality of the evidence offered, and conformity to legal rules of evidence shall not be necessary."

A common thread runs through these guidelines. The arbitrator is to serve the parties in accord with the procedures designed by the parties within established professional guidelines, and to provide a full and fair hearing so that the parties can present their evidence without inappropriate interference or intervention. In other words, unless the evidence record is in serious jeopardy, it appears from these general guidelines that advocates should be allowed to use their brushes, palettes, and paint to complete their desired fact portrait.

Control of the Hearing

An integral aspect of building the evidence record is an arbitrator's control of the hearing. As already indicated, the hearing is the vehicle through which the evidence record is built and from which the ultimate decision and award will flow. As stated by Sam Kagel, the hearing "can be legalistic or informal; strictly conducted or free-wheeling. But at all times it should be under control of the arbitrator."[25]

As part of this responsibility the arbitrator should discourage personal attacks, improper tactics such as abusive cross-examination, argumentative questioning, witness badgering, shouting at witnesses, and intimidation.[26] Acrimonious exchanges and advocate abuse of the hearing process must be equitably and firmly addressed with authority.

Both advocates and arbitrators agree that the arbitrator must "run the hearing in a professional manner" and that the advocates must conduct their presentations in an orderly and equally professional manner, absent bitter and caustic remarks or personal invective.

The Advocate as an "Indirect Witness"

Most experienced arbitrators have developed an approach when faced with inappropriate conduct by an advocate. The first consideration, however, is whether the conduct is indeed "inap-

---

[25]Kagel, Anatomy of a Labor Arbitration (Washington: BNA Books, 1961), 79. *See also* Jaffee, *The Arbitration Hearing—Avoiding a Shambles,* in Proceedings of the 18th Annual Meeting, National Academy of Arbitrators, ed. Dallas L. Jones (Washington: BNA Books, 1965), 76.

[26]See Scheinman, Evidence and Proof in Arbitration (Ithaca, N.Y.: ILR Press, 1977), 1 ff.; Haughton, *Running the Hearing,* in Arbitration in Practice, ed. Arnold Zack (Ithaca, N.Y.: ILR Press, 1984), 46.

propriate." Assuming arguendo that it is properly determined to be inappropriate, advocates should keep in perspective, whether they desire it or not, that their advocacy may affect belief in the evidence and arguments presented. As described in one trial advocacy text for the judicial forum, the advocate is "an indirect witness" who may face in an indirect manner the divining rod of credibility.[27]

On the Field at Curtis School—An Analogy

The most common complaint raised by advocates to this arbitrator is that arbitrators are reluctant or fail to make clear and definitive rulings on disputed matters during the building of the evidence record. As one commentator described this situation, "the arbitrator may be in charge of the proceeding but does not take charge."[28] In other words, too much is allowed into the evidence record. Rulings are reserved, and the weight to be accorded certain evidence is postponed to the posthearing scale in the arbitrator's office, where probative weights are attached in privacy.

By way of illustration, let me make a brief personal detour. I had occasion to referee a fourth grade girls' soccer game, in which my daughter was an active participant. The outcome of the game determined which team would move to the finals. The referee did not show, and I was asked to referee the game. After making the full disclosures necessary, a type of *Commonwealth Coatings* disclosure,[29] I took to the field with my borrowed whistle. The whistle was blown and the game commenced. It is one thing to view an athletic contest from the sidelines, but it is quite another to be in the middle enforcing the rules before a live audience of highly partisan observers.

To make a long story short, I can inform you with great assurance that you must make immediate, definitive, and clear decisions even if you may not have seen everything. Even when you are absolutely certain on a call, one side will release a chorus of uncomplimentary words. Parents with their little "alter egos" running on the playing field have no patience with equivocation. There is no time for protracted colloquies or "I'll take it under

---

[27]Given, Advocacy: The Art of Pleading a Case, §2.07 (Trial Practice Series, 2nd ed.) (New York: McGraw-Hill, 1985).

[28]*Supra* note 6 at 223.

[29]*Commonwealth Coatings Corp. v. Continental Casualty Co.* 393 U.S. 145 (1968).

advisement," or "I'll give it the weight it deserves," or "It's too close to call." Enough said!

Clear and definitive rulings provide a window into the arbitrator's thoughts, and most advocates seem to appreciate this opportunity.

Profile of an Arbitral Advocate

As one final consideration in today's discussion, it seems appropriate that the significant features of the arbitral advocate be portrayed—a type of profile.[30] The hearing context for this profile is as follows: a grievance arbitration in the private sector with reasonably competent advocates, and the arbitrator selected in an ad hoc manner.

It takes little for the arbitral advocate to swing into a domineering role. The arbitral advocate has the attitude that intervening heavily in the advocate's presentation is an acceptable exercise of arbitral discretion. Minimum justification, if any, is required.

The arbitral advocate thinks nothing of calling witnesses who are not called by the parties. Rather than the exception, this is normal and routine. The arbitral advocate does not find it unthinkable to introduce a new theory for the advocates, because that is the theory the arbitral advocate finds most appealing or appropriate. If there is a question by the advocates as to this new theory, an immediate classroom is set up to educate.

Being dissatisfied with direct and cross-examination, the arbitral advocate takes over the questioning of witnesses, often with the approach of an investigative reporter on "60 Minutes" or an inquisitor from the Spanish Inquisition period. Parenthetically, it takes a truly strong advocate to object to the form or content of the arbitral advocate's questions. This same arbitral advocate makes comments during the hearing which demonstrate he or she has already reached findings and conclusions, often before one side has even started to present its evidence.

If so moved, the arbitral advocate will force mediation or settlement when neither side requests or even indirectly makes comments which could reasonably be construed as suggesting

---

[30]Davey, *What's Right and What's Wrong With Grievance Arbitration*, 28 Arb. J. 209, 224 (1973).

this approach. The justification is that this is "in the best interests of the parties." It may very well be, but!

After intervening during the advocate's presentation, the arbitral advocate declares, "I've heard enough!" At this point the arbitral advocate turns to the opposing advocate and asks him or her to proceed, "if you have anything to add to the contrary."

In a discharge case the arbitral advocate will turn to the union at 1:30 p.m. and state that the union may proceed with its evidence, but that a plane must be caught at 3:00 p.m., and there are no available dates within the forseeable future to resume the hearing. It is hoped that the arbitrator will not rule against the union on the basis of the sufficiency of the evidence.

Not an attractive profile, even if one attempts to mask certain aspects in whole or in part with euphemistic titles, such as "educator-facilitator."[31]

Abuse of Discretion—Examples

Given a rights grievance in the private sector with reasonably competent advocates and an arbitrator selected on an ad hoc basis, the following are examples of abuses of discretion, listing the most serious first:
 (1) introducing a new theory into the hearing;
 (2) calling witnesses not called by the parties;[32]
 (3) making comments during the hearing which clearly demonstrate a predetermination of the matters in dispute;
 (4) forcing mediation or settlement; and
 (5) taking over the direct and cross-examination of witnesses.

Other Discretionary Aspects

Certain evidentiary and procedural rulings by arbitrators during the building of the evidence record do not neatly fit on either continuum identified today. Such rulings nonetheless should be illustrated:
 (1) Should the employer be allowed to call the grievant as the first witness in a discharge case?

---

[31]*Supra* note 13.
[32]*See* Gosline, *Witnesses in Labor Arbitration: Spotters, Informers and Code of Silence*, 43 Arb. J. 44, 50 (1988).

(2) Should the arbitrator allow into the record evidence of postdischarge misconduct by the grievant?

(3) Should the arbitrator allow into the hearing room the grievant's personal attorney when his or her presence is objected to by either or both sides?

(4) Should witnesses be excluded from the hearing?

The answers to these questions require the exercise of arbitral discretion; however, a reading of the texts and articles in the field indicates that positions and practices have evolved. Advocates look for certainty, and arbitrators look for the preferred view as expressed in the texts. As to the four illustrative questions, there appears to be a majority view and a minority view.

The real question is whether these preferred or majority views should be codified as a type of "Code for the Exercise of Discretion." If such a code were developed, it would remove some of these difficult discretionary calls and bridle the would-be arbitral advocate. It would provide greater certainty, uniformity, and consistency in building an evidence record and could function in a manner similar to the Rules of Evidence in the judicial forum. Reviewing courts in vacature actions could easily identify errors and abuses; thus, they could add this code to their "rationality," "essence," and "public policy" tests.

This possibility is mentioned to illustrate positions represented to me by advocates in the past. This moves the hearing on the style continuum toward legalism, a direction I feel is not in the best interests of the arbitration process. In my judgment, the "Code for the Exercise of Discretion" should be appropriately buried with full honors.

Final Troubling Aspects

As already noted, the traditional labor-management arbitration hearing and the building of the evidence record within that hearing are guided in large measure by an arbitrator's exercise of discretion. The arbitrator is governed by very general guidelines, and these guidelines are subject to the arbitrator's own interpretation and application. Circumstances and guidelines applicable in a particular case will dictate where the arbitrator will be located on the involvement continuum and the style continuum. Extremes are always dangerous and attempting to legislate control over the extremes is equally treacherous ground.

Mutual acceptability and selection of arbitrators, one of the hallmarks of this dispute-resolution forum, may be the best control over abuses and aberrant behavior in the exercise of arbitral discretion; however, "prudent activism" should not be confused with arbitral advocacy. It is granted that they are degrees of intrusiveness.

No one would question the responsibility of the arbitrator to ask clarifying questions, to request of an advocate that the witness be allowed to testify and not the "indirect witness" during direct examination, or that compound, complex, or unintelligible questions be corrected in order that a "yes" or "no" answer stands in response to such questions. "Prudent activism" would call for arbitral intervention to arrest these situations and make the evidence record clear and complete.

The final troubling area in this excursion into the exercise of arbitral discretion, which may or may not be troubling to many of you, is the real possibility that two very different evidence records can be built by two different arbitrators located at the extremes or close to the extremes on the involvement continuum and/or the style continuum in the same case. Differences as to credibility determinations and probative weight considerations are expected. Differences on procedural rulings are also expected. Are differences in the evidence record caused by expansive arbitral intervention into the advocates' role to be expected?

It is difficult enough to have the potential of different awards from the same factual situation based on credibility, probative value, and procedural rulings. Should the advocates have to face the arbitral advocacy variable as well?

The judicial forum gained some assurances in this regard through the Rules of Evidence and civil procedural requirements. The arbitration forum has not followed this lead. Should a "Code for the Exercise of Discretion" be resurrected so quickly! I would certainly hope not, as I just buried it a few pages back! If creeping legalism is dangerous, this code is even more dangerous. However, I do not view insisting on a well-built evidence record to be a legalistic approach.

What then is the solution to the arbitral advocate and movement on the involvement continuum in that direction? The solution I offer today is one used by Greek and Roman playwrights who got snarled in a plot and could not extricate themselves by the final curtain—*deus ex machina*. This theatrical phrase calls for the gods or a god to enter the scene and, through the magic only gods can create, straighten things out.

I hope that during the following discussion groups, you can assume the *deus ex machina* role and address possible bounds to the exercise of arbitral discretion in the building of the evidence record.

II. A MANAGEMENT VIEWPOINT

RICHARD L. MARCUS*

Alluding to what he describes as "the Darwinian approach," Joseph Gentile has observed that "continued survival as an arbitrator . . . requires adaptation to . . . changing hearing circumstances." As a management advocate whose clients' fortunes and perceptions of their counsel's talents may be significantly influenced by arbitral decisions rendered by members of this august body, it would no doubt be most prudent for me to avoid heretical proposals. That having been said, I will nevertheless express a thesis which will, I fear, be rejected as totally unacceptable by many of you.

The parties to a collective bargaining agreement have made their deal. In any but the interest arbitration context (and, it can be argued, in that context as well), one side is claiming that the other is not living up to its part of the bargain. Given this basic format, there are sound legal and practical reasons to suggest:

First, the party making such a claim is duty bound to prove it or accept the consequences.

Second, the arbitration process has been in place long enough and employers and unions have become sophisticated enough to know the ground rules and to understand and appreciate all of their ramifications.

Third, it is both presumptuous and inappropriate for any arbitrator to assist either the charging party in presenting its proofs or the charged party in defending against them via what we would all be ready to condemn as "arbitral advocacy."

I would go further to suggest that the end result is no more palatable if produced under the guise of arbitral activism or discretion, or under the rubric of "fact gathering" or "making a

---

*Sonnenschein, Carlin, Nath & Rosenthal, Chicago, Illinois.

complete record," no matter how well intentioned or where, on Gentile's "continuum line," such an exercise falls.

The rationale for my thesis can be explained as follows:

First, unlike a judicial proceeding, there is essentially no opportunity for review of an arbitration proceeding. If there were any doubts on this score, many recent court decisions have effectively dispelled them.[1] As Judge Richard Posner of the Seventh Circuit said not too long ago:

> [W]e want to make clear that we take seriously the twin proposi-
> tions that (1) the reviewing court's function (whether the district
> court's, or this court's) is at an end when it concludes that what the
> arbitrator did was interpretation of the contract, and (2) when in
> doubt the court must find that it was interpretation. We do not want
> to be plagued by cases in which companies or unions refuse to
> comply with arbitration awards merely because they think the
> arbitrator clearly misinterpreted the collective bargaining agree-
> ment. If parties to collective bargaining contracts are unhappy with
> arbitration awards they can bargain for a different method of select-
> ing arbitrators, or for panels of arbitrators, trial or appellate.[2]

There is, in short, no effective way to set aside an award which is the product of arbitral advocacy in even its most virulent form.

Second, unlike most judicial proceedings, when arbitration is over, the parties are still living with each other. Accordingly, if either or both parties are dissatisfied with the results produced by arbitration proceedings, they have the wherewithal to change any or all operative elements of those procedures, either ad hoc (interim arrangements) or permanently (through negotiations). We have all seen contract provisions of this kind: e.g., restrictions against posthearing briefs, prohibitions against par-ticipation by attorneys, specific allocations of burden of proof, and use of mediation-type processes in lieu of formal arbitration proceedings. Indeed, the parties can decide and, in some cases, have decided to abandon the arbitration process altogether.

The reasons which underlie adoption of these changes are myriad. Most important, such provisions come about because the basic system—collective bargaining—works very well and, by its very nature, is designed to accommodate these myriad needs. Since arbitration is only one (albeit important) element of that

---

[1]*See, e.g., Paperworkers v. Misco,* 484 U.S. 29, 126 LRRM 3113 (1987); *Pack Concrete, Inc. v. Cunningham,* 866 F.2d 283, 130 LRRM 2490 (9th Cir. 1989); *Berklee College of Music v. Teachers Local 4412,* 858 F.2d 31, 129 LRRM 2465 (1st Cir. 1988); *Daniel Constr. Co. v. Electrical Workers (IBEW) Local 257,* 856 F.2d 1174, 129 LRRM 2429 (8th Cir. 1988).

[2]*Ethyl Corp. v. Steelworkers,* 768 F.2d 180, 187, 119 LRRM 3566 (7th Cir. 1985).

system, it is vitally important that arbitrators refrain from imposing their own conceptions of how it should work and whether, in
the arbitral mind, it is "fair" for it to work one way as opposed to
another.

Even if a discharge grievant's claim is rejected, the parties who
have codified their faith in the arbitral process are still together;
and, I submit, that is what matters most. Their relationship is
intact and, if they believe that the process produces unfair
results, they can change that process at any time. As for the
discharge grievants, the "just cause" criteria written or imputed
into the contract are properly shaped by the parties' intentions
and by the very procedure which the parties have adopted to
apply them, including most significantly the actions taken by the
parties at the arbitration hearing manifested by their own
choices as to what evidence to produce and how to produce it.
These contractual just cause criteria and the methods by which
they are tested, whether vague or specific, are subject to revision
at any time the signatory parties choose. As for the grievant and
the arbitrator, the very definition of contractual just cause criteria must be considered as governed by reference to what the
contractual parties consider at that time to be relevant and
material. Given the Supreme Court's holdings, there is little
reason for the arbitrator to be overly concerned with or deferen-
tial to "just cause" rights dehors the contract. There clearly are
forums available for the adjudication of those rights.[3]

Third, the suggestion that arbitral activism at the hearing is
justified by the absence of pretrial discovery procedures does not
hold up under scrutiny. The parties clearly have the right to
demand information at the various steps of the grievance procedure and at any time prior to arbitration. Refusal to produce
such evidence may be actionable under the NLRA.[4] Testimony
concerning the refusal of a party to produce information should
be and, in my experience, is considered relevant at the hearing.
As relevant testimony, it can properly be accorded significant
weight by arbitrators in reaching conclusions and rendering
awards.

More specifically, I am suggesting the following guidelines for
arbitral conduct and demeanor in labor arbitration proceedings:

---

[3]See, e.g., Lingle v. Magic Chef, Norge Div., 486 U.S. ___, 46 FEP Cases 1553 (1988);
McDonald v. City of West Branch, Mich., 466 U.S. 284, 115 LRRM 3646 (1984); Alexander v.
Gardner-Denver Co., 415 U.S. 36, 7 FEP Cases 81 (1974).
[4]Island Creek Coal Co., 289 NLRB No. 121, 129 LRRM 1244 (1988).

(1) I agree fully with Gentile that the arbitrator need not and should not tolerate abuse of witnesses or demeaning conduct of advocates. In this connection let me add that I have often told associates that the arbitration result for which they should strive (and the best they can hope to accomplish) is a disgruntled grievant telling fellow employees that the case would have been won but for the stupid arbitrator who messed up or didn't understand the case. If the result is the same person saying the case would have been won but for the sleazy company mouthpiece who wouldn't let the story be told, the management advocate hasn't won very much. There will be a day of reckoning (called contract negotiations).

(2) Let the parties present as much or as little evidence as they desire, in whatever form they choose. It is infinitely more desirable—and, I submit, far more faithful to the terms of the arbitrator's engagement—to issue an award saying, "The record fails to disclose" than to ask at the hearing, "What are the facts?"

To put it bluntly, I strongly disagree with Gentile's contention that "some degree of arbitral activism is triggered when the arbitrator perceives an inability in the advocates to build a quality evidence record." Indeed, I believe that the error of this statement is proven by his follow-up observation that "this perception may not be shared by the participating advocates." If the parties' chosen representatives are satisfied with the record they have developed, it is in fact for their purposes (and, I submit, for all properly relevant purposes) a "quality evidence record," and it is wholly inappropriate for the arbitrator to conclude otherwise.

(3) I have no quarrel with the principle that arbitrators are not bound by federal or state rules of evidence. On the other hand, arcane as some of these rules may be, there are significant, legitimate reasons for judges and arbitrators alike to disregard certain proffered evidence, most notably blatant hearsay. Hearsay is (a) inherently unreliable, (b) there is no practical way for hearsay to be effectively rebutted, and (c) hearsay often raises additional issues or matters which, at best, are insignificant (but prolong the proceeding) or, at worst, saddle the parties with the dilemma of having to decide whether to seek out additional evidence to rebut testimony which the arbitrator has "let in for whatever it's worth."

(4) If, in the most extreme case, you find after the presentations by both sides that you simply do not understand the *issue* of

the case, make your dilemma known to the advocates, requesting either an oral explanation or an elucidation in the briefs (if there are any to be filed). I would urge that this request be used very sparingly. The distinction between conceptual difficulty with the issue and curiosity concerning facts that may crucially affect the outcome is a difficult one to draw. But it is most important that the arbitrator make the distinction; for while failure to understand the issue will likely result in disservice to both parties, inquiry concerning even crucial facts can and should be perceived as either (a) a disservice to the one party whose case is lost because of the arbitrator's production of evidence which the other side failed to adduce on its own, or (b) a disservice to one or both parties who, for reasons of their own, simply did not want such evidence adduced at all.

[*Editor's note*: The Union Viewpoint was presented by Gilbert Cornfield, Cornfield & Feldman, Chicago, Illinois.]

III. WHOSE HEARING IS IT ANYWAY?

GEORGE NICOLAU*

It's always difficult, at least for me, to speak to an audience such as this. The expectation is that something profound will be said. But I have no profundities, just the experiences and views of one arbitrator.

When you think of it a bit, the question before us—"Whose Hearing Is It Anyway?"—is a fascinating one. It's simply loaded with tension, tension that goes far beyond the subsidiary questions we intend to address.

Let me, by way of introduction, dwell on that thought for a moment. We've all been schooled in the maxim that we're the creature of the parties and that the process is theirs. Yet, we also know that arbitrators "may vary the [hearing's] normal procedure," that they are the sole judges of the "relevance and materiality of the evidence offered" and that the parties are required—are *required*, mind you—to "produce such additional evidence as the arbitrator may deem necessary to an understanding and determination of the dispute."[1]

---

*Member, National Academy of Arbitrators, New York, New York. This paper was presented at the Academy's Continuing Education Conference in Milwaukee, Wis., October 30, 1988.
[1]The quoted portions are from Rules 26 and 28 of the American Arbitration Association's Voluntary Labor Arbitration Rules, as amended and in effect January 1, 1988.

Imagine, if you will, how the tension inherent in these very different arbitral guideposts (the arbitrator as the parties' creature versus the arbitrator as envisioned in the AAA Rules) is heightened when you are a young, relatively new, and inexperienced arbitrator who walks into the hearing room to find relatively experienced, sophisticated, and sometimes jaded advocates who picked you because they thought they could con you or, failing that, push you around.

You are the creature of the parties, of course. If it wasn't for them—if they hadn't selected you—you wouldn't be there. But, in a very real sense, at least in my view, the hearing is not theirs, but yours. Some may disagree, but as our esteemed Academy President well knows, that's baseball.

Surely, you bow to the parties to the extent that they have a procedure on which they agree and to which your dissent or distaste is not so basic as to impel you to take the next plane out of town. If, for example, you can live with a two-sided clock that allows each party only a half-hour on a discharge case of an employee with 20 years of service, so be it. I wouldn't suggest or recommend that you do any such thing, but to some, such a procedure might be acceptable.

My point, however, goes beyond time limits or mere matters of mechanics. Our goal, in those cases where truth is an issue, is the *search* for truth. And in all cases our goal must be an orderly procedure, one most conducive to a marshalling of *all* the facts and *all* the arguments necessary to a full understanding of the case, an understanding that will reveal to you what is necessary to a reasoned and fair disposition of the dispute.

This is not always easy, my friends. Often enough, one side or the other doesn't want you to know that much. If you did, the answer to the ultimate question the parties have put to you might be much clearer than it first appeared. Apart from exercises in obfuscation, there are all kinds of folks out there, more each day it seems, who don't think of arbitration as an extension of the collective bargaining process or as a "cooperative endeavor," but as a substitute for the courtroom or the football field where witnesses and even clients are expendable casualties of the battle of the moment, and Vince Lombardi's credo of combat holds sway. They too are not overly interested in the truth or the most reasonable and appropriate answer, but strive primarily for victory, often irrespective of the cost in labor relations terms.

Let me suggest to you that the process might be theirs, but the hearing should be yours. As the contract reader and the decision maker, you are entitled under the AAA Rules, under our Code, and plain common sense, to an orderly hearing and all the evidence you deem necessary.

For the newer arbitrators, taking control of the hearing is a delicate and, some think, a dangerous task. After all, a good deal, if not everything, rides on acceptability. But you have to do it if our goals—the search for truth, an orderly process, and the facts one needs for a fair and reasoned disposition—are to be attained. The trick is to be quietly, but determinedly assertive. If you exercise that assertiveness with tact and skill, with what Jack Dunsford has described as "mandarin courtesy," most parties, I venture to say, will think no less of you; some may indeed be grateful.

While gently taking control of the hearing is by no means painless in the early stages of a career, it becomes less difficult as you progress from case to case. This is not only because you become more comfortable with experience, but also because the parties react to that experience. Jack Dunsford wisely recognized the phenomenon at work in such circumstances, as he has recognized a number of other things many of us see but don't adequately perceive. He described it this way:

> As the reputation and degree of acceptability possessed by the arbitrator grow in the marketplace, his conduct, rulings, and decisions at the hearings may be taken as representing the expected standard of performance. The parties may then begin to orient their understanding of the process to the actions of the established arbitrator.[2]

It's what might be called the reverse Hawthorne effect—that which is observed changes the behavior of the observer. Or it might be dubbed as the "You've been around a long time and have a helluva good reputation, so you must know what you're doing" syndrome.

One example of this was vividly brought home to me when attorneys for both sides in a longstanding collective bargaining relationship independently advised that they liked to select me as an arbitrator. The reason each one gave was that with some

---

[2]Dunsford, *The Role and Function of the Labor Arbitrator*, 30 St. Louis U.L.J. 109, 113 (1985).

other arbitrators his adversary tended to get out of control and behave in an obnoxious manner. I perceive myself as a pussycat. Apparently, if these two attorneys are to be believed, that's not the image that's received.

In any event, whatever image you project, try never to forget, the hearing is yours. Remember too, what Tom Roberts' good friend Peter Ueberroth is fond of saying, "Authority is ten percent given and ninety percent taken."

Obnoxious Advocates

There is no place in an arbitration hearing for obnoxious advocates. They contribute nothing to the proceeding. In my view, they subvert it. Moreover, they damage the relationship and the very concept of arbitration, for such behavior serves only to confirm what many suspect: that arbitration is not really designed to advance understanding or to give everyone a "fair shake," but to reward the cunning or the clever or those with the sharpest killer instinct.

The trick is to get the obnoxious advocate to stop. There are various techniques; which one you use is largely a matter of judgment, though the gradual escalation of pain is generally the preferable tactic. There is the "let's have a talk in the hallway" approach, where you can appeal to notions of honor or, that failing, instill anxiety or fear. There's the direct confrontation in the hearing room, perhaps gentle at first, then increasing in severity and, in the end, if it comes to that, the "arbitrator's walkout" during which you say over your shoulder something like, "We'll resume when you advise that you're ready to conduct yourself in an appropriate and civil manner."

It's hard, I fear, to deal with obnoxious advocates without lecturing. Try as you might, there are times when no alternative is left if your hearing, *your hearing,* is going to proceed in the fashion you need.

Unequal Representation

At first blush, this issue seems a strange candidate for the topic "Whose Hearing Is It Anyway?" but it's not.

While the hearing is yours, the presentation of the case is not. The issue of unequal representation highlights that distinction.

The question, of course, is how far you should go to aid a party whose representation is inadequate.

There is, I suspect, no unanimity among us. Some would go further than others. I think it evident, however, that you can't take over the case or suggest what a party should do or what arguments should be made. Nor, in my view, should you. As long as both sides understand the procedures (educating the uninitiated in procedures I consider my job), this arbitral restraint applies even if one side is represented by an attorney and the other is not and even if one side is unrepresented, as we commonly understand that term.

What you can do in these situations, to go back to what I said before, is make certain that you have enough for an informed decision. If you do, that should be the end of it. If you don't, then you have to ask yourself where the gaps are and how you can close those gaps and get what you need without taking over a presentation or favoring one side. While what you do to close those gaps may have the effect of aiding a presentation, that is not its purpose. Its purpose is to give you what you need for an informed judgment and, in my opinion, you have a right, indeed a duty, to do that.

Having made that point, I must also say that there's an area with respect to this issue where I might be more assertive even if I have, at that moment, everything I really need for the decision. Where I see something happening or not happening that might jeopardize the finality of the award, something, for example, affecting the duty of fair representation, I might be inclined, if I can, to take steps to eliminate that possible infirmity. Absent that consideration, however, if I have enough for a decision, I leave presentation to the parties.

Sequestering Witnesses

I really don't see sequestration as an issue. If such a motion is made and I'm satisfied, after the shortest of inquiries, that witnesses will be testifying about the same event or events, they are excused. The grievant may stay, of course, as well as one representative from each side other than counsel. Once a sequestered witness testifies, that witness may stay for the remainder of the proceeding regardless of whether rebuttal testimony is expected.

There is one other matter I'd like to comment on before I close. It's tangentially related to sequestration and certainly germane to our overall topic: It is the tendency of the party who does not have the burden of going forward to reserve its opening statement until the other party's case has been presented. In a discipline case the union representative often reserves, treating the matter as a criminal trial and behaving as if there had been no discussions during the grievance procedure. In a contract interpretation case company counsel will frequently seek to forgo an opening, saying that the company wants to know just what the union's case is before revealing its position.

I hope it doesn't show at the hearing, but I bristle at such tactics. They don't advance the process. Arbitration is not a game of surprises. Each party's position should have been revealed in the grievance procedure. To forgo that is to forgo the opportunity for settlement, which is what the grievance procedure is all about.

Apart from that, failing to reveal one's position is a disservice to you as arbitrator and to the party one represents. If you are kept in the dark regarding a party's position, you may spend time concentrating on irrelevancies and miss the whole point that party is seeking to make or never fully appreciate its significance.

More than wasting your time by letting you peer into ultimate blind alleys is the disservice such tactics perpetrate on the client. More often than not, you come into the proceeding knowing little or nothing about the case. The opening statement is *the* opportunity to grab and focus your attention, to shape and color the perspective, to paint the picture, to create an almost indelible impression. To throw that opportunity away is a basic mistake of advocacy.

Thus, you will find me saying on occasion, "I understand your viewpoint, counsel, but don't you want to tell me just a little bit about what I should be looking for?" It usually works and everyone's the better for it.

CHAPTER 6

THE CODE AND POSTAWARD ARBITRAL DISCRETION

CHARLES M. REHMUS*

Some issues that come before this Academy, like old soldiers, never die, nor do they fade away. The original *Code of Ethics for Arbitrators* was jointly prepared and published by the Academy and the American Arbitration Association (AAA) in 1951. It provided in Part II, Section 5.a, that an award "should reserve no future duties to the arbitrator except by agreement of the parties." It has been suggested to me by one of our experienced members that the origin of this sentence was perhaps an earlier, undated AAA booklet on arbitration procedures that specified: "The power of the arbitrator ends with the making of the award."[1]

Public criticism of this arbitral version of the doctrine of *functus officio* first began, as far as I am able to ascertain, at our 17th Annual Meeting in 1964. Our late colleague, Peter Seitz, argued there that when the record is incomplete, justice and fairness require that no final decision be made until all the facts are known. Noting that permanent umpires with continuing jurisdiction have few problems in this area, Seitz contended that even ad hoc arbitrators should not hesitate to retain jurisdiction if additional facts or even experience with an operation are needed.[2] The primary vehicle by which he accomplished this objective was an interim award, which he then followed by a final award when all the facts became known. Opposition to this position was voiced in that same session by a management advo-

---

*Member, National Academy of Arbitrators; Adjunct Professor of Law, University of San Diego Law School, Poway, California.
    [1]Labor Arbitration: Techniques and Procedures (New York: American Arbitration Ass'n, ca. 1947), 21.
    [2]*Problems of the Finality of Awards, or Functus Officio and All That*, in Labor Arbitration: Perspectives and Problems, Proceedings of the 17th Annual Meeting, National Academy of Arbitrators, ed. Mark L. Kahn (Washington: BNA Books, 1964).

cate, the late Jesse Freidin, who somewhat intemperately objected that if the parties think a decision can be reached, it is not up to us to decide otherwise. Our duty is simply to rule against the party who fails to meet its factual burden of proof.

Eight years later at our 25th Annual Meeting, the issue was again taken up by another member, Lou Crane. His position was that while an arbitrator might be justified in unilaterally retaining jurisdiction in back pay cases where there is no evidence in the record about interim earnings, in all other cases he considered retention of jurisdiction without the parties' specific permission to be an abuse of arbitral discretion.[3]

During that same year, 1972, the Academy, the AAA, and the Federal Mediation and Conciliation Service (FMCS) established a joint committee to revise and update the 1951 Code. The committee met frequently during 1972 and 1973, preparing eight different drafts of a new Code. Each of these continued to retain the specification that without the parties' agreement an arbitrator's award should "reserve no further duties." The eighth draft was distributed for discussion at our Members Meeting in 1974. The transcript of that session is 150 pages long. A full one-sixth of it, 25 pages, is devoted to discussion of the single sentence regarding "no further duties." Five members spoke in favor of retaining the sentence while nine favored its deletion. The flavor of the discussion may be recalled by quoting two distinguished members no longer with us. Philip Marshall spoke for retaining the sentence, saying, "This is an important canon of ethics that should be continued," if we were to "avoid unethical grasping" for future business. Bob Howlett strongly disagreed, saying, "an arbitrator is derelict in his duty in a discharge or seniority case if he fails to reserve jurisdiction to settle back pay or relative placement issues." Many of our members who spoke that day or later wrote to the committee admitted that even if they had not sought the parties' permission, they quite often retained some jurisdiction in one or another type of case. I thought that Bill Eaton best summarized the whole discussion in true arbitral style when he concluded, "It seems to me we have created a past practice which supersedes the language of the old Code."[4]

---

[3]*The Use and Abuse of Arbitral Power*, in Labor Arbitration at the Quarter-Century Mark, Proceedings of the 25th Annual Meeting, National Academy of Arbitrators, eds. Barbara D. Dennis and Gerald G. Somers (Washington: BNA Books, 1973).

[4]The quotations in this paragraph are from the transcript of the Members Meeting, Tuesday, April 23, 1974.

Apparently the committee agreed. The ninth draft no longer contained the controversial "no further duties" sentence. Instead, the new Code of Professional Responsibility which the Academy, the AAA, and the FMCS then approved, in Section 6.D.1 states only, "No clarification or interpretation of an award is permissible without the consent of the parties."[5] As experts in construing bargaining history and contract language, what are we to make of this evolution in the Code? That it is discretionary whether we retain jurisdiction or even ask the parties, provided it is not for the purpose of clarifying or interpreting an award?

The Law and the Practice

My haphazard survey of colleagues' practices and our published awards leads me to believe that perhaps half of us read the "no clarification . . . without the consent of the parties" to mean that we may not retain jurisdiction unless we ask the parties' permission before we do so. But the timing of such a request troubles some. To ask at the beginning of the hearing is to make a request at a time when it can hardly be refused. The Code does not permit us to force the parties to make an irrevocable commitment about publication before they see our award. Why then should we be permitted to force their commitment on retention of jurisdiction before they see it? But to ask them if we may retain jurisdiction at the end of the hearing is even worse. Late in a hearing day a management advocate once responded to my question about retaining jurisdiction, "So you've decided against me before I've written my brief?" A late request is wrong because it may lead both advocates and grievants to conclude that we have reached an answer at a time when we are still genuinely in doubt.

To avoid these kinds of problems, some of us exercise our discretion by neither asking for nor retaining jurisdiction. This road, however, can lead to problems when the parties fail either to give us complete information at the hearing or later to agree on the implementation of the remedy we ordered. They may then wind up in court. It is true that in every such case that I have

---

[5]*Code of Professional Responsibility for Arbitrators of Labor-Management Disputes*, National Academy of Arbitrators, American Arbitration Association, Federal Mediation and Conciliation Service, 1974.

seen, absent some malfeasance on the arbitrator's part, the court had no hesitation in returning the award to the original arbitrator for completion or clarification.[6] In *Enterprise Wheel* the Fourth Circuit rejected the argument that *functus officio* prevented the resubmission of back-pay determinations to the original arbitrator. It said this doctrine "should not be applied today in the settlement of employer-employee disputes."[7] When *Enterprise Wheel* reached the Supreme Court in the *Steelworkers Trilogy*, specifically with regard to the back-pay issue, the Court said, "We agree with the Court of Appeals . . . that the amounts due the employees may be definitely determined in arbitration. . . ."[8]

Returning to current practice, others of us, because we feel the parties should not have to go to court to get our awards completed or clarified, without asking the parties' consent appear simply to retain jurisdiction. Following *Enterprise Wheel*, courts have often held that arbitrators did not exceed their authority when they retained jurisdiction over aspects of a dispute.[9] The Second Circuit recently remanded to Arbitrator Ted Kheel a case in which he retained jurisdiction 10 years ago, asking that he now clarify his views on an issue that the court conceded he "apparently did not foresee."[10] Courts also have often insisted that arbitrators continue to have jurisdiction despite the arbitrators' conclusion that they were *functus officio*.[11] Whatever the uses of *functus officio* at law, courts have little patience or use for it in arbitration.

The common law rule that arbitrators have no authority to modify or correct an award because of *functus officio* has also been modified by statute. The Uniform Arbitration Act (and many states have adopted it or some variant) permits us, upon timely application from only one party, to correct miscalculations of figures; evident mistakes in our descriptions of persons,

---

[6]*E.g., Hanford Atomic Metal Trades Council v. General Electric*, 353 F.2d 302 (9th Cir. 1965); *Electrical Workers (IBEW) Local 494 v. Brewery Proprietors*, 289 F.Supp. 865, 69 LRRM 2292 (E.D. Wis. 1968); *Safeway Stores v. Teamsters Local 70*, 83 Cal.App. 430, 147 Cal. Rptr. 835, 99 LRRM 2928 (1978).
[7]*Enterprise Wheel & Car Corp. v. Steelworkers*, 269 F.2d 327, 332, 44 LRRM 2349 (4th Cir. 1959).
[8]363 U.S. 593, 599, 46 LRRM 2423 (1960).
[9]*E.g., Teamsters Local 509 v. Richmond Chase Corp.*, 191 Cal.App. 2d (1961); *Department of Public Safety (Alaska) v. Public Safety Employees Ass'n*, 732 P.2d 1090, 125 LRRM 2116 (Alaska 1987).
[10]*New York Bus Tours v. Kheel*, 864 F.2d 9, 130 LRRM 2277 (2d Cir. 1988).
[11]*E.g.*, cases cited in note 6, *supra.*

things, or property; or imperfections of form. But such corrections may not affect the merits of our decision.[12] This statutory authority can still create problems for us, however.

Suppose that you were presented a case in which the employer had rejected the bids of over 20 senior bargaining unit members for three higher-paying bus operator positions in favor of three part-time operators without seniority. The union alleges that this violates the contractual seniority rights of the grievants and asks as a remedy that you decide which of them should have been given the three vacancies. You decide that the union is contractually correct and award the jobs to Smith, Jones, and Brown, together with back pay to each. After you mail out the award, the union politely writes you that the record showed two Browns had bid and you, apparently mistakenly, had awarded the job to Junior rather than Senior Brown. It asks that you correct your error. After checking the record you discover in dismay that the union is correct. You have erroneously described the individual whom you meant to have the job. But the employer writes to object, stating that it has carried out your award. Should you correct your mistake? Even if it changes the bottom line of your award? An analogous issue is now before the Committee on Professional Responsibility and may lead to a Code supplement.

As I noted earlier, after making an affirmative award many of us routinely retain jurisdiction to resolve back pay, seniority placement, or other types of problems. These may be problems we do not foresee but know from experience may arise, or problems that our record does not allow us adequately to address at the time we make our original award. However we characterize such an incomplete award, we return it to the parties, hoping that they can settle any problems that arise, but retaining jurisdiction to resolve them if the parties do not. To return to where I began, despite the criticism his view had received, Peter Seitz continued to make use of interim awards throughout his long and distinguished career.[13] Several of us to whom Russell Smith was mentor in Michigan follow his example and routinely retain jurisdiction to resolve the problems that may arise after our awards if the parties cannot. The Michigan Employment Relations Commission in my time recommended strongly to arbitrators we appointed that they should retain

---

[12]Uniform Arbitration Act, Sections 9, 13.
[13]Seitz, *Substitution of Disciplinary Suspension for Discharge*, 35 Arb. J. 27 (1980).

limited jurisdiction over affirmative awards after the Michigan courts criticized us for not suggesting that they do so.[14]

According to one regional study[15] and my own casual look through volumes of published awards, retention of jurisdiction with or without the parties' consent seems to take place in 10 to 20 percent of all affirmative awards.[16] Among the noteworthy types of jurisdictional retention I have read are: "until the date when the remedy is implemented," "while the parties attempt to negotiate a remedy," "in the event the parties seek clarification," and "in the event the parties fail to agree on the administration of the remedy awarded." Several of these retention phrases seem to skirt rather narrowly the Code's ban in Section 6.D.1 on clarification without a joint request. Perhaps in the retentions I quoted a joint request for clarification is implied by the use of the plural "parties." But retention of jurisdiction is often found without use of "both," "parties," or a "joint" request. I then wonder how the arbitrator intends to handle what must surely come sooner or later—a request for clarification from a single party, objected to by the other. The arbitrator must then accede to the request or refuse, and the parties may end in court in either case. This may explain why the Code forbids us from complying with a unilateral request for clarification.

Most surprisingly, I have found reference to two awards in which the arbitrator retained jurisdiction despite an objection to his doing so by one of the parties.[17] I also know of two cases in which the arbitrator *refused* to retain jurisdiction though both parties requested that he do so; one of them is mine.[18] Such refusal is based on the consideration or fear that what the parties really desire is to have the arbitrator participate in the enforcement of the award. An example of this is a recently published award in which the arbitrator retained jurisdiction to decide

---

[14]*E.g.*, *Opinion Explaining Decision, West Bloomfield Board of Education* (unpublished) (Alexander, 1975).

[15]*Retaining Jurisdiction*, Study Time (New York: American Arbitration Ass'n, July 1980).

[16]*E.g.*, *Overly Co.*, 68 LA 1343 (E. Jones, Jr., 1977); *Providence Medical Center*, 77-1 ARB ¶8191 (Conant, 1977); *Riverdale Plating Co.*, 71 LA 43 (D. Peterson, 1978); *Consolidated Aluminum*, 78-1 ARB ¶1918 (Bailey, 1978); *Holland Plastics*, 74 LA 69 (Belcher, 1980); *Western Airlines*, 74 LA 923 (Richman, 1980); *Bay Area Rapid Transit*, 18 Lab. Arb. in Gov't No. 4090 (Koven, 1988); *City of Ottawa, Ill.*, 18 Lab. Arb. in Gov't No. 4093 (E. Alexander, 1988); *Sweet Life Foods*, 359 Lab. Arb. Awards 10 (Bornstein, 1989); *Butler Paper Co.*, 359 Lab. Arb. Awards 11 (Weiss, 1989).

[17]*Supra* note 15.

[18]*Uarco, Inc.*, 43 LA 1060 (Koven, 1964); *Wilmington Transp. Co.*, (unpublished) (Rehmus, 1988).

"any issue raised by either party over compliance with this award."[19] Section 6.E.1 of the Code states that retention for this purpose is beyond the arbitrator's responsibility.

The danger when an arbitrator ignores Section 6.E.1 and retains jurisdiction for compliance or enforcement purposes is exemplified by an arbitrator whom I shall refer to by the eponymous name Smith. The Social Security Administration and AFGE were faced with 1000 or more grievances under their national agreement, all dealing with aspects of the conduct of union training or business at federal expense and while in federal pay status. The parties and Smith agreed that all of these grievances involved only 29 basic issues, on each of which Smith rendered an opinion and award. He went further, however, and agreed to retain jurisdiction to apply and enforce his award in the many hundreds of individual grievances that remained. It appears that he did so on some mistaken theory that the law of his state encouraged or required him to do so. Enforcement proved an impossible task. Four years and over $43,000 in time charges later Smith was not finished. He continued to render new oral and sometimes *ex parte* enforcement decisions, some of which even modified or went well beyond the issues in his original award.

At long last the Federal Labor Relations Authority (FLRA) looked closely at an agency motion to remove Smith and ordered that new arbitrators be selected to clean out this Augean stable.[20] In a herculean 80-page opinion Ira Jaffe began the job, but Sol Yarowsky, David Kaplan, and Donald Goodman have all had to render additional awards in the continuing effort to set this matter aright. At this point the situation can best serve as a monument to the wisdom of the authors of our present Code, who warned us against any attempt to enforce or participate in the enforcement of our awards.

The Federal Sector

This incident brings me to the federal sector. It will come as no surprise to those of you who arbitrate there to hear that the federal view of arbitral *functus officio* is chaotic. The FLRA routinely hears appeals from one or both parties in about 20 per-

---

[19]*Dow Jones & Co.*, 360 Lab. Arb. Awards 1 (Eisenberg, 1989).
[20]*Social Security Admin. and AFGE*, 33 FLRA No. 87 (1988).

cent of arbitration awards in the federal sector.[21] It has recently decided that *functus officio* is alive and well in cases coming before it. In 1987 Academy member Jerry Ross found that "where the record is incomplete due to the failure of the parties to cite applicable law . . . I find that my jurisdiction under the [Civil Service Reform Act] encompasses correction of the Award to bring it into conformance with FLRA precedent."[22] The Authority disagreed, upholding the Defense Department's objection, and ruled that once an award is rendered arbitrators lack jurisdiction to reopen the matter, even when neither agency nor union has properly informed them of applicable law. The FLRA cited traditional case precedents on *functus officio* and comfortably noted, "The failure of the parties to identify applicable law may make an arbitrator's task more difficult, but it does not confer jurisdiction on an arbitrator to change an award in an attempt to make the award consistent with the Statute."[23]

The Office of Personnel Management (OPM) is charged with enforcing the civil service laws and has the statutory right to review and, if necessary, obtain judicial review of the acts of both the Merit Systems Protection Board and the FLRA.[24] Three months after the FLRA decision affirming *functus officio* that I just described, the OPM came to the exact opposite view.

Another of our members, Arthur Berkeley, reinstated an employee whom NASA had removed from service. Neither NASA nor the union appealed his decision to the FLRA. Nevertheless, OPM, which receives copies of all federal arbitration awards, asked Berkeley to reconsider his award. He refused to do so on the basis that he was *functus officio* and thus without authority to reconsider the merits of his award without a joint request from the parties, which the union refused to give. At OPM's request the Justice Department then petitioned the Court of Appeals for the Federal Circuit to order Berkeley to reconsider and reverse his error in interpreting the Civil Service Reform Act (CSRA). The Justice brief contended, "when [*functus officio*] is invoked to deny a request by the Director of OPM for review of an arbitral award, it is in direct conflict with

---

[21]Frazier, *Arbitration in the Federal Sector*, 41 Arb. J. 70 (1986).
[22]Quoted in *Overseas Fed'n of Teachers (AFT) and Department of Defense Dependents Schools, Mediterranean Region*, 32 FLRA 410 (1988).
[23]*Id.*
[24]5 U.S.C. 1103.

federal law. . . ."[25] The brief continued, "the doctrine of *functus officio* simply must give way to the requirement in section 7703(d) [of CSRA] that arbitrators address the merits of OPM reconsideration requests."[26]

To compound the confusion, while this difference of opinion is awaiting resolution by the court, the FLRA came down with a second opinion in which it said that, of course, *functus officio* doesn't *always* apply to federal awards. Arbitrator Kinoul Long declined to consider a request for attorney's fees that was made after his award was rendered leaving him, he decided, without jurisdiction. This time the Authority said that nothing in the Back Pay Act or OPM regulations required that remedial requests for attorney fees must be made before the record closed. Hence this arbitrator's decision that he was *functus officio* was wrong and he was required to consider and act upon the postaward request for an additional remedy.[27]

Federal sector grievance arbitration reminds me of a line from *Through the Looking-Glass*. With regard to *functus officio* it's just as Humpty-Dumpty said, "When *I* use a word, it means just what I choose it to mean—neither more nor less."

Concluding Recommendations

My conclusion from the foregoing is that we arbitrators remain divided to this day about when, if ever; how; and for what purposes we may retain jurisdiction after making an award. Many, perhaps a majority, of us read the Code to mean that we may retain jurisdiction only with the consent of both parties. Many among this group appear seldom to request that they be given such consent. This is understandable, for *functus officio* has its virtues. It protects us from long telephone calls and the indignant protests of those who, having presented and lost ill-thought-out cases, might otherwise importune us for reconsideration. Blessedly, the award puts the dispute to bed and lets sleeping dogs and arbitrators lie. Those who render only final awards seem never to doubt that they have answered all questions asked of them in words over which reasonable men and women would never differ.

---

[25]Petitioner's Brief, *Horner v. Corrado*, Appeal No. ___ at 6 (Sept. 21, 1988).
[26]*Id.* at 16. At this writing, the decision in this case is pending.
[27]*Philadelphia Naval Shipyard and Philadelphia Metal Trades Council*, 32 FLRA 417 (1988).

But what of those whose collective bargaining experience has taught that such clarity is God-given and all too rarely man-made? Many of this group have never fully understood or agreed with the Academy's inhibition on retention. They (and I include myself among them) believe that we are not really *functus officio* until our job is finished. We realize that it makes good sense to let the parties try first to resolve issues that they really know more about than we do. We welcome savvy advocates who ask at the hearing that we retain jurisdiction when the circum-stances suggest that it may be appropriate. But what if they don't and, for whatever reason, we haven't asked? In such cases, when we finally decide that an affirmative award is appropriate, are we powerless? At the time of award a request to retain jurisdiction may be refused by a newly disappointed loser. Yet the winner's remedy may be jeopardized if the parties can't agree on each aspect of it and the same bad loser, a stickler for *functus officio*, refuses to let us complete our award and finish the job. Must the parties then litigate, perhaps re-arbitrate? We think not, so we retain jurisdiction.

The danger that such reservation may lead to a violation of the language or intent of Section 6 of the Code (or worse, may appear to be a boarding-house reach for further business) can in my opinion be avoided, even in the absence of prior agreement, if we take three simple precautions. First, I believe that any retention of jurisdiction should be only until a date specific and that not long ahead. This has two virtues. It tells the parties and anyone else who cares that we are not reaching, particularly if, as I do, we retain jurisdiction for no more than 60 or 90 days. Short retentions force the parties to get together and finish the job if they can. A refusal to meet can be handled by the winner's timely request to the arbitrator for further specification or hearing. In any event, no good is served by letting these things drag on.

The second precaution I commend to those who retain juris-diction is that they do so for as specific a purpose as possible. Precise words, such as "In the event the parties fail to agree, jurisdiction is retained to determine the grievant's placement in the B Street warehouse seniority list," are certainly preferable if specificity is at all possible. Language such as "until the admin-istration of this award is completed" is a black hole from which no light escapes.

Third, and perhaps controversial to some, I think we should accept no further remuneration following a preliminary or incomplete award. Unless the parties ask for additional hearing days to present their positions on unresolved issues, I have never changed for a supplementary or final award. My *functus* may not be *officio*, but my financial interest in the matter is over. The few hours it may take me to participate in a conference telephone call, or read letters of argument and then prepare a short final award, are minimal and noncompensable. And properly so. If one or both parties genuinely do not understand what I intended, or if I fail to think through all possible ramifications of my award, I failed to do my initial job properly.

Those of us who do not regularly ask both parties' consent but nonetheless sometimes conclude we must retain jurisdiction should, I think, accept such cautionary limitations. If we do so, I believe we fulfill the parties' expectations of us. At the same time we will avoid exceeding the reasonable limits of the slight postaward discretion granted us by the Code.

Discussion—

DENNIS R. NOLAN*

The time-honored doctrine of *functus officio* has several faces: It is a rule of law, of prudence, of loyalty, and of ethics. Charles Rehmus has tackled the last of these. His paper is at once thorough, tolerant, reasoned, and fair. More surprisingly for a scholarly paper, he writes concisely and with an unusually fluid prose style. As well as casting light on a relatively obscure topic, Rehmus adds much to our knowledge by explaining how and why the drafters of the second code dropped the provision that an award "should reserve no future duties to the arbitrator except by agreement of the parties."[1] That change was of great practical importance because it permitted retention of jurisdiction, provided that the arbitrator complied with other ethical obligations.[2] In short, and apart from any disagreements one

---

*Member, National Academy of Arbitrators; Roy Webster Professor of Labor Law, University of South Carolina, Columbia, South Carolina.

[1]*Code of Ethics for Arbitrators*, Sec. II.5.a (1951).

[2]The most pertinent of the other requirements of the *Code of Professional Responsibility for Arbitrators of Labor-Management Disputes* (1974) are Secs. 6.C ("The award should be definite, certain, and as concise as possible"), 6.D.1 ("No clarification or interpretation of an award is permissible without the consent of both parties"), 6.E.1 ("The arbitrator's responsibility does not extend to the enforcement of an award"), and 6.E.2 ("An arbitrator should not voluntarily participate in legal enforcement proceedings").

might have about the *substance* of Rehmus' paper, it is a pleasure to read and a model for all of us to follow.

Rehmus addresses a question that has bedeviled arbitrators for several decades: whether and under what conditions an arbitrator may ethically retain jurisdiction once he has rendered a decision on the merits of a grievance.[3] While granting the legitimate points of those opposed to retention of jurisdiction, Rehmus concludes that arbitrators may (and perhaps should) do so, but only for a short period, for a specific purpose, and for free. With one exception and one reservation, I strongly agree with his analysis and conclusions.

To resolve the most difficult ethical questions of *functus officio*, one must go back to the purposes of the ethical rule. *Functus officio* has three objectives: first, to avoid undermining the principle of finality; second, to avoid delay; and third, to avoid the appearance of arbitral overreach—the impression of what Rehmus, in a typically pithy phrase, terms "a boarding-house reach for further business." As long as the arbitrator accomplishes these objectives, retention of jurisdiction does not violate any ethical canon.

My one disagreement with Rehmus' paper concerns his third recommendation, that arbitrators work for free on any supplemental opinions not requiring additional hearing days. This recommendation attempts to satisfy the third of the rule's objectives, the appearance of arbitral overreach. If Rehmus is proposing some sort of *de minimis* rule, for example that we should not charge for a few minutes spent clearing up a simple point of confusion, no one would disagree. If he intends more than that, many if not most of us would surely differ with him. Some supplemental work involves a large amount of time. When that is

---

[3]The most prolific discussant of this question was the late Peter Seitz, whose seminal 1964 paper Rehmus cites. See also his other major piece on the subject, *Substitution of Disciplinary Suspension for Discharge (A Proposed "Guide to the Perplexed" in Arbitration)*, 35 Arb. J. (No. 2) 27 (1980). Seitz also wrote a brief letter on the subject to Study Time (New York: American Arbitration Ass'n, January 1981), 3–4.

Among the best of the other writings are Busch, *Does the Arbitrator's Function Survive His Award?*, 16 Arb. J. 31 (1961); Dilts, *Award Clarification: An Ethical Dilemma?*, 33 Lab. L.J. 366 (1982); Elkouri & Elkouri, How Arbitration Works, 4th ed. (Washington: BNA Books, 1985), 283–285; Fairweather, Practice and Procedure in Labor Arbitration, 2d ed. (Washington: BNA Books, 1983), 579–583; Jones, *Arbitration and the Dilemma of Possible Error*, 11 Lab. L.J. 1023 (1960); Scheiber, *The Doctrine of Functus Officio With Particular Relation to Labor Arbitration*, 23 Lab. L.J. 638 (1972); and Werner & Holtzman, *Clarification of Arbitration Awards*, 3 Lab. Law. 183 (1987). The AAA Study Time published three short articles on retention of jurisdiction by arbitrators: *Retaining Jurisdiction* (July 1980), 1; *More on Retaining Jurisdiction* (October 1980), 1; and *Final Comments on Retaining Jurisdiction* (January 1980), 3.

the case, arbitrators should be paid for their time even as other workers are.

Similarly, if Rehmus is proposing a rule of humility, that we should not charge the parties for correcting our own errors, no one would disagree with him. Rehmus hints that supplemental work may be required only because of the arbitrator's lack of clarity. If so, the humble arbitrator would likely decline to charge the parties. If he intends more than to caution us to be humble, however, his argument is unpersuasive. Most supplemental work is likely to concern things like the calculation of back pay—work necessitated by the parties' decision not to introduce evidence on that question until the arbitrator has determined that some back pay may be due. In that situation there is no reason for the arbitrator to work for free. To the contrary, if the arbitrator did so, the parties would be likely to get what they paid for.

Ethically, then, arbitrators may retain jurisdiction as long as they craft the retention provision to avoid relitigation of the merits (thus satisfying the first of the rule's objectives), to limit the duration of jurisdiction (thus satisfying the second of the rule's objectives), and to exclude any possible assertion of jurisdiction over new issues or new cases (thus satisfying the third of the rule's objectives).[4] Indeed, in many cases retention will best serve the parties' own interests by providing a speedier and cheaper means of resolving disputes over the award than going to court or filing a new grievance before a new arbitrator. If the retention itself is ethical, payment for the supplemental work is equally so.

The one reservation I have with Rehmus' paper concerns its scope—or rather its lack of scope. As I said, he deals with only one narrow part of the interface between *functus officio* and arbitral ethics, the retention of jurisdiction. This may well be the simplest part, too, because (at least arguably) retention to resolve remedial disputes is not a "clarification or interpretation" proscribed by Section 6.D.1 of the new Code. A full analysis of the ethical dimensions of *functus officio* will have to await another occasion, but I can mention briefly four ethical issues Rehmus

---

[4]In this connection, I commend Rehmus for his criticism of the most flagrant piece of arbitral overreaching I have encountered, the infamous series of awards by Arbitrator Smith in his *Social Security Administration* cases.

did not address, and suggest how an arbitrator might deal with them.

First, there is the matter of the arbitrator's issuance or completion of a partial award. Much of the criticism of Peter Seitz's recommendation that arbitrators issue "interim awards" misses the point, because the doctrine of *functus officio* does not even come into play until the arbitrator issues something purporting to be a "final" award. Given the occasional alternatives of issuing a final award on an incomplete record or of making no award at all until some subsidiary issues are resolved, issuance of an interim award is not only ethical but also wise. Once an arbitrator has rendered an interim award, nothing in Section 6.D.1 prohibits its completion.[5]

Second, there is the problem of correcting obvious errors, for instance, typographical errors involving dates or computational errors involving back pay. Some might find that any change in the written award violates *functus officio*, but it is more accurate to view these corrections as mechanical ones intended to make sure that the writing corresponds with the arbitrator's intention: they do not *change* the award, but merely assure its accurate expression. Moreover, Section 9 of the Uniform Arbitration Act expressly permits the arbitrator to make these sorts of corrections,[6] so an arbitrator in a case governed by the Uniform Act may interpret the agreement as incorporating that authority.

Third, there is the matter of remand by a court or administrative agency. As Rehmus mentions, courts and the Federal Labor Relations Authority are increasingly likely to bounce awards back to arbitrators for clarification rather than undertake the job themselves.[7] If the court or Authority does so in the smoothest

---

[5]Partial awards may run into Sec. 6.C.1's direction that the award be "definite, certain, and concise as possible," but the two weasel words at the end of that quote leave the arbitrator a lot of room.

[6]Section 9 reads as follows:

Section 9. (Change of Award by Arbitrators.) On application of a party or, if an application to the court is pending under Sections 11, 12 or 13, on submission to the arbitrators by the court under such conditions as the court may order, the arbitrators may modify or correct the award upon the grounds stated in paragraphs (1) and (3) of subdivision (a) of Section 13. . . .

The referenced paragraphs of Section 13(a) are these:

(1) There was an evident miscalculation of figures or an evident mistake in the description of any person, thing or property referred to in the award.

(3) The award is imperfect in a matter of form, not affecting the merits of the controversy.

[7]There is ample statutory authority for such remands, including Sec. 9 of the Uniform Arbitration Act, Sec. 10 of the United States Arbitration Act, 9 U.S.C. Sec. 10 (1982), and Sec. 301 of the Labor-Management Relations Act, 29 U.S.C. Sec. 185 (1982).

possible way, by ordering *the parties* to resubmit the case to the arbitrator, there is no ethical problem because the arbitrator then has the consent of both parties, although the "consent" of one of the two might exist only because of the court's order.[8]

If the court or Authority purports to remand the case directly to the arbitrator, there is indeed an ethical problem. Most arbitrators would have little difficulty in resolving that problem, however, even assuming they perceived it. They might assume that the contract implicitly incorporated the relevant law, or that the statute superseded the contract, or that by returning to the arbitrator the objecting party waived its claim of *functus officio*. Should the objecting party renew its claim, though, the arbitrator should consider very carefully whether he or she may ethically proceed. Unless the arbitrator was a party to the litigation, the court has no power over him or her, and the court order thus would not trump the Code's prohibition.

Finally, and most disturbingly, there is the problem of a request from a single party for clarification beyond the correction of evident errors. Absent some supervening authority, the arbitrator cannot ethically grant this request. This is what I term the "hard core" of *functus officio*. To act on such a request would violate Section 6.D.1 of the Code as blatantly as one could imagine.

But what if there is some arguable supervening authority? For example, Section 9 of the Uniform Arbitration Act provides: "On application of *a party* . . . the arbitrators may modify or correct the award . . . for the purpose of clarifying the award" (emphasis added). Before acting on that authority, the arbitrator should be very sure the statute applies to the case. South Carolina's version of the Uniform Arbitration Act, for example, expressly excludes "arbitration agreements between employers and employees or between their respective representatives unless the agreement provides that this chapter shall apply. . . ."[9]

If arbitrators find that the statute does apply, they may conclude that a contract negotiated against that legal background

---

[8]This may have been the situation in the most egregious case cited by Rehmus, *New York Bus Tours v. Kheel*, 864 F.2d 9, 130 LRRM 2277 (2d Cir. 1988). Although the arbitrator was a named defendant, he did not appear in the appeal. The real dispute was between the two parties, and the court's order directing the district court to "remand to the arbitrator" might be an infelicitous way of expressing its direction to the parties themselves.

[9]S.C. Code Sec. 15-48-10(b)(2) (1988 Cumulative Supplement).

impliedly incorporates the statute, but that is a lawyer's argument, not an arbitrator's. It treads very close to the borderline of conduct permitted by the Code. The prudent arbitrator, trying to avoid brinkmanship, might reasonably decline to exercise jurisdiction without joint consent, even if the law would permit a clarification. The statute may make lawful an arbitrator's clarification on the request of a single party, without necessarily making it ethical.

Perhaps my reservation is too demanding. One could easily present a paper on any of these issues, and authors are free to choose their own battleground. Within his chosen field, Rehmus has superbly illuminated the problem and has given us solid and sensible guidance on how to resolve it. For that his hearers and later readers owe him thanks.

FRANCIS X. QUINN*

There can be no argument that an arbitrator who retains jurisdiction solely to make more money is unethical. While Charles Rehmus' parenetic analysis of postaward arbitral discretion makes use of past codes to accuse, condemn, and urge repentance, he is precisely on target when he condemns "grasping for cases." The record indicates that more and more arbitrators show their bad manners and bad ethics in "extending their boarding-house reach."

The Code of Professional Conduct for Arbitrators of Labor-Management Disputes can be used to praise, advise, implore, and encourage.[1] However, such parenesis will succeed only if genuine consensus exists about what is right and wrong, about what is ethical and what is not.

The Code of Professional Conduct for Arbitrators presents a fundamental problem. The Code seems interesting and relevant when it abandons the ephemeral realm of theory and abstract speculation and gets down to practical questions, such as those raised by Rehmus. However, if we treat the questions of postaward discretion as something entirely new, novel, or newfangled, we may lose the best way of finding the answers.

---

*Member, National Academy of Arbitrators, Tulsa, Oklahoma and Philadelphia, Pennsylvania.
    [1]*Code of Professional Responsibility for Arbitrators of Labor-Management Disputes*, National Academy of Arbitrators, American Arbitration Association, and Federal Mediation and Conciliation Service, 1974.

Rehmus reported the public criticism of versions of *functus officio*. Peter Seitz, of happy memory, summed it up well when he said, "When the record is incomplete, justice and fairness require no final decision be made until all the facts are known."[2]

The founding fathers of this Academy regularly affirmed that, although each case must be viewed together with all its unique circumstances and from the view or intention of the presiding arbitrator, there are principles of ethics; there are norms of behavior; there are responsibilities to the profession, to the parties, and to the administrative agencies. Listen to the minutes of our very first meeting in 1947, when there were only two committees: one for membership, and the other called the "Ethics Committee."

> In truth the arbitration process is capable of infinite variety and no code of ethics or standards should be drawn so narrowly as to inhibit the possibility of varying the process to fit the present needs and desires of the parties and of the public. . . .
> In summary, we are agreed on certain basic canons of ethics for arbitrators embodying concepts of decency, integrity, and fair play.[3]

Decency, integrity, and fairness became the recurring theme in 1952 and 1953, and in the eight drafts of the Code that led to our present qualifications of honesty, integrity, impartiality, and general competence.

In 42 years there have been 20 opinions issued by the Ethics Committee, now known as the Committee on Professional Responsibility and Grievances. You are familiar with the topics: no advertising, full disclosure, rules concerning the publication of awards, the use of interns, decency, integrity, and honesty.[4] The science of ethics also speaks to us.

As one reads the Code, one has to remember the distinctions made in Ethics Course 101. There is a difference between law and ethics, between the law and the Code of Professional Responsibility. One hopes they are in accord. Ethics and the Code demand more than the law. And if perchance they are not

---

[2]*Problems of the Finality of Awards or Functus Officio and All That in Labor Arbitration,* in Labor Arbitration: Perspectives and Problems, Proceedings of the 17th Annual Meeting, National Academy of Arbitrators, ed. Mark L. Kahn (Washington: BNA Books, 1964).

[3]McKelvey, *Ethics Then and Now: A Comparison of Ethical Practices,* in Arbitration 1985: Law and Practice, Proceedings of the 38th Annual Meeting, National Academy of Arbitrators, ed. Walter J. Gershenfeld (Washington: BNA Books, 1985).

[4]*Opinions 1–19.* National Academy of Arbitrators Committee on Professional Responsibility and Grievances, 1989.

in accord, Ethics 201 reminds us of the rights and duties of conscience.

Ethics is interested in doing the good, seeking justice and equity. If you studied Aristotle carefully, you know that he wrote a treatise on arbitration and ethics. In that treatise he affirmed the principle of *epieikeia*, or equity. Ethicists ever since have been quoting Aristotle, affirming that we are rational animals, and *epieikeia*, or equity, is the principle that looks to the meaning of the law giver, or code author.

> Equity makes allowance for human weakness, looking not to the law but to the meaning of the law giver, not to the act but to the intention, not to the part but to the whole, not to what a person is at the moment, but to what he is as a rule. Equity remembers benefits received rather than benefits conferred; it is patient under justice, it is readier to appeal to reason than force, to arbitration than to law. For the arbitrator looks to what is equitable, whereas the judge sees only the law; indeed arbitration was devised for no other words than to secure the triumph of equity.[5]

Ethics 301 affirms the fundamental reasonableness of *epieikeia*; namely, no code of professional conduct can foresee all circumstances. The drafters of the Code in their eight versions presumed to address ordinary contingencies. *Epieikeia* attempts to interpret the mind and will of those who drafted the Code. Indeed, Rehmus is on strong ground when he announces that, "no clarification or interpretation of an award is permissible without the consent of both parties." That's what Part 6.D.1 says. *Epieikeia* affirms that if a situation arises wherein the observance of that canon would be hurtful, it should not be observed. For example, can or should an arbitrator correct evident clerical mistakes or computational errors in an award upon request by one party or on the arbitrator's own initiative? You know what Part 6.D.1 of the Code says: "No clarification of an award is permissible without the consent of the parties."

Suppose an arbitrator awards back pay to some employees as remedy for failure to assign them to particular overtime work and rejects the claim of certain other named employees. After the award issues, the union informs the arbitrator that the award mistakenly identifies one of the employees entitled to back pay and that the amount of back pay awarded to another employee

---

[5]Aristotle, *Nicomachean Ethics*, in The Works of Aristotle, ed. W.D. Ross (Oxford, Clarendon Press, 1962), Book VI, Ch. 3.

was incorrect due to an arithmetic miscalculation by the arbitrator. In both instances the cited errors are evident from the undisputed facts. The union asks for a corrected award. The company says the award is final and binding, and does not consent to the arbitrator's issuing a corrected award.

In these circumstances, correction of the identity of one of the employees entitled to back pay and of the arithmetic error in calculation, does not constitute a clarification or interpretation within the meaning of Part 6.D.1. Where obvious clerical or computational mistakes have been made, they should be subject to correction. Rectifying the arbitrator's carelessness in identifying grievants, making arithmetic calculations, or proofreading, are not clarifications or interpretations. To permit such obvious errors to be binding on the parties would impose unfair burdens and would be detrimental to the arbitration process and deleterious to honesty, integrity, fairness, and impartiality. Of course, the arbitrator should ensure each party the right to be heard before any such correction is made.[6]

Functus officio does not bar correction of clerical mistakes or obvious computational errors. Rehmus reminds us that the Academy has an inhibition on retention, but that we are not really *functus officio* until our job is finished. His conditions of short retention, not more than 90 days with specific purpose spelled out, are admirable. His suggestion to accept no further remuneration is admirable, but service pro bono is hardly necessary. Sometimes a financial burden is conducive to getting the parties to finish the job. He is true to the Academy tradition in warning us about the ethical cautionary limitations embodied in the Code.

When the final draft of the Code of Professional Conduct was adopted, the Academy was fortunate to have authors well experienced in arbitration practice and in ethical precepts. Names like William Simkin and Ralph Seward were and are synonymous with honesty, integrity, and good judgment. Past chairmen of the Ethics Committee, Richard Mittenthal, Alexander Porter, Howard Cole, William Fallon and Arthur Stark, demonstrate the continuing premium the Academy places on fairness, equity, and prudence.[7] With the Academy's burgeon-

---

[6]*Opinion No. 20*. National Academy of Arbitrators Committee on Professional Responsibility and Grievances, 1989.

[7]*Dissemination and Enforcement of the Code of Ethics*, in Arbitration 1988: Emerging Issues for the 1990s, Proceedings of the 41st Annual Meeting, National Academy of Arbitrators, ed. Gladys W. Gruenberg (Washington: BNA Books, 1989).

ing membership, now nearly 700 members, and the *Directory of U.S. Labor Arbitrators* reflecting nearly four times that number, we need more reflection on the Code and arbitral discretion with the same depth and light that Rehmus has given.

May I remind you that Aristotle concluded his long discussion of the arbitrator and ethics by equating ethics with the inside of the nest. Our Code reminds us of the principles with which our ethical nest is built. It is catastrophic if we dirty our own nest.[8]

We are impartials whose profession demands integrity, impartiality, and general competence. Happily, in the good judgment you exercise in procedural matters and in substantive decisions, you usually meet those qualifications. Don't maintain jurisdiction unless it is necessary. You're the best judge of that.

---

[8]Kagel, *Legalism—and Some Comments on Illegalisms—in Arbitration*, in Arbitration 1985: Law and Practice, Proceedings of the 38th Annual Meeting, National Academy of Arbitrators, ed. Walter J. Gershenfeld (Washington: BNA Books, 1985).

CHAPTER 7

OTHER ARBITRAL ISSUES

I. THE PREDICTABILITY OF GRIEVANCE ARBITRATION AWARDS: DOES ARBITRATOR EXPERIENCE MATTER?

PERRY A. ZIRKEL*
ROBERT J. THORNTON**

There is a considerable body of evidence showing that labor and management exhibit a strong preference for experienced, rather than inexperienced, arbitrators in grievance disputes. At the same time, however, some studies have shown that arbitration awards do not seem to vary according to the experience of the arbitrators.

The purpose of this study is to investigate more deeply the nature of the preference given to experience as a factor in arbitrator selection. Specifically, we seek to ascertain whether there are differences in the awards expected by labor and management in cases decided by inexperienced arbitrators and, if so, in what ways these awards are expected to differ from those handed down by experienced arbitrators. For the purpose of analyzing these questions, we used a sample of 232 labor and management representatives and asked them to predict the arbitrators' awards for a number of common arbitral cases. With respect to the sample size and the number of cases analyzed, we believe that this study is the largest undertaken on the subject.

Prior Research

As noted above, studies of the acceptability of arbitrators to labor and management have consistently found that previous

---

*Member, National Academy of Arbitrators; University Professor of Education and Law, Lehigh University, Bethlehem, Pennsylvania.
**Professor of Economics, Lehigh University, Bethlehem, Pennsylvania.
The authors wish to thank Mario Bognanno, Ed Pereles, and Vern Hauck for some of the suggestions in the Conclusion section.

experience is a significant factor in arbitrator selection. In a series of 35 interviews in 1967, Eaton discovered a general preference among the parties for "expert" arbitrators.[1] Similarly, based on a sample of 34 union and management representatives in 1971, King found that both sides expressed more favorable attitudes toward experienced arbitrators than toward their inexperienced counterparts.[2] The resistance to inexperienced arbitrators was much higher among the management representatives, however.

In a multiple regression analysis, Primeaux and Brannen found that the number of cases which their sample of 104 arbitrators handled in a given period was strongly and significantly related to their past experience—the implication again being that labor and management exhibit a marked preference for experienced arbitrators.[3] On the basis of interviews with 26 labor and management representatives, Rezler and Petersen discovered that experience was the most highly rated criterion considered in the selection of arbitrators.[4] Briggs and Anderson's survey of arbitrators found that visibility characteristics, such as number of awards published, were significantly related to acceptability, as measured by current caseload.[5]

From a subsequent survey of 36 labor and management representatives, Lawson also deduced that arbitral experience was an important factor in the arbitral selection process.[6] More recently, Nelson surveyed a group of 74 labor and management representatives and found that arbitrator experience received the highest ranking among the criteria used to select arbitrators.[7] The preference for experience was particularly strong within the management group. Most recently, the role of arbitral experience in the selection process was put in question by Berkeley's study, but his results are not presented fully enough to make an informed determination.[8]

---

[1]Eaton, *Labor Arbitration in the San Francisco Area*, 48 LA 1381 (1967).
[2]King, *Management and Union Attitudes Affecting the Employment of Inexperienced Labor Arbitrators*, 48 Lab. L.J. 23 (1971).
[3]Primaux & Brannen, *Why Few Arbitrators Are Deemed Acceptable*, 98 Monthly Lab. Rev. 27 (1975).
[4]Rezler & Petersen, *Strategies of Arbitrator Selection*, 70 LA 1307 (1978).
[5]Briggs & Anderson, *An Empirical Investigation of Arbitrator Acceptability*, 19 Indus. Rel. 163 (1980).
[6]Lawson, *Arbitrator Acceptability: Factors Affecting Selection*, 36 Arb. J. 22 (1981).
[7]Nelson, *The Selection of Arbitrators*, 37 Lab. L.J. 703 (1986).
[8]Berkeley, *Arbitrators and Advocates: The Consumers Report*, in Arbitration 1988: Emerging Issues for the 1990s, Proceedings of the 41st Annual Meeting, National Academy of Arbitrators, ed. Gladys W. Gruenberg (Washington: BNA Books 1989), 300–301. He

Why does there exist such a strong preference for experienced arbitrators? The evidence here is mixed, but King observed that the decisions of inexperienced arbitrators were often considered to be "unpredictable."[9] Further, his observation that management representatives were particularly resistant to inexperienced arbitrators[10] was borne out by Nelson's finding that inexperienced arbitrators were more likely to reinstate the grievant, at least in the single hypothetical discharge case which he tested on his sample of arbitrators.[11] Primeaux and Brannen have argued that management and labor perceive experienced arbitrators as more likely to be "fair" in their awards.[12] Whatever the reasons, the preference for experience exists and is quite strong.

But does arbitrator experience really make a difference in actual award outcomes? Empirical research on this question has put the efficacy of the experience criterion somewhat in doubt. For example, in his early study of discharge cases, Teele noted that "busy" and "less busy" arbitrators were remarkably similar in terms of the bases for their awards.[13] In his widely cited "experiment" in 1965, Fleming observed that 75 percent of his law students came to the same decisions as experienced arbitrators, a finding which led Fleming to conclude that experience in arbitration does not necessarily make a difference in the award granted.[14] In another interesting experiment, Westerkamp and Miller found that attorneys could not distinguish the decisions of experienced arbitrators from those of the inexperienced.[15] More recently, Heneman and Sandver found that experience-related variables, such as membership in the National Academy of Arbitrators and previous experience as a labor or management employee, were not significantly related to

---

found that prearbitration background was the most important characteristic and that NAA membership was relatively unimportant. However, he did not report the specific results for most of the variables, including number of awards issued.

Although our focus is grievance arbitration, similar findings have been obtained in studies of interest arbitration. *See, e.g.,* Bloom & Cavanagh, *An Analysis of the Selection of Arbitrators*, 86 Am. Econ. Rev. 408 (1986).

[9]*Supra* note 2 at 27.

[10]*Id.* at 25–26.

[11]*Supra* note 7 at 707.

[12]*Supra* note 3 at 30.

[13]Teele, *The Thought Processes of the Arbitrator*, 17 Arb. J. 85 (1962).

[14]Fleming, The Labor Arbitration Process (Urbana: Univ. of Ill. Press, 1965), 81. In a second experiment, Fleming found that two attorney assistants without any arbitration experience reached the same result as he, based on the same case materials. *Id.* at 86.

[15]Westerkamp & Miller, *The Acceptability of Inexperienced Arbitrators: An Experiment*, 22 Lab. L.J. 763 (1971).

award outcome.[16] And most recently, Thornton and Zirkel found that the decisions of grievance arbitrators did not seem to be significantly related to the experience of arbitrators.[17]

In the sections that follow, we delve more deeply into the nature of this apparent preference for experience. Given that experienced arbitrators are preferred even though the actual decisions do not appear to be a function of experience, just what are the perceptions of labor and management? Do they expect different awards from experienced versus inexperienced arbitrators? Does management, for example, see inexperienced arbitrators as more inclined to uphold a grievant's case, as Nelson's limited evidence suggests? Or does the preference simply reflect a feeling that the awards of inexperienced arbitrators tend to be more "unpredictable"? Finally, do there seem to be differences between labor and management in their perceptions of either the inclinations or the unpredictability of inexperienced arbitrators?

Method

For the purpose of analyzing the questions above, the authors gathered a random sample of 200 labor and 200 management representatives from the active national records of the American Arbitration Association. Each of the representatives was sent a questionnaire and was asked to predict the arbitrator's award for a number of common arbitral cases.

The survey instrument provided two grievance arbitration scenarios, each with two additional factual variations.[18] Each scenario was approximately 300 words in length and consisted of the facts of an actual case. The two factual variations of each scenario were constructed by adding two material facts—one in the grievant's favor and one in the company's favor.

The first scenario was a just cause dismissal case based on excessive absenteeism. The company had a no-fault attendance

---

[16]Heneman & Sandver, *Arbitrators' Background and Behavior*, 4 J. Lab. Res. 115 (1983).
[17]Thornton & Zirkel, *The Consistency and Predictability of Grievance Arbitration Awards*, 43 Indus. & Lab. Rel. Rev. 294 (Jan. 1990).
Further, providing peripheral support was a study reporting that members of the NAA tended to be notably more experienced than nonmembers but which found no evidence that their awards would differ from those of nonmembers. Sprehe & Small, *Members and Nonmembers of the National Academy of Arbitrators: Do They Differ?* 39 Arb. J. 25 (1984).
[18]The survey instrument contained the same six case situations used in the companion study by Thornton & Zirkel, *supra* note 17.

policy that had been only recently enforced, resulting in the grievant being progressively disciplined. After several months of satisfactory attendance, the grievant called in sick. However, he was reportedly seen at a local bar, resulting in his termination. Based on Scott and Taylor's study,[19] the following two alternative factual variations of the first scenario were then presented:

- the fact that the company had not conducted an impartial investigation prior to the employee's dismissal;
- the fact that the company had been consistently strict for the past several years in enforcing its attendance policy.

The second scenario was a contract interpretation case based on modified seniority. The grievant had applied for a promotion to a posted position, but an outside applicant with considerably more experience and training was selected for the job. The contract put a priority on company seniority for applicants deemed to be qualified by a management committee and was ambiguous as to whether a trial period was required. Based on the work of Elkouri and Elkouri,[20] the two alternative factual variations for this scenario were:

- the fact that the contract contained a nondiscrimination clause and the grievant was a member of a minority group;
- the fact that the contract clearly required a trial period for qualified applicants.

All in all, the two scenarios, each with two factual variations, resulted in a total of six cases for the survey instrument.

The 200 labor representatives and 200 management representatives to whom the instrument was sent were divided beforehand into two equal subsamples. The members of one subsample were asked to predict the awards which they would expect for each of the above six cases from a "relatively experienced" arbitrator. "Relatively experienced" was defined to characterize "an arbitrator who had decided at least 20 cases this past year and at least 100 cases in his/her career." This definition was largely based on the previous research discussed in the prior section. The members of the other subsample were asked to predict the awards which they would expect for each of the six

---

[19]Scott & Taylor, *An Analysis of Absenteeism Cases Taken to Arbitration: 1975–1981*, 38 Arb. J. 61 (1983).
[20]Elkouri & Elkouri, How Arbitration Works, 4th ed. (Washington: BNA Books, 1985), 625–628 and 643–645.

cases from a "relatively inexperienced" arbitrator, with "relatively inexperienced" having the obverse definition.

After first being field tested on nine respected members of the labor-management community, the survey instrument was mailed to the 200 labor and 200 management representatives. The instrument was accompanied by an American Arbitration Association cover letter that referred to the purpose of the study as "part of our efforts to understand and improve the profession of arbitration." This unobtrusiveness, along with an accompanying promise of confidentiality, was provided to minimize effects relating to social desirability. Two follow-up mailings were sent to initial nonrespondents. Usable responses were obtained from 232 (58 percent) of those to whom the instrument was sent—108 from the labor group and 124 from the management group.

Results and Discussion

Table 1 presents information on the distributions of the expected awards for the full sample of 232 respondents. Of the sample, 109 respondents had been presented with the "inexperienced arbitrator" assumption, and 123 with the "experienced arbitrator" assumption. The table is broken down in the following fashion. The columns represent the six case variations discussed earlier—the two principal scenarios and the two factual variations of each scenario. The rows contain the distribution of awards which the respondents predicted would be made by the arbitrator. The three possibilities for the awards were: 1) expect grievance to be upheld, 2) expect grievance to be partially upheld and partially denied (split award), and 3) expect grievance to be denied. Each major row grouping thus compares the distribution of awards expected from an inexperienced arbitrator versus the distribution of awards expected from an experienced arbitrator. For example, in the original grievance involving just cause dismissal, 12.0 percent of those respondents asked to predict how an inexperienced arbitrator would rule expected the grievance to be upheld, while only 6.5 percent of those respondents predicting how an experienced arbitrator would rule expected the grievance to be upheld. The layout of the table makes it easy to compare the expected awards for the six cases by assumed arbitrator experience level.

First of all, it can be seen from Table 1 that there is a fairly substantial degree of variability—i.e., unpredictability—in the

Table 1
Distribution of Awards Expected from Inexperienced Versus Experienced Arbitrators, Full Sample (n = 232)*

	Original Just Cause Scenario	No-Impartial-Investigation Variant	Strict Adherence-to-Policy Variant	Original Contract-Interpretation Scenario	Minority-Group Variant	Trial Period Variant
Percentage Expecting Grievance to be Upheld by:						
Inexperienced Arbitrator	12.0	23.9	12.8	55.1	57.8	69.7
Experienced Arbitrator	6.5	22.0	12.2	52.0	54.5	78.1
Percentage Expecting Split Award from:						
Inexperienced Arbitrator	63.9	55.0	28.4	11.9	12.8	11.0
Experienced Arbitrator	68.3	55.3	23.6	8.1	8.9	7.3
Percentage Expecting Grievance to be Denied by:						
Inexperienced Arbitrator	24.1	21.1	58.7	33.0	29.4	11.3
Experienced Arbitrator	25.2	22.8	64.2	39.8	36.6	14.6
	$x^2 = 2.14$ ($p = 0.34$)	$x^2 = 0.16$ ($p = 0.92$)	$x^2 = 0.83$ ($p = 0.66$)	$x^2 = 1.67$ ($p = 0.43$)	$x^2 = 1.84$ ($p = 0.40$)	$x^2 = 2.15$ ($p = 0.34$)

*The values in the table in any one column represent the percentages of respondents in the respective assumed arbitrator-experience categories expecting the various award outcomes.

awards expected for both assumed levels of experience. Since the data are nominal data, conventional measures of dispersion (such as the standard deviation) are inappropriate. However, a simple, yet satisfactory, indicator of the degree of dispersion is the percentage of responses differing from the modal response. In each of the six cases, an award other than the modal award was expected by from 25 to 50 percent of the respondents. In other words, the arbitral awards for these cases exhibit a large element of unpredictability. But the important point here is that the degree of unpredictability of the awards is unrelated to the assumed experience level of the arbitrator. On average, about 40 percent of the respondents expected an award other than the modal award to be given by an unexperienced arbitrator, while about 38 percent expected an award other than the modal award from an experienced arbitrator. King's claim[21] that experienced arbitrators are preferred because their decisions are more "predictable" is not strongly supported by the evidence which we see here.

However, it can be inferred from the first four rows of the table that the inexperienced arbitrator was perceived as more likely either to uphold the grievance or to split the award than the experienced arbitrator. This was so for five of the six cases, the sole exception being the trial period variant of the contract interpretation case. This finding, of course, is consistent with that of Nelson,[22] who saw inexperienced arbitrators as more likely to reinstate the grievant. However, it should be noted that the differences are in most cases fairly small. And as the X^2 values at the bottom of each column indicate, the award distributions do not differ significantly by assumed experience at conventional significance levels.

We next analyzed the expected award distributions separately for the labor and the management representatives. This was done to see whether any of the differences in the expected awards could be attributed to the orientation of the respondents. In Table 2, we have listed the award distributions predicted by the labor representatives. As in the case of the full sample, there is a considerable degree of variability in the awards expected, with again from 25 to 50 percent of the respondents expecting an award other than the modal award. However, the awards

---

[21]*Supra* note 9.
[22]*Supra* note 11.

Table 2

Distribution of Awards Expected from Inexperienced Versus Experienced Arbitrators, Labor Representatives Only (n = 108)*

	Original Just Cause Scenario	No-Impartial-Investigation Variant	Strict Adherence-to-Policy Variant	Original Contract-Interpretation Scenario	Minority-Group Variant	Trial Period Variant
Percentage Expecting Grievance to be Upheld by:						
Inexperienced Arbitrator	10.0	28.0	8.0	60.0	66.0	76.0
Experienced Arbitrator	12.1	36.2	8.6	62.1	65.5	84.5
Percentage Expecting Split Award from:						
Inexperienced Arbitrator	68.0	54.0	28.0	16.0	16.0	10.0
Experienced Arbitrator	63.8	44.8	29.3	3.4	5.2	8.6
Percentage Expecting Grievance to be Denied by:						
Inexperienced Arbitrator	22.0	18.0	64.0	24.0	18.0	14.0
Experienced Arbitrator	24.1	19.0	62.1	34.5	29.3	6.9
	$x^2 = 0.23$ ($p = 0.89$)	$x^2 = 1.03$ ($p = 0.60$)	$x^2 = 0.04$ ($p = 0.98$)	$x^2 = 5.58$ ($p = 0.06$)	$x^2 = 4.52$ ($p = 0.10$)	$x^2 = 1.63$ ($p = 0.44$)

*The values in the table in any one column represent the percentages of respondents in the respective assumed arbitrator-experience categories expecting the various award outcomes.

expected from an inexperienced arbitrator were no more "unpredictable" than those expected from an experienced arbitrator.

Interestingly, as an examination of the table will show, there is no strong indication of a perceived "leaning" of experienced arbitrators toward upholding the grievance. It is true that in five of the six cases the labor representatives expected an experienced arbitrator to be more likely to uphold the grievance than an inexperienced arbitrator. Conversely, in four of the six cases the labor representatives also expected a slightly higher percentage of experienced arbitrators to deny the grievance. Generally the difference was not substantial, however; and in most cases again the X^2 values indicate that the expected award distributions do not differ significantly by assumed experience level.

Table 3 shows the award distributions expected by the subsample of management representatives. Here the results are particularly interesting. First, the same substantial degree of award unpredictability is evident on the part of management. However, in five of the six cases the management respondents expected the inexperienced arbitrator to be more likely to uphold the grievance than the experienced arbitrator. In several cases (particularly the original just cause scenario) the difference is quite substantial. Conversely, in five of the six cases the experienced arbitrator was seen by management representatives as more likely to deny the grievance. However, only once do the distributions of expected awards differ significantly by assumed experience level (p = .03 for the original just cause scenario).

Taken together, Tables 2 and 3 reveal that the expectations of labor and management with respect to arbitral awards are somewhat dissimilar. The labor representatives perceived only limited differences between experienced and inexperienced arbitrators with respect to the tendency to uphold or deny a grievance. However, management representatives saw experienced arbitrators as less likely to uphold a grievance and more likely to deny it. Although the differences are for the most part not statistically significant, the pattern that shows management representatives expecting a more favorable award from experienced arbitrators for most of the cases is still striking. Since arbitration awards do not in fact seem to vary according to the experience of the arbitrators, our results suggest that the preference for experience may be due to a mistaken perception, at least on the part of management. In any case, our findings square

Table 3

Distribution of Awards Expected from Inexperienced Versus Experienced Arbitrators,[1] Management Representatives Only (n = 124)

	Original Just Cause Scenario	No-Impartial-Investigation Variant	Strict Adherence-to-Policy Variant	Original Contract-Interpretation Scenario	Minority-Group Variant	Trial Period Variant
Percentage Expecting Grievance to be Upheld by:						
Inexperienced Arbitrator	13.8	20.3	17.0	50.9	50.9	66.4
Experienced Arbitrator	1.5	9.2	15.4	43.1	44.6	72.3
Percentage Expecting Split Award from:						
Inexperienced Arbitrator	60.3	55.9	28.8	8.5	10.2	11.9
Experienced Arbitrator	72.3	64.6	18.5	12.3	12.3	6.2
Percentage Expecting Grievance to be Denied by:						
Inexperienced Arbitrator	25.9	23.7	54.2	40.7	39.0	23.7
Experienced Arbitrator	26.2	26.2	66.2	44.6	43.1	21.5
	$x^2 = 6.95$	$x^2 = 3.09$	$x^2 = 2.19$	$x^2 = 0.95$	$x^2 = 0.50$	$x^2 = 1.48$
	$(p = 0.03)$	$(p = 0.21)$	$(p = 0.34)$	$(p = 0.62)$	$(p = 0.78)$	$(p = 0.48)$

[1]The values in the table in any one column represent the percentages of respondents in the respective assumed arbitrator-experience categories expecting the various award outcomes.

nicely with King's earlier observation[23] that the resistance to inexperienced arbitrators was higher among management than among union representatives. Our findings also at least partially overlap with those of Nelson, who found that inexperienced arbitrators are more likely to uphold the grievant's case.[24]

Conclusion

With regard to awards in grievance arbitration, the experience factor may be largely a myth. Both labor and management have a pronounced preference for experienced arbitrators. Nevertheless, other research reveals that the parties cannot distinguish between the awards of experienced arbitrators and those of inexperienced arbitrators. More importantly, experience does not seem to be significantly related to arbitral outcomes.

Although generally improving notably upon previous research, the design of the present study has limitations. Most involve tradeoffs with the need for economy and variety in the presentation of the case situations. For example, the abbreviated scenarios provide the distilled facts, but not the full flavor of "real world" cases. Similarly, the factual variations may have produced a carryover effect on the responses to the extent that respondents may have thought, based on the alternating structure, that certain responses were expected.

The line drawn between arbitral experience and inexperience, although generally an accepted standard, was a limited definition; more numerous categories might have produced more robust results. Moreover, including possible interaction variables, such as the previous labor-management experience of the arbitrator and the extent of prior arbitral selection experience of the respondents, would have been useful. Similarly, asking the respondents for estimated indices of the closeness of the case and the confidence of the prediction would have increased the richness of the results. Finally, the effect of the unobtrusive technique, where the respondents did not readily know that the study was comparing expectations for inexperienced versus experienced arbitrators, is subject to speculation.

---

[23]*Supra* note 10.
[24]*Supra* note 11.

Nevertheless, the present study adds to the array of empirical evidence against the preference for arbitral experience by finding substantial variability in award expectations, a variability that was not significantly linked to the experience of the arbitrator. Although there was some tendency for management to expect experienced arbitrators to be more likely to rule in its favor, this finding was outweighed by the general lack of statistically significant differences between the expected awards of inexperienced versus those of experienced arbitrators.

Perhaps the experience factor is important in other ways than the actual or expected outcome of the case. It may be that experienced arbitrators are more skillful in conducting the hearing, although Sprehe and Small's study revealed only limited differences between members and nonmembers of NAA with respect to the conduct of the hearing.[25] It may be that experienced arbitrators are more efficient than inexperienced arbitrators, but Bognanno and Smith's survey results do not show overall economic advantages for using nonexperienced arbitrators.[26] It may be that experienced arbitrators are more coherent and cogent in their opinion writing, although Westerkamp and Miller's exploratory study seems to suggest otherwise.[27] It may be that the thought processes of experienced arbitrators are more predictable, but the studies to date[28] have not included comparisons based on experience, and the thought process is secondary to the persuasiveness and accuracy of the award.

Perhaps the most likely explanation is that experience is important because the parties and their clients/constituencies think it is important. The ultimate cornerstone is selection of an individual arbitrator, based on the interaction of various factors including, but not at all limited to, arbitral experience. As long as the persons doing the selecting believe that experienced arbitrators are more predictable and otherwise preferable (e.g., politically defensible), experience as an arbitrator will be impor-

---

[25]Sprehe & Small, *supra* note 17.

[26]Bognanno & Smith, *Demographic and Professional Characteristics of Arbitrators in North America*, in Arbitration 1988: Emerging Issues for the 1990s, Proceedings of the 41st Annual Meeting, ed. Gladys W. Gruenberg (Washington: BNA Books, 1989), 284.

[27]*Supra* note 15.

[28]*See, e.g.*, Hauck & South, *Arbitrating Discrimination Grievances: An Empirical Model for Decision Standards*, in Proceedings of the 39th Annual Meeting, Industrial Relations Research Association, ed. Barbara D. Dennis (Madison, Wis.: IRRA, 1987) (also appearing in 16 Pol'y Stud. 511 (1988)); Cain & Stahl, *Modeling the Policies of Several Labor Arbitrators*, 40 Acad. Mgmt. J. 140 (1983).

tant, whether or not it is justifiable on an objective basis. The results of this study and the authors' earlier, companion study challenge the "experience myth" in relation to actual and expected arbitration outcomes. Is this preference a bias? Is there a bias against finding out?

II. REMEDIES, TROUBLED EMPLOYEES, AND THE ARBITRATOR'S ROLE

MARVIN F. HILL, JR.*
ANTHONY V. SINICROPI**

Background: The "Just Cause" Standard

The standard of review for most, if not all, discharges is that of "just cause." The term "just cause" is generally held to be synonymous with "cause," "proper cause," or "reasonable cause." While there is no uniform definition of just cause, a sampling of arbitral opinion indicates some basic notion of fundamental fairness as the underlying criterion for evaluating dismissals.

Arbitrator William Belshaw, in *Hiram Walker & Sons, Inc.*,[1] sustained the dismissal of a fork lift operator—a capable, intelligent, long-term employee (25 years)—who was found to be under the influence while on the job. Belshaw noted that "he [the grievant] blew the deal not once but twice [the grievant had one other alcohol-related incident], and, despite that, made a really insufficient effort to either solve the problem or save his job (the same thing)." What is particularly instructive is the arbitrator's analysis and approach in ruling as he did. Addressing the concept of just cause, Belshaw had this to say:

> There are many definitions of "just cause." All of them, however, sooner or later, get back to some evaluation of industrial punishment in the light of mores, those behavioral rules that structure a society, like it or not. And it is a very individual process, in arbitration, at least, because the determiner is, indeed, both single and final.

---

*Member, National Academy of Arbitrators; Professor of Industrial Relations, Northern Illinois University, DeKalb, Illinois.
**Member, National Academy of Arbitrators; John F. Murray Professor of Industrial Relations, University of Iowa, Iowa City, Iowa. This paper is a version of a paper presented at the Academy's Continuing Education Conference in Milwaukee, Wisconsin, October 30, 1988.
[1]75 LA 899, 900 (Belshaw, 1980).

In years of exposure and study and thought, both to and of the bad as well as the good, some conclusions have inevitably emerged, and one of them is a definition of what "just cause" probably is, for here and now. It seems to be that cause which, to a presumably-reasonable determiner (is there one here?), appears to be (not necessarily is), fair and reasonable, when all of the applicable facts and circumstances are considered, and are viewed in the light of the ethic of the time and place. That's a mouthful, in words, but it really is only, bottom-line, another expression of the now-common expression, "fair shake."

In sustaining the discharge the arbitrator stated in a footnote that "there has been no ignoring of the modest, single-letter showing of the grievant's rehabiliatory efforts. They seemed both little and late."

Perhaps the most often-quoted statement of the criteria used by advocates and arbitrators is in the form of a series of questions provided by Arbitrator Carroll Daugherty.[2] [Editor's note: Daugherty's Seven Tests are enumerated in the Addendum to John Dunsford's presentation in Chapter 3.]

In *Ritchie Industries*,[3] Arbitrator Raymond Roberts outlined the usual standards for nondisciplinary discharge as follows:

1. That the cause or reason for nondisciplinary discharge substantially impairs the employment relationship.
2. That the cause has been chronic or, by its inherent nature, clearly will be so.
3. That there is no reasonable prognosis that the cause will be removed in a reasonable period of time.

The common link in most decisions is this: Any determination of just cause requires two separate considerations: (1) whether the employee is guilty of misconduct, and (2) assuming guilt, whether the discipline imposed is a reasonable penalty under the circumstances of the case. Further, the universal rule in grievance arbitration is that the employer must carry the burden of proof of just cause in a discharge case.

Remedies, Just Cause, and the Troubled Employee

Thomas Miller and Susan Oliver, in a paper presented at the 1989 Annual Meeting of the Academy, query whether

---

[2]*Enterprise Wire Co.*, 46 LA 359, 363–364 (Daugherty, 1966); *Grief Bros. Cooperage Corp.*, 42 LA 555, 558 (Daugherty, 1964).
[3]74 LA 650, 655 (Roberts, 1980).

arbitrators apply traditional concepts of just cause to troubled employees who engage in misconduct or unsatisfactory job performance. They point out that troubled employees argue that they would not have engaged in the misconduct warranting discipline, but for their alcohol or chemical dependency problem. Also, employees maintain that their successful treatment following termination should justify mitigation of the discharge penalty. The authors note that a review of airline arbitration decisions indicates that there is a divergence of opinion among arbitrators as to whether the alcohol or chemical dependent employee who has engaged in misconduct should be subject to the traditional just cause standard. Miller and Oliver, citing Denenberg & Denenberg, *Alcohol and Drugs: Issues in the Workplace*,[4] submit that many arbitrators have adopted three approaches in deciding discharge cases where alcohol or chemical dependency is asserted as a defense:

1. *Traditional Corrective Discipline Model.* Arbitrators using this approach uphold discipline or discharge without regard to an employee's claimed alcoholism or chemical dependency so long as the employer has properly adhered to all pertinent disciplinary requirements.

2. *Therapeutic Model.* Under the therapeutic model, alcoholism or chemical dependency is viewed as an illness warranting opportunities to recover, including leaves of absence and rehabilitation. An employee's subsequent failure to refrain from misconduct or to correct performance deficiencies is not viewed as cause for discipline, but rather as indicating the need for additional treatment.

3. *A Modified Corrective Discipline Model.* This approach takes a middle ground between the traditional corrective discipline model and the therapeutic model. Arbitrators advocating this approach view alcoholism or chemical dependency as an illness, and will routinely allow one "second chance" after there has been some opportunity for rehabilitation. However, should there be a subsequent failure to correct the behavior, the employee will be held fully accountable.

The authors assert that arbitrators adjudicating airline cases appear to limit their approach to either the traditional corrective discipline or the modified corrective discipline models. We submit that arbitrators reach the same result in nonairline cases.

Under what conditions is an arbitrator likely to apply the corrective discipline model to a discharge case involving a "trou-

⁴Miller & Oliver, *Just Cause and the Troubled Employee: Management Viewpoint*, in Arbitration 1988: Emerging Issues for the 1990s, Proceedings of the 41st Annual Meeting, National Academy of Arbitrators, ed. Gladys W. Gruenberg (Washington: BNA Books, 1989), 40–41, citing Denenberg & Denenberg, Alcohol and Drugs: Issues in the Workplace (Washington: BNA Books, 1983), 3.

bled" employee? When a troubled employee is reinstated, does it follow that a conditional remedy will issue? In *Crewe v. United States Office of Personnel Management*,[5] the U.S. court of appeals considered a claim under the Rehabilitation Act of 1973.[6] In discussing alcoholism the court stated:

> At the outset there can be little doubt that alcoholism is a handicap for the purposes of the Act. The Attorney General of the United States has so concluded, 43 Op. Att'y Gen. 12 (1977); the federal agency charged with implementing the Act (the Merit Systems Protection Board) has agreed, *Ruzek v. General Services Administration*, 7 M.S.P.B. 307 (1981); *Rison v. Department of the Navy*, 23 M.S.P.B. 118 (1984). Commentators also agree, Richards, "Handicap Discrimination in Employment: The Rehabilitation Act of 1973", 39 Ark. L. Rev. 1, 9-10 (1985); Comment, "Hidden Handicaps: Protection of Alcoholics, Drug Addicts, and the Mentally Ill Against Employment Discrimination Under the Rehabilitation Act of 1973 and The Wisconsin Fair Employment Act", 1983 Wisc. L. Rev. 725 (1983); and the federal courts have concurred. *Whitloc v. Donovan*, 598 F. Supp. 126, 129, 36 FEP Cases 425 (D.D.C. 1984), aff'd without opinion, 790 F.2d 964, 45 FEP Cases 520 (1986).[7]

Later in the same opinion the court noted:

> In determining whether to hire persons with a prior history of alcohol abuse the federal government has adopted the following policy:
>
> In considering applicants for federal employment who have a history of alcoholism . . . the Office of Personnel Management will make its determination on the basis of whether or not the applicant is a good employment risk. In such cases, the length of time since the last abuse of alcohol . . . is less important than the steps taken by the applicant to obtain treatment of his or her illness through medical care, rehabilitation, and similar actions.[8]

Arbitrators have recognized the potential for successfully overcoming the debilitating effects of alcoholism and other disabilities "subject to cure," even after repeated relapses by the employees. In *Thrifty Drug Stores Co.*,[9] the arbitrator agreed with the union that relapses in the treatment of chronic alcoholism were a common occurrence and that the main problem in alcohol treatment was getting patients to accept that they had a problem. Arbitrator Edward Peters ruled that "the grievant should be given yet another opportunity to demonstrate that he

---

[5]834 F.2d 140, 45 FEP Cases 555 (8th Cir. 1987).
[6]29 U.S.C. §701–794.
[7]*Supra* note 5, 45 FEP Cases at 556.
[8]*Id.* at 557.
[9]56 LA 789, 794 (Peters, 1971).

has managed to acquire an acceptable control over his problem." What is particularly interesting is that the arbitrator did not formulate a conditional remedy of any kind, but simply reinstated the grievant with all contractual benefits, but without back pay. He noted that if the employee still retained the illusion that he could handle one or two drinks, "then the outcome of this arbitration will accomplish no more than to defer for a few weeks or months his inevitable termination."

In *City of Buffalo*,[10] the grievant, an account clerk stenographer and a 15-year employee, was found intoxicated at work and given a leave of absence to be hospitalized, after which she enrolled in Alcoholics Anonymous (AA). She was then discovered drunk at work again and discharged. In reducing the penalty to a two-month suspension, the arbitrator concluded:

> Taking into consideration B--'s employment and her willingness to faithfully attend Alcoholics Anonymous and group therapy with the Alcoholism Clinic, the penalty of discharge is too severe.[11]

In *Chrysler Corp.*,[12] an employee was dismissed for reporting to work under the influence. The record indicated that the grievant had been repeatedly admonished and penalized for alcohol abuse at work. Arbitrator Gabriel Alexander, in overturning the dismissal, credited the grievant's postdischarge rehabilitation and reasoned:

> [T]he evidence shows clearly that since he was discharged, Grievant has done the sort of things that an alcoholic should do. He placed himself under the care of his physician. He joined Alcoholics Anonymous, and has regularly attended its sessions. He has taken help from a church, and from an alcoholic treatment center maintained by the City of Detroit. Representatives of those agencies and his doctor have issued written statements to the effect that he is doing well. No contradictory evidence was submitted on that point. Accordingly, the Chairman concludes that Grievant has been making progress on the road towards control of his addiction.[13]

What is interesting is that the arbitrator rejected the employer's plea that the employee had ample opportunity to reform his conduct before he was dismissed and that, therefore, no mitigating significance should be accorded his subsequent efforts. No conditional remedy was ordered by Alexander

---

[10]59 LA 334 (Rinaldo, 1972).
[11]*Id.* at 337.
[12]40 LA 935 (G. Alexander, 1963).
[13]*Id.* at 936.

although the facts arguably called for one. In all these cases reinstatement was ordered after the employee suffered a relapse.

The significance of an employee's demonstrating a strong desire to rehabilitate which affects the arbitrator's award is seen in *Armstrong Cork Co.*[14] The employee was discharged after his third absence from work because of a drinking problem. The arbitrator ruled that:

> The violation occurred not because of an indifference toward the Company rules but because [the Grievant] was emotionally and physically sick. He testified that he was an alcoholic and this fact must be taken into account in assessing the punishment. . . .
>
> * * *
>
> Since the discharge, the uncontradicted evidence is that B-- not only has joined Alcoholics Anonymous but has regularly attended its meetings and has not had a drop to drink. In view of the fact that it is now more than eight months since his discharge this is impressive evidence of a serious effort at self-rehabilitation.[15]

In ordering reinstatement, the arbitrator imposed the following conditional remedy:

> * * *
>
> B-- is directed to supply the Company Personnel Manager with written verification from his Alcoholics Anonymous group chairman of his attendance at Alcoholics Anonymous meetings. This will be done on a monthly basis for six months.
>
> If B-- is AWOL during said six months period, the full history upon which the Company relied in this case shall be considered in imposing punishment notwithstanding any Company policy to remit penalties occurring beyond the allowed time limits.
>
> At the end of six months, without being on AWOL, B-- is to be treated in the normal way under the contract and Company rules.[16]

In *Texaco, Inc.*,[17] a 20-year employee with two prior alcohol-related suspensions was discharged for coming to work under the influence. Following the discharge he met with a physician, attended AA, and was given medication. He had eight months of sobriety before the arbitration hearing. In ordering reinstatement, Arbitrator Paul Prasow stated that there was no quick cure for alcoholism and that the alcoholic needed support. Though

---

[14]56 LA 527 (Wolf, 1971).
[15]*Id.* at 529–530.
[16]*Id.* at 530–531.
[17]42 LA 408 (Prasow, 1963).

there was a risk, the possibility of recovery could provide great benefits to the alcoholic, his family, the company and society.

While not forming a conditional remedy (the arbitrator simply ordered reinstatement without back pay), Prasow noted in his opinion that he hoped the grievant would continue his rehabilitation, and "that any future deviation from strict sobriety on the job will warrant immediate termination."[18]

Similarly, in *Pacific Northwest Bell Telephone*,[19] the arbitrator noted that postdischarge efforts at rehabilitation are relevant in evaluating whether just cause for discharge exists and the severity of the penalty. In the arbitrator's words:

> [I]f the discharged employee proves after this discharge that he has a significant chance for recovery, the officials must have misjudged him and have given him too severe a penalty. The arbitrator even if he upholds the officials' charge, may reduce the penalty to give the offender another chance.

Harter cited with approval a decision by Arbitrator Louis Kesselman as follows:

> Before an alcoholic is disciplined or discharged Kesselman would require:
> (1) that the employee be informed as to the nature of his illness.
> (2) he must be directed or encouraged to seek treatment.
> (3) he must refuse treatment or
> (4) he must fail to make substantial progress over a considerable period of time.[20]

The remedy was drafted as follows:

> [T]he Employer may have the option to retire the Grievant on a service pension.
> . . . [T]he Employer may restore the Grievant to duty subject to involuntary retirement if he should miss work because of drinking, if he should drink on the job, or if he should be arrested for driving under the influence of alcohol.[21]

* * *

There is no question that postdischarge rehabilitation is a determinative factor in reinstating a discharged alcoholic or drug abuser.[22]

---

[18]*Id.* at 412.
[19]66 LA 965, 973 (Harter, 1976).
[20]*Id.* at 973, citing *American Synthetic Rubber Corp.* 71-1 ARB ¶8070 (Kesselman, 1973).
[21]*Id.* at 975.
[22]*See, e.g.,* Greenbaum, *The "Disciplinator," the "Arbichiatrist," and the "Social Psychotrator": An Inquiry into How Arbitrators Deal With a Grievant's Personal Problems and the Extent to Which they Affect the Award,* 37 Arb. J. 51, 59–61 (1982).

In short, even if the grievant took no rehabilitative efforts before termination, where the misconduct at issue occurs because of a condition subject to "cure" rather than from willful misconduct, arbitrators will consider whether the grievant has taken the necessary steps to be "cured" and use this as a mitigating factor in determining whether discharge is appropriate.[23]

A more difficult case is where the troubled grievant is offered an Employee Assistance Program (EAP) before conduct resulted in termination but refuses management's help. Generally, an employee has less chance of getting a sympathetic ear from an arbitrator if help was offered by management but the employee rejected it.[24]

To what extent must employees cooperate with management in admitting that they have an alcohol or drug problem? In *General Telephone Co. of Illinois*,[25] Arbitrator John Sembower held that a telephone serviceman who would not admit that he was an alcoholic was not refusing to cooperate with the alcohol rehabilitation program he had agreed to attend as a condition of an earlier reinstatement. Interesting is the question posed by Sembower and the implications for an arbitrator who, as a condition to reinstatement, orders the grievant to attend Alcoholics Anonymous:

> [T]he theorem of those who work with alcoholics rehabilitation, particularly Alcoholics Anonymous, that it is an essential prerequisite to any effective treatment that a patient acknowledge that he is an alcoholic is put to the acid test. It is all very well with those individuals who voluntarily subscribe to a program such as Alcoholics Anonymous be required to acknowledge at the outset that they are alcoholics, but what of the person who, like this Grievant, is

---

[23]Koven & Smith, Just Cause: The Seven Tests (San Francisco: Coloracre Publications, 1985), 216–217. *See also Veterans Admin. Medical Center*, 83 LA 51 (Denson, 1984) (under Alcohol Abuse Act employer required to provide opportunity for alcoholic employees to obtain treatment of their drinking problem before taking disciplinary action); *Greenlee Bros.*, 67 LA 847 (Wolff, 1976) (ordering conditional remedy of reinstatement and six-month leave of absence so employee can place himself in rehabilitation center); *Land O' Lakes*, 65 LA 803 (Smythe, 1975) (grievant reinstated provided he undertake treatment to cure drinking problem; failure to resolve drinking problem negates reinstatement); *Monte Mart-Grant Auto Concession*, 56 LA 738 (Jacobs, 1971) (holding discharge for just cause, but according grievant medical leave for alcohol treatment).

[24]*See* Koven & Smith, Alcohol-Related Misconduct (San Francisco: Coloracre Publications, 1984), 144–152; Loomis, *Employee Assistance Programs: Their Impact on Arbitration and Litigation of Termination Cases*, 12 (2) Emp. Rel. L.J. 275, 277 (1987): "Arbitrators are split about how to handle such situations. Some arbitrators have ruled that an employee must be reinstated, with the condition that the employee participate in an EAP. Other arbitrators have held that, once an employee has been terminated, he or she may not use the employer's rehabilitation program as a crutch to regain employment."

[25]77-2 ARB ¶8481 (Sembower, 1977).

precipitated into such a program somewhat or wholly against his will. Must he also be required to admit that he is an alcoholic as an indicia of his "cooperation" with such rehabilitative efforts?[26]

If an arbitrator is convinced that the grievant has a reasonable chance to succeed in becoming a useful employee (the term often used is "salvageable"), a conditional remedy may be issued.[27] Reinstatement may be conditioned upon the occurrence of a future event (condition precedent). Thus, an employee may be reinstated after successfully completing a six-week alcohol abuse or EAP program. Alternatively, an arbitrator may provide for reinstatement; but, if some event or condition materializes in the future (e.g., the grievant fails to continue professional counseling), the remedy is no longer binding on management (condition subsequent). Arbitrators who issue conditional remedies must make clear the exact nature of the condition—whether a condition precedent or subsequent is being imposed.

Sometimes, an arbitrator will form a remedy with both conditions. Thus, Arbitrator Jeffrey Winton, in *General Telephone Co. of Indiana*,[28] issued the following remedy for an employee who had been accused of reporting under the influence:

> The grievant will be reinstated to his job on the day he meets the following conditions and his continued employment will be dependent on continuing them:
> 1. Proof of enrollment in a hospital administered alcoholism program.
> A. It will be either an inpatient or outpatient program as the hospital recommends and he will continue with the program until released by the hospital.
> 2. Weekly attendance at Alcoholics Anonymous (AA) meetings for one year.
> 3. Reporting to work under the influence of alcohol even if it causes very limited physical or mental impairment, shall be cause for immediate discharge.[29]

Implications for the Future

It is fair to query what the future might hold for "troubled" employees' chances in the arbitral forum, especially in those

---

[26]*Id.* at 5088.

[27]For a variety of reasons, we are on record urging arbitrators to proceed with caution in drafting conditional remedies. *See* Hill & Sinicropi, Remedies in Arbitration (Washington: BNA Books, 1980), 48–50.

[28]86-1 ARB ¶8013 (Winton, 1985).

[29]*Id.* at 3057.

cases where the therapeutic or modified-corrective-discipline model is urged as a defense or as a mitigating factor in a discharge case. When attempting to speculate, one should not overlook the fact that, in general, arbitrators have not been at the forefront of social change for employees with serious personal problems, alcohol or drug dependencies, or other personal disabilities asserted as the direct cause of misconduct or unsatisfactory job performance, although arbitrators may follow legal, social, or industrial norms once the door is opened. It seems safe to conclude that as the parties adopt new policies to deal with troubled employees, arbitrators will react and formulate appropriate remedies when it is determined that there is a nexus between the employee's problem and the conduct at issue. They are, however, unlikely to plow new ground and adopt expansive policies and remedies (read therapeutic model) which have not been contemplated by the parties.

A factor of significance in this regard is the so-called "common law of the shop." From Archibald Cox and John Dunlop[30] to Harry Shulman[31] to Justice William O. Douglas[32] to the present, this phrase has been important to advocates and arbitrators. But we believe it is appropriate to reexamine the relevance of this concept, at least as it applies to troubled employees. As labor arbitration has expanded from blue-collar, private sector manufacturing to white-collar, public sector service industries, the common law of the shop is no longer a homogeneous concept. The variety of norms advocates urge arbitrators to accept or reject increases. This development may make "arbitral authority" or arbitral trends less discernible. What is arbitral authority for airlines may not be authority for steel.

It should be noted, however, that the absence of homogeneity may not be bad. In fact, it may be good. Arbitration is not for the most part a public institution. It is still a private forum owned and shaped by the parties. Thus, arbitrators should not plow

---

[30]Cox & Dunlop, *The Duty to Bargain Collectively During the Term of an Existing Agreement*, 63 Harv. L. Rev. 1097, 1116–1117 (1950): "[A] collective bargaining agreement should be deemed, unless a contrary intention is manifest, to carry forward for its term the major terms and conditions of employment, not covered by the agreement, which prevailed when the agreement was executed."

[31]*Ford Motor Co.*, 19 LA 237 (Shulman, 1952).

[32]In *Steelworkers v. Warrior & Gulf Navigation Co.*, 363 U.S. 574, 46 LRRM 2416, 2419 (1960), Justice Douglas declared: "The labor arbitrator's source of law is not confined to the express provisions of the contract, as the industrial common law—the practices of the industry and the shop—is equally a part of the collective bargaining agreement although not expressed in it."

new ground and venture blindly into areas not contemplated by the parties in their bargaining relationship. To the extent that the parties adopt and apply changes in the way troubled employees are treated, arbitrators may properly make decisions reflecting these values. To go beyond that boundary, however, is to effect a disservice to the parties' on-going relationship.

Admittedly, this is a conservative view of the arbitrator's role, but it has been the role that has made arbitration successful and a viable alternative to economic warfare. Arbitration does not exist for the benefit of arbitrators who desire to apply their own models of legal, social, or medical justice; it exists for the benefit of the parties. Although arbitrators are actors in an ongoing drama, they should never strive for top billing in providing assistance that was never contemplated by the parties themselves.

III. LIFE AFTER MISCO

R. WAYNE ESTES*

In its 1987 *Misco*[1] decision, the United States Supreme Court focused attention on the requirements for a reviewing court vacating a labor arbitration award on the basis of the award's being contrary to public policy. The Court limited this judicial action to situations in which the public policy violated is "well defined" and ascertainable by reference to "laws and legal precedents." The Supreme Court indicated that the violation of "general considerations of supposed public interests" will not suffice as a basis for vacating an award.[2]

Equally important to the Court's ruling on public policy vacation was its basic endorsement of the 1960 *Steelworkers Trilogy*

---

*Member, National Academy of Arbitrators; Professor of Law, Pepperdine University, Malibu, California. This paper was presented at the Academy's Continuing Education Conference in Milwaukee, Wis., October 30, 1988.
    [1]*Paperworkers v. Misco*, 484 U.S. 29, 126 LRRM 3113 (1987). For a general discussion of the impact and meaning of the *Misco* decision, *see* Wayland, Stephens & Franklin, *Misco: Its Impact on Arbitration Awards*, 39 Lab. L.J. 813 (1988); Parker, *Judicial Review of Labor Arbitration Awards: Misco and Its Impact on the Public Policy Exception*, 4 Lab. Law. 683 (1988); Berlowe, *Judicial Deference to Grievance Arbitration in the Private Sector: Saving Grace in the Search for a Well-Defined Public Policy Exception*, 42 U. Miami L. Rev. 767 (1988); Roebker, *Public Policy Exception to the General Rule of Judicial Deference to Labor Arbitration Awards*, 57 U. Cin. L. Rev. 819 (1988); and Dunsford, *The Judicial Doctrine of Public Policy: Misco Reviewed*, 4 Lab. Law. 669 (1988).
    [2]*Paperworkers v. Misco, supra* note 1, 126 LRRM at 3119.

decisions[3] in regard to the scope of judicial review of labor arbitration awards. As earlier indicated in its 1986 *AT&T Technologies* decision,[4] the Court agreed with the *Trilogy* decisions as to the limited role of the courts in reviewing labor arbitration awards and noted that "[c]ourts thus do not sit to hear claims of factual or legal error by an arbitrator as an appellate court does in reviewing the decisions of lower courts."[5] The Court restated the doctrine of the *Enterprise Wheel* decision[6] of the *Trilogy* that while awards must draw their "essence" from the labor agreement, a reviewing court cannot strike down an award simply because the court disagrees with the arbitrator's decision.[7]

Public Policy Challenges Since *Misco*

Two 1988 decisions of federal circuit courts of appeals provide illustrations of judicial application of the *Misco* public policy standards.

In its *Stead Motors*[8] decision, the Ninth Circuit found that *Misco* standards for public policy were satisfied by a district court in vacating an award reinstating an employee who had been discharged for not properly tightening the lugs on a motor vehicle wheel. The court recognized the requisite violated public policy in the safety requirements of the California Vehicle Code and the statute creating the California Bureau of Automotive Repair.[9]

The Third Circuit engaged in a stricter quest for a violated public policy in its *U.S. Postal Service v. National Association of Letter Carriers* decision.[10] An arbitrator had reinstated an employee who fired gunshots into his supervisor's unoccupied vehicle. A district court vacated the award, finding a violation of a public policy against permitting an employee to direct physical violence at a supervisor and ruling that the arbitrator had mis-

---

[3]*Steelworkers v. American Mfg. Co.*, 363 U.S. 564, 46 LRRM 2414 (1960); *Steelworkers v. Warrior & Gulf Navigation Co.*, 363 U.S. 574, 46 LRRM 2416 (1960); *Steelworkers v. Enterprise Wheel & Car Corp.*, 363 U.S. 593, 46 LRRM 2423 (1960).
[4]*AT&T Technologies v. Communications Workers*, 475 U.S. 643, 649, 121 LRRM 3329 (1986).
[5]*Paperworkers v. Misco, supra* note 1, 126 LRRM at 3117.
[6]*Steelworkers v. Enterprise Wheel & Car Corp., supra* note 3.
[7]*Paperworkers v. Misco, supra* note 1, 126 LRRM at 3118.
[8]*Stead Motors of Walnut Creek v. Machinists Lodge 1173*, 843 F.2d 357, 127 LRRM 3213 (9th Cir. 1988). *See* Parker, *supra* note 1 at 702.
[9]*Id.* at 359.
[10]839 F.2d 146, 127 LRRM 2593 (3d Cir. 1988). *See* Parker, *supra* note 1 at 702.

construed the "just cause" standard for discharge that was set out in the labor agreement. The circuit court criticized the district court's "second-guessing" of the arbitrator's evidentiary findings and construction of the contract and found that the district court had failed to establish a violated public policy in keeping with the *Misco* standards.[11]

Looking Ahead

What can be expected in regard to further judicial review of labor arbitration awards? Many courts apply the *Trilogy* standards with great care and consistency. In reading opinions from other courts, it appears that sometimes ways around the Supreme Court *Trilogy-Misco* judicial review criteria are sought. If the public policy route had been used in the past to implement broader judicial review of awards, the restrictive *Misco* public policy limitations may mean that any increased judicial scrutiny of labor arbitration awards now may be based upon other theories.

While it is unwise to judge motivations, particularly judicial motivations, it is difficult to resist the conclusion that some judges may not be totally supportive of the *Trilogy* originated and *Misco* endorsed concept of a very limited judicial role in reviewing labor arbitration awards. In some instances, one can sense a lack of total judicial appreciation of the basic policy favoring arbitration finality and recognizing grievance arbitration as the desired method of resolving disputes arising under labor contracts. In other instances, it is apparent that some judges have a very restrictive concept of when an award derives its "essence" from the labor agreement.

Judicial review approaching an examination of the merits of the underlying dispute and the "correctness" of the award is sometimes noted. Consider the following observations made in recent decisions about characteristics of an award that may subject it to judicial vacation:

1. "Arbitrary or capricious."[12]
2. Not "'rationally inferable' in 'some logical way'" from the contract.[13]

---

[11]*Id.* at 148 and 149.
[12]847 F.2d 775, 778, 128 LRRM 2842 (11th Cir. 1988).
[13]*Manville Forest Prods. Corp. v. Paperworkers*, 831 F.2d 72, 74, 126 LRRM 2895 (5th Cir. 1987).

3. "Irrational."[14]
4. "[T]he grosser the apparent misinterpretation, the likelier it is that the arbitrators weren't interpreting the contract at all."[15]

If greater judicial activity develops in scrutiny of the essential merits of awards, the basic thrust of the *Trilogy* review standards may be undermined even though these standards continue to be endorsed by the Supreme Court.

The *S.D. Warren* Decisions

Two 1988 First Circuit Court of Appeals decisions involving the S.D. Warren Company and the United Paperworkers International Union have prompted discussion and examination.[16] These cases are sometimes referred to as *Warren I*[17] and *Warren II*.[18] In both cases, discharges had occurred for drug related offenses under a contract that contained both a just cause standard for discharge and a set of disciplinary rules under which the drug related offense was cause for discharge. The arbitrators in both awards found an ambiguity in the agreement language and other company publications concerning whether discharge was mandatory for the offense. Considering past practice by the employer in instances in which discharge had not always followed the rule infraction, the arbitrators found that standard just cause tests for discharge had not been satisfied, and they reinstated the employees. Two different panels of the First Circuit found that the discharges were proper under the contract, and the awards were vacated. Essentially, the courts in *Warren I* and *Warren II* found that an ambiguity had not existed in the contract language and that the arbitrators had exceeded their authority in fashioning a remedy other than discharge for the rule violation.

---

[14]*Independent Employees Union of Hillshire Farm Co. v. Hillshire Farm Co.*, 826 F.2d 530, 533, 125 LRRM 3435 (7th Cir. 1987).

[15]*Hill v. Norfolk & Western Ry.*, 814 F.2d 1192, 1195, 124 LRRM 3057 (7th Cir. 1987).

[16]*See* Alleyne, *The Law and Arbitration*, Chronicle, Oct. 1988, at 3 (National Academy of Arbitrators); *Circuit Court Reaffirms S.D. Warren Decision*, Study Time, No. 2, at 1 (American Arbitration Association 1988); *Circuit Judge Raises Questions About S.D. Warren Ruling*, Study Time, No. 3, at 1 (American Arbitration Association 1988); Parker, *supra* note 1 at 700.

[17]*S.D. Warren Co. v. Paperworkers Local 1069*, 845 F.2d 3, 128 LRRM 2175 (1st Cir. 1988).

[18]*S.D. Warren Co. v. Paperworkers Local 1069*, 846 F.2d 827, 128 LRRM 2432 (1st Cir. 1988).

However, in *Warren II* one of the judges filed a concurring opinion that actually is a dissent. Circuit Judge Coffin reasoned that, at least arguably, the arbitrator could have found an ambiguity in the contract language, and in view of the employee's past practice in regard to the rule violation, the arbitrator arguably might have found a lack of proper cause for the discharge.[19]

Judge Coffin concluded that under *Trilogy-Misco* standards for judicial review, the award should not have been vacated. Judge Coffin, in discussing both *Warren I* and *Warren II*, ended his "concurring" opinion:

> I would conclude that, in both cases, the arbitrator was "arguably construing or applying the contract and acting within the scope of his authority." *Misco*, 108 S.Ct. at 371. Therefore, the fact that we might be "convinced he committed serious error does not suffice to overturn his decision." *Id.*[20]

Increased Judicial Scrutiny of Merits?

More intensive judicial examination of arbitrators' findings of "ambiguity" in contract language and increased attention to the "plain meaning" of contract clauses could result in judicial expansion of the *Trilogy* "essence" test.[21] Such inquiries could bring about judicial review that is closer to an examination of the merits of disputes than apparently was intended under the *Steelworkers* and *Misco* decisions.

A wide and distinct division among the circuits may be required before the Supreme Court agrees to hear another case relative to the application of the *Trilogy* standards of judicial review of labor arbitration awards. In the meantime, more attor-

---

[19]*Id.* at 833.

[20]*Id.*

[21]Following the presentation of this paper, Academy member William Murphy made the following comment:

Despite the Supreme Court's reaffirmation and amplification in *Misco* of its *Enterprise Wheel* language on the power of the arbitrator to interpret the contract, the *Misco* opinion contains a real joker. That is the statement that "The arbitrator may not ignore the plain meaning of the contract. . . ." The plain-meaning rule, despite all criticisms and ridicule, refuses to die. The Supreme Court and other courts continue to apply it, and I wager almost all arbitrators have used it to explicate a result. It was predictable that the Court's recognition of the rule in *Misco* would provide the justification for the refusal of lower courts to enforce an award. This was precisely what the First Circuit did in *S.D. Warren II*. The joker permits a court to hold that the contract language is "plain" even though an arbitrator has held that it is ambiguous. Unless the Supreme Court puts a stop to it, we can be sure that *S.D. Warren II* is not the last decision to reverse an award under the plain-language joker.

Estes, *Life After Misco*, Chronicle, Mar. 1988, at 4 (National Academy of Arbitrators).

neys for losing parties in arbitration may advise their clients to test the waters of their circuits in attempts to use an expanded "essence" test as a basis for vacating awards. Even if unsuccessful, such litigation could have the effects of undermining labor arbitration finality and adding burdens to an already crowded court system.

CHAPTER 8

UNIQUE PROBLEMS AND OPPORTUNITIES OF PERMANENT UMPIRESHIPS—A PANEL DISCUSSION

I.

ARNOLD ZACK*

There are two kinds of permanent umpireships—the major and the minor. The major kind is when you know you are the umpire and you actually do hear cases; the minor kind is when you don't know you're a permanent umpire until somebody calls you in the fifth year of your umpireship and tells you that your name has been listed in the contract as the permanent umpire but there have been no cases to arbitrate until this time.

A couple of months ago I got a call from a client in Massachusetts for an arbitration, but they called back and told me that a terrible mistake had been made, that I had been on the permanent panel under the previous contract, but that my name had been taken off the list when the new contract was signed. I hadn't known I was named in the previous contract and, of course, had never had a case.

We've all been lured with the glamour of a permanent umpireship, the socializing, stories about the grand masters participating in the parties sponsored by the auto and other industries. Prospects of a steady income, the security, the longevity of the relationship, the financial arrangements—that image was the goal of every arbitrator when I joined the Academy in 1962. The status of permanent umpires even at the Academy meetings was enormous, but these goals are not achieved by all of us. For example, just as I was about to join Saul Wallen in 1956, he learned that he was being fired as permanent umpire for General Motors because he had decided an issue one way

---

*Member, National Academy of Arbitrators, Boston, Massachusetts.

while Harry Shulman at Ford had decided it another way. By that time he had invested about 75 percent of his work time in GM, and it represented a very critical portion of his income. After that he told me he would never spend more than a third of his time in a permanent umpireship because he could not afford to lose the income when it ended. So there comes a time when people lose their umpireships.

Usually you lose an umpireship for deciding the "crucial" case, as happened in Wallen's experience. I had a similar situation. In one umpireship I was told by both parties that if I decided against either one, it would be my last case. And that's exactly what happened. There is always that kind of pressure. There is also the possibility that you won't be fired, but for six or eight months while working out your contract you'll be in the very uncomfortable position of attending hearings when one or both parties would rather not have you there.

Umpireships have also been lost for another reason—scorecard keeping. I was umpire for a tire and rubber company and mediated most cases before me, so that 102 grievances were settled, leaving me with eight to arbitrate. The union said they just couldn't settle those because of political and fair representation problems. The union lost all eight and the membership insisted that they fire me. So mediation may be a cause of demise. There are also political changes within the union. Cleaning house may mean getting a new umpire, without regard to whether the umpire has acted fairly.

Now, are umpireships appealing on other grounds? Do they really entail a lot of money? I can't believe that companies and unions would be willing to throw away a lot more money on a permanent umpireship than they would pay for an ad hoc relationship. Their rationale would be to save money or at least pay no more than they have to for going to arbitration. Sometimes you have more cases, sometimes less; it's a gamble. Of course, frequent-flyer privileges may be one of the benefits. But the time spent in getting to some of these places often outweighs those benefits. The out-of-the-way places where some of these plants are located makes it very difficult, and it takes hours to get back to civilization again. The time, the energy, the exclusion of opportunities to work elsewhere are costs.

Some of the relationships I have had have been very enjoyable. They have given all concerned satisfaction with the fun and camaraderie. But there is a down-side to that as well because sometimes the parties may feel they own you, that they can call you and complain about your awards hoping that you will tilt toward them in the next case. That is something you don't face with ad hoc arbitration.

As to the enduring relationships, a lot do last. I don't mean to bad-mouth umpireships, but the average duration is said to be about three years. Involvement tends to create a dependency to the exclusion of other work. Then when you're fired, it takes quite a while to build up your practice again. And there's always that doubt about why the parties fired you. Some of our distinguished members have come to these meetings and asked around about whether anybody knew why they were fired. Apparently there is always a nagging feeling that if they had done something different, the umpireship would have lasted longer. It's a pretty hurtful situation.

I think ad hoc arbitration is a much more satisfying way to go. You have more freedom—freedom of scheduling, freedom to reject cases you don't want. For example, I like to take summers off. Under an umpireship that was very difficult. You have your choice of clients to deal with; you don't have to live out a contract. You can choose your locations, travel where you want; it's a much more comfortable arrangement, with more control.

Everybody wants to be loved and wanted. The costs may be particularly painful when you lose an umpireship, both financially and professionally. Losing one is not the end of the world. There is a round robin of people serving on umpireships, going from one to another. But at the bottom line, if people didn't lose umpireships, none of us would get them.

II.

Elliott H. Goldstein*

This paper will focus on what the parties get out of a permanent umpireship as the device of choice to resolve contractual disputes. The issues facing advocates and neutrals in such a relationship will be discussed in light of the opportunities afforded by a permanent umpireship, as well as the difficulties such a structure may create. The paper is intended to highlight some of

---

*Member, National Academy of Arbitrators, Chicago, Illinois.

the many positive aspects of an umpireship as the institution has developed and the unique issues that are likely to surface when such a relationship has been adopted.

Comparisons and Salient Characteristics

One purpose of the panel today is an attempt to grapple with the differences between the permanent umpire relationship and standard arbitration practice, including the negative aspects of a permanent relationship, such as the hurt engendered when an arbitrator is terminated by one or both parties, a reduction in the freedom of scheduling of cases, and the issues of excessive party control and too much concern for maintaining acceptability, feelings that the institutional structure itself may help to create in a particular umpire. Fellow panelist Arnold Zack has discussed what he perceives are the overwhelmingly negative aspects of a permanent umpireship. On the other hand, I believe a permanent umpireship has many positive characteristics, both for the umpire and for the parties. Otherwise, umpireships would have fallen into disuse or been eliminated over time. Simply put, the device must be serving some institutional need for the parties in industries where it continues to be commonly used, and it must satisfy at least some interest of arbitrators, because umpireships are still thought to give prestige and to be desirable appointments.

It is my assumption that the basic arbitration model, that is the ad hoc appointment, requires that the hearing be conducted in a manner allowing the participants to present the case fully to the arbitrator. It is usually far better in an ad hoc case that the arbitrator hear too much rather than too little. Thus the arbitrator commonly encourages the parties to present the case in a comprehensive fashion. All concerned must be satisfied that the issues have been fully aired.

In the case of a permanent umpireship, less encouragement is necessary to make sure the parties present all issues or angles surrounding each issue, when the only motivation is a concern that participants be fully heard. Objections on the grounds of lack of relevancy or materiality therefore may be sustained after the arbitrator comprehends the issues and the subject matter of the dispute. The focus of the inquiry may be more quickly directed at the basic elements of the case, but the proceedings still achieve accurate results in an efficient manner acceptable to the parties.

That standard, i.e., that the procedural integrity of the process must be weighed against the accuracy of the results, the efficiency of the proceedings, and the acceptability of the process and results by the parties, was articulated by Roger Abrams in an article published in 1977.[1] Abrams' thesis is that the integrity of the arbitral process increases as structural devices permitting fuller review by courts of law are added, so long as efficiency and acceptability are not at the same time decreased causing the parties not to use the process. In other words, Abrams' basic arbitration model must include: (1) an unbiased adjudicator, (2) who conducts a hearing in an informal yet orderly manner, (3) protecting the rights of the grievant, (4) in a proceeding for which a record is made; (5) the arbitrator must render a reasoned decision, so that (6) a court can meaningfully review the proceeding to ensure the integrity of the arbitral process.[2]

This thesis (that the integrity of the arbitration process is enhanced by procedural structures or devices permitting courts to review the proceedings) is directly contradicted by Reginald Alleyne in a recent article.[3] Alleyne rejects "the wide gap that often separates the simplicity of an arbitration issue and the complexity of the hearing employed to resolve it."[4] It is his thesis that resisting "creeping formalism," often brought about by the use of lawyers and legal procedures, is the desirable goal for both the parties and the arbitrator. I agree.

History

At the heart of the idea of a permanent umpireship is the fact that umpires were first chosen where mass justice was needed, i.e., in the clothing manufacturing industries, such as hosiery, in the 1920s, and then in the mass production industries that were organized by the CIO unions in the 1930s. These industries included steel, auto, rubber, electrical products, and petroleum refining. In the early development of arbitration, permanent umpireships were more common, at least in the sense that a higher percentage of total cases heard came out of disputes

---

[1]Abrams, *The Integrity of the Arbitral Processes*, 76 Mich. L. Rev. 231 (1977).
[2]*Id.* at 243.
[3]Alleyne, *De-Lawyerizing Labor Arbitration*, 50 Ohio St. L.J. 93 (1989).
[4]*Id.* at 93.

where the parties had engaged a permanent umpire rather than made an ad hoc selection. The basic idea was that cases heard before an umpire could be handled in less time than cases where the parties and the arbitrator were not familiar with each other and where for each case procedural ground rules had to be arranged, or at least discussed, between the advocates and the neutral.

Other procedural differences flowed from the permanence of the relationship. For example, because the same arbitrator was hearing *all* cases brought under a particular labor contract, consistency of result in cases with similar issues could be expected. An umpire got to know the bargaining history between the parties and the background and peculiarities of a specific industry. By custom and practice attorneys were less involved as advocates in the presentation of cases before a permanent umpire. Because of the great number of cases to be decided, procedural requirements could be kept simple, and a specific number of days for hearing before the same unbiased, skilled, and experienced adjudicator could be assured.

In short, the structure permitted the development of a system to do "mass justice" with a minimum of procedural requirements, and yet decisions were made by an individual familiar with the bargaining relationship in a context where consistency was clearly a primary value for both the advocates and the neutral. These circumstances persist today.

The history of umpireships was discussed in some detail in an article by Dennis Nolan and Roger Abrams, who indicated that permanent umpireships developed early, especially in the clothing industry.[5] George Taylor was engaged as a permanent umpire in the hosiery industry in the 1920s, for example. However, the real growth of umpireships occurred when the mass production industries were organized in the 1930s for the CIO unions. To use the words of Nolan and Abrams:

> These new industrial unions developed contract administration systems which differed significantly from those in the older craft unions. Multi-step grievance procedures became commonplace and the newer contracts often limited the scope of the arbitrator's authority. These developments encouraged manufacturers and unions alike to move from grudging acceptance of *ad hoc* arbitration to voluntary establishment of permanent arbitration machinery.[6]

---

[5]Nolan & Abrams, *American Labor Arbitration: The Early Years*, 25 Fla. L. Rev. 373 (1983).
[6]*Id.* at 418.

Nolan and Abrams note that Taylor engaged in a hybrid system of mediation and grievance arbitration when he functioned as permanent umpire for the hosiery industry and later at General Motors. He rarely wrote formal opinions, and when he did they were extremely brief. He used the device of showing his draft opinions to the advocates for both sides prior to issuing an opinion and award, to make sure that the language did not cause the parties problems or have an effect in areas beyond the precise issue presented. He conducted hearings with a minimum of formalism. He believed that the labor contract was only a skeleton and not the complete agreement between the parties, and that the mediated results of the disputes arising under the agreement which were "decided" by him directly added to the totality of the bargain and became an integral part of the collective bargaining agreement.

By 1940 the permanent umpireship system had been adopted at General Motors. The development of the GM system was discussed by Gabriel Alexander at the 12th Annual Meeting of the Academy in 1959.[7]

It was Alexander's view that the 1940 agreement between GM and the UAW expressly restricted the umpire to handling grievance disputes rather than interest issues. Moreover, the contract clauses dealing with arbitration expressly limited arbitrators to interpreting the written agreement. The office of the "umpire" and the procedures and structure of the GM-UAW arbitration model were developed under the first four permanent umpires, including Taylor as the second umpire. The system did become "legalistic," at least to the limited extent that certain basic elements of arbitration procedure deemed essential to the achievement of accurate results were incorporated. The model was crafted so that a privately appointed neutral disposed of disputes in an informal yet orderly manner, decided cases from a "record," permitted confrontation between grievant and the employer, all with the result that the arbitrator made a reasoned decision in writing based on the evidence adduced on the record.

It is a truism that, from the time of its ascendency as the nearly exclusive means of resolving disputes over the meaning of collective bargaining agreements, labor arbitration has been por-

---

[7]Alexander, *Impartial Umpireships: The General Motors-UAW Experience*, in Arbitration and the Law, Proceedings of the 12th Annual Meeting, National Academy of Arbitrators, ed. Jean T. McKelvey (Washington: BNA Books, 1959).

trayed as a simple and expeditious procedure. There is obviously real tension between that goal and the ever-growing legalism and resulting increase in cost and time before a final decision in ad hoc cases. Umpireships have retained this simpler structure better than ad hoc grievance arbitration. Grievance hearings were intended to be swiftly reached and swiftly conducted; nonlawyer representation for both sides was the rule rather than the exception. These attributes were considered desirable in all arbitration. In my view, they are still deemed a "must" where a permanent umpireship exists. However, it is clear that in ad hoc arbitration, quite different development has occurred.

A majority of the legal trappings have not been grafted on the permanent umpire system, as distinguished from ad hoc cases. Perhaps the reason that the parties and the neutrals often reach the same conclusion that the system works faster and more efficiently than an ad hoc selection has a great deal to do with the fact that procedures have been kept simple. The role of precedent, when a substantial body of decisions has been issued interpreting language of the labor contract existing between the parties, helps to ensure consistency, which is a prime value in this relationship. Extensive objections for reasons other than relevancy or privilege are not often honored or even tolerated. In many umpireships as many as three or four cases are heard in a single day. No great loss in accuracy or fairness results from this system put in place specifically to emphasize efficiency, knowledge of the particular bargaining history, and consistency in overall decision making.

Recommendations

There are common characteristics in decision making when a permanent umpireship is involved. Initially, these are the need for mass justice because there are thousands of employees involved in multiplant units in the mass production industries of our nation; a central or national agreement that needs to be consistently enforced at numerous locations; clear restrictions on the umpire limiting his or her decisions to interpreting the written agreement and deciding only the issue presented; and a strong desire by the parties for consistent interpretation and application of the labor contract.

In an umpireship the assumption that formalism is essential in labor arbitration proceedings, perhaps best articulated by Abrams,[8] has been rejected and been found invalid to the extent that its across-the-board application to this kind of arbitration hearing has not happened. This makes a great deal of sense, especially considering the relative simplicity of the usual issues in dispute. The fact is perhaps that there is no need to "delaw-yerize" a permanent umpireship. It is both the symptom and cause of its vitality, along with the fact that consistency is easier to maintain where there is a "permanent" arbitrator in place.

Accordingly, to the extent that the system takes into account institutional needs in making particular choices of procedures, there should be adherence to what is already being done, in accordance with Alleyne's recommendations summarized as follows:

Needless and counter-productive formalism in labor arbitration should be avoided whenever possible;

Objections to documents should go only to weight, after the documents have been properly marked and admitted into evidence. Post-testimony comments on evidence, either through the oral summation at the conclusion of the hearing, or in the advocate's brief, should be pointed to the basis for devaluating the evidence, including written documents and not the technical issues of admissibility;

Objections to questions and testimony should be limited to relevancy or materiality and questions of privilege. Such common objections as form of question, best evidence, lack of foundation, and hearsay should be uniformly rejected;

The burden of proof and persuasion should be on the party filing the grievance in all matters except discipline cases and, where discipline is involved, the Employer should be obligated to go forward and to sustain the burden of proof. The quantum of proof standard should be that the arbitrator is convinced that the facts are as contended for by the particular party;

The parties should have broad control of the order desired for the calling of witnesses (except the individual neutral must determine for his or herself whether a grievant can be called as an adverse witness in a discipline or discharge case).[9]

These are keys to an effective arbitration proceeding when the neutral is a permanent umpire. I would suggest that these recommendations be considered in the conduct of ad hoc arbitration. Ultimately, a rejection of formalism, a respect for bargaining history, and the need for predictability and consis-

---

[8]*Supra* note 1.
[9]*Supra* note 3 at 107.

tency will help to return arbitration to its declared purpose of resolving disputes through an expeditious and informal procedure while providing accurate and acceptable results to the parties. The assumption that formalism is necessary to help courts to review arbitration decisions, even if true, cannot outweigh the harm done by the rejection of the basic values which caused the adoption of arbitration. The parties do a better job in presenting a case to a neutral if they have actively and carefully assessed the case on the merits, and do not become bogged down in issues of admissibility of evidence. Use of simple procedures may result in more settlements, since the focus will be back on the actual issues in dispute. The rejection of formalism should cut down the number of cases that end up in arbitration. All these results are to be encouraged if this system is to be maintained in the future. Umpireships are accordingly a useful model or example for the entire arbitration process.

III.

JAMES J. SHERMAN*

Serving as permanent umpire provides some unique experiences. Some are pleasant and even exhilarating, others are quite unpleasant and frustrating. But, all such experiences are educational, providing new insights into the variety of ways people perceive the process of collective bargaining and especially arbitration.

One of my more rewarding experiences has been with the School System of Pinellas County, Florida. This is the second largest school district in Florida. It employs about 7,000 teachers and 3,500 support personnel. What is unusual about this experience is the fact that I am the only arbitrator the school board and the teachers have ever known. And this goes back 22 years.

When this relationship (the board, the teachers, and my role as arbitrator) began, there was no public employee bargaining law in Florida and the status of my award was clearly only advisory. With this in mind, I routinely arranged to have a meeting with the parties wherein I had an opportunity to mediate and generally test the limits of what rulings might be seen as acceptable. I

*Member, National Academy of Arbitrators, Tampa, Florida.

guess you could say that I was practicing "med-arb," although this was before I was aware that there was a term to describe the process.

In 1974 Florida passed a collective bargaining law for public employees, and arbitration awards became final and binding. I should say, almost final and binding, because the law so clearly favors the school boards, especially where personnel assignments are concerned, that every award favoring the teachers is a potential case for the courts.

Arbitrators who hear teacher cases are in general agreement that labor relations in most schools are less than ideal. Teachers are notorious and articulate complainers; school boards are protective to a fault of their management rights, and both teachers and school boards will go to court on the slightest provocation. In spite of this potential for excessive arbitration and litigation, my case load, at least in recent years, is quite low (between five and ten cases a year), and none of my awards has ever been challenged in court.

There are several possible explanations for this atmosphere of relative harmony. I believe the most important contributing factor is the procedure we follow. I still meet with the parties after the hearing to explore settlement opportunities and, more importantly, to send up "trial balloons" relative to possible rulings. This is important because it gives the parties an opportunity to remind me of relevant precedents, and to point out the problems that a particular ruling might present to their relationship sometime in the future. Then, as I face the task which is often quite difficult in any permanent umpireship, namely, maintaining a semblance of consistency while providing a reasonable resolution of the grievance and looking to the future, the task becomes much more manageable.

In light of this experience, I would recommend to any school board that it give some thought to trying a permanent umpire because school boards change, superintendents are quite transient, and advocates come and go with great regularity. As a result, there tends to be little stability in the relationship between the two groups (administrators and teachers) who are relatively permanent employees of the school system. In my opinion a permanent umpire tends to be more consistent in providing contract interpretations, and this helps the advocates to settle grievances short of arbitration. In my case, I have survived several school superintendents, countless new advocates, and about a dozen school board elections, which leaves me as the only permanent decision maker standing between the administrators and the teachers.

I held another umpireship that provided some valuable insights into the internal politics of the company and the union. For the first year or more of this umpireship, the union won the vast majority of cases that reached arbitration. Then came the telephone call which I had been expecting. I was asked to meet with the corporate vice president for human relations and his union counterpart. I thought to myself, "If they want to fire me, why can't they tell me over the phone and save us all a trip?" But it did not turn out that way. Instead, the company representatives informed me that he had read every one of my decisions and that he would have decided them exactly as I did. He commented, "The local facilities are not taking their responsibilities seriously enough, and I intend to do something about it." Whatever he did, it worked. Indeed, it worked too well. Either the message was too strong or the local company representatives overreacted, as often happens. For the next year the union never won a single arbitration case. So, I knew my days were numbered.

In spite of this long unbroken string of losses for the union, I might have survived for a while longer had it not been for some internal union politics. The local unions resented any type of international control and requested ad hoc arbitration. The international wanted a permanent umpire and a board to participate in and review all decisions. As a compromise, the local accepted the permanent umpireship but with the assurance that there would be no board. This seemed like a reasonable accommodation. But almost immediately I received a call from the international union directing me to send all of my decisions to them for "approval" before releasing them to the local. By this directive the international union violated its agreement with the locals and created a board—in this case, a clandestine board.

I did not appreciate being placed in this position, but I thought "It's none of my business—that's how things are done in unions." And I could have lived with this arrangement except that whoever was supposed to review and eventually approve my decisions for the union took forever to respond. As a result, I often returned to a particular local facility to hear a series of cases and had to face hostile local union officers, demanding to know when I planned to give them decisions in hearings which were held three or four months before.

One of my umpireships was the most rewarding while it lasted, and the saddest experience when it ended. It was rewarding because the three-person board worked to near perfection. It was a sad day when it ended because, in the eight years we served together on the board, we had become close friends as well as colleagues. The board's success was due primarily to the integrity of these two men. Both were deeply and sincerely religious. This was manifest in all our dealings. In our discussion of grievances, they would not shade the truth, much less deviate from it. And each was knowledgeable and highly respected within his own organization. Working with such a board, it was possible to solve problems, which at some point had seemed insoluble, because neither man was afraid to express his opinions and defend them, however unpopular they may have been within his own organization.

A lesson I learned from this experience was that, once the board had a statement of the facts that we could rely upon, a resolution of the grievance was almost a certainty. I became convinced that, when the company and union select persons such as this to serve on a board of arbitration, they are making a wise choice, since the board's decisions tend to be not only more consistent but also more reasonable. This encourages settlement of disputes before they reach arbitration, which engenders an atmosphere of mutual trust and respect throughout the collective bargaining relationship.

Finally, reflecting upon all the collective bargaining relationships I have known, I would describe the ones having permanent umpireships as more effective in dealing with employee complaints than those relationships that rely upon ad hoc arbitration. However, I must admit, I am not certain that the umpireship system created, or even contributed to, this comparative advantage. It may well be that, because the relationship was mature and stable, the parties opted for a permanent umpire, someone who would be more consistent and more predictable. In other words, when I think about permanent umpireships and mature collective bargaining relationships, I am convinced that they are related, but I do not know which is cause and which is effect.

CHAPTER 9

ARBITRATION IN THE AIRLINES

I.

DANA E. EISCHEN*

I will give a brief legal and historical overview of arbitration in the airline industry to set the scene for the presentations of the other panel members. As most of you know, this industry is covered by the Railway Labor Act (RLA) and not by the National Labor Relations Act (NLRA). The reason why the airlines ended up under the RLA rather than under the NLRA is a curious accident of personalities and history. The story, as I understand it, goes this way.

The Airline Pilots Association, formed in 1931, had as its first president David L. Behncke, a United Airlines pilot. From the beginning he was in favor of coverage under the Railway Labor Act. Probably not even thinking about grievance arbitration, he was in favor of compulsory mediation for settlement of interest disputes, which was attractive to a fledgling labor union. The airline industry for the most part was indifferent about the RLA. In fact, experience with the National Labor Board, the precursor of the NLRB, had so disaffected airline management that they too were willing to accept any viable alternative.

In 1936 Title II of the Railway Labor Act was amended to provide for coverage of airlines, including the establishment of the National Air Transportation Adjustment Board (NATAB) similar to the National Railroad Adjustment Board. The amended Railway Labor Act provides for NATAB, a system with two members each from industry and labor, giving the National Mediation Board discretion to create and implement NATAB with the same jurisdiction and authority as the railroad Boards of Adjustment and with the same government subsidy and administration.

---

*Member, National Academy of Arbitrators, Ithaca, New York.

With this statutory structure there is an overlay of judicial gloss imposing compulsory arbitration of minor disputes, i.e., grievances. In 1957 a decision by the U.S. Supreme Court[1] essentially held that in minor disputes there is compulsory arbitration. Under the RLA there is no right to self-help or a strike over grievances, contrary to the interpretation of employee rights under the NLRA. (I apologize to the more sophisticated members of the audience for an oversimplification of this distinction.) This removal of the right to strike has been used by some as an explanation for the federal subsidy, whereby the government pays for arbitration in the railroad industry. This appears to be a latter-day rationalization, however, developed some 20 years after passage of the statute; but it is suggested that this is a quid pro quo for giving up the right to strike.

Parties in the airline industry chose not to follow that model. With the government subsidy, no economic incentive to settle, and no right to self-help, there have been lots of problems in the railroad industry with grievance arbitration. The airlines have never pressured the National Mediation Board to establish the National Airline Transportation Adjustment Board, but instead have established their own system boards of adjustment through negotiation. Arbitration is still a statutory mandate, but the vehicle is through collective bargaining rather than through a statutory NATAB. Because of the pluralism in the airline industry, there is a wide variety of structures and processes.

Two common factors are: (1) tripartitism, which results in sometimes three, sometimes five, or as many as seven members on arbitration boards, with one chair and an equal number of partisan members; and (2) a systemwide jurisdiction, whereby the collective bargaining agreement covers the entire airline nationwide. This also determines the jurisdiction of the boards of arbitration, which are permanent features of the relationship rather than ad hoc structures.

This has been a very brief historical and legal background of arbitration in the airline industry. Now let me review what the other speakers are going to be talking about:

Seth Rosen of the Air Line Pilots Association will discuss the variety of structures and procedures, including the wide range of formality and informality and the historical development of

---

[1]*Chicago River & Indiana R.R. v. Railroad Trainmen*, 353 U.S. 30, 39 LRRM 2578 (1957).

these boards, emphasizing the effects of deregulation as well as some of the substantive issues.

John Hedblom of United Airlines will speak generally about the tripartite system, its advantages and disadvantages, and then add his perspective as a management representative in evaluating the arbitration process as it relates to the complex cases with which this industry abounds, especially with reference to integration of seniority lists and mergers.

Mary Clare Haskin of the Association of Flight Attendants is going to bring a unique perspective to this discussion in her role as grievance chairperson at United Airlines. She will cover the administration of tripartite boards with specific reference to cost effectiveness, arbitrator selection, scheduling, and case screening prior to arbitration.

Martin Soll of Eastern Airlines will talk about the arbitrator's role on a tripartite board, what the parties have a right to expect from the neutral, and what conduct is unacceptable. He will also discuss stress and overload in the system, its causes, and how to deal with it.

II.

SETH D. ROSEN*

I have been a practitioner under the Railway Labor Act for many years and came to it from a background under the National Labor Relations Act. While a student taking labor law, I can remember that the Railway Labor Act was merely a footnote and was never covered on any examination during my period at George Washington University where I took all the labor law courses. I came to the Air Line Pilots Association (ALPA) in 1971, and I'm a product of a somewhat mixed career there since we represented both pilots and flight attendants when I first arrived. It was then a heavily regulated industry. I've gone through the ebb and flow of the industry over a long period of time. I ended up in Washington at headquarters. I have had the pleasure of working at every airline that we represent. That now

---

*Director of Representation, Air Line Pilots Association, Washington, D.C.

consists of 46 carriers, each one with its separate bargaining unit and each one with its separate system board of adjustment.

When I started representing flight attendants at Western Airlines in 1971, we handled five discharge cases in one four-member system board of adjustment quarterly meeting and resolved all the cases. In fact, that was the pattern of most of the boards at that time. We seldom went to a five-member board because we settled most of the cases with the four-member board.

The two four-member system boards I'm going to talk about today are good examples of that approach. United Airlines was first organized by ALPA in 1940. The very first agreement we had with a major carrier was with American Airlines some 50 years ago. Shortly thereafter all the major carriers were organized, the last of which was Eastern Airlines.

Each agreement established a system board of adjustment. In order to maintain stability in the transportation industry, one of the underlying premises of the Railway Labor Act was to provide for the prompt and orderly settlement of all disputes growing out of grievances or involving the interpretation or application of agreements covering rates of pay, rules, or working conditions. When Title II of the Railway Labor Act was added, that language was incorporated into Section 204 to detail how broad the jurisdiction of the system board was in resolving disputes.

Although there is a distinction between major and minor disputes, the courts have determined that disputes arising out of the employment contract are minor disputes subject to the arbitration process under the system board procedures for resolution by the parties. The trend has been changing somewhat and some precedents have been challenged, especially regarding finality of system board awards. I need not talk to the Academy about the importance of the finality of the arbitration process.

When the industry first started, it was a small industry with a small work group. There was a closeness among all the people in the airline, and that attitude spilled over in the conduct of the system boards. United is a good example. They have always had a formalized procedure with rules and transcripts, but a very active four-member board that resolved practically all disputes. Over time things changed so that in 1968 it became more formalized. The collective bargaining agreement permitted either party to request initially that the case go to a five-member board. Since that time every case goes to an arbitrator.

It was similar during those formative years at Eastern Airlines. It wasn't until 1982 that a provision allowing bypassing the board by either party was negotiated into the contract. Previously, they had a marvelous success rate with only the four-member system board without requiring the services of a neutral. Over 75 percent of all cases at Eastern were resolved at the board level. That active process continues even today, up to the time of the strike, except for complex contract interpretation and discharge cases.

We have seen a trend toward more formalized relationships through the arbitration process, following the trend overall in labor relations matters. We are becoming a very litigious people. There has been an increase in formalism rather than the relaxed process that prevailed with four-member boards.

There is one key ingredient that makes the four-member board system work, and that is trust. There also must be a lot of independence and authority entrusted to the people who are presiding as board members. The people on both sides of the table have political considerations to deal with, but it is only when those people are free to exercise their will in a fair and just manner, without being subject to recrimination by either side, that such a structure can work.

That system still does work at some airlines, for example at Delta (although the trend lately has been toward having neutrals enter more and more disputes). Until a few years ago there was never an arbitration at Delta, but now we have two or three arbitrations a year. Most carriers and pilot groups are now moving toward a five-member board with an arbitrator. I think that is a very negative trend. I think people are better off working out their own problems, coming up with their own solutions, and living with those decisions.

When you deal with pilot jobs, you are dealing with a multi-million dollar career with all the legal considerations that go with it. So what we've seen is a much more technical handling of the cases with transcripts, discovery, subpoenas. Even the composition of the board is changing. Now at United, Northwest, and other places, we see lawyers being inserted on the boards instead of only management and union representatives. If the company puts a lawyer on the board, we have to counter by doing the same thing to protect our interests. That tends to break down the process—the informality, the free-flowing dialogue between board members, and the ability to give the arbitrators what they want in terms of assistance from the board, namely, an understanding of the property and how things work, not a lot of lawyer arguments and relitigation in executive session, but some common sense being brought to the situation.

When you add to this the duty-of-fair-representation problems unions face, with employees bringing in outside counsel and companies bringing in outside counsel instead of internalizing the matter and keeping it in the family, there is bound to be more acrimony and a more confrontational environment. This is part of the changing society—changing labor relations starting with PATCO in 1981 and other significant factors. Once there is instability and a contentious environment, the ability to resolve disputes in a local and friendly fashion is bound to erode. Eastern and United are models of that.

When United Airlines came into deregulation in 1978, the United pilots supported the company in its desire to have Congress enact deregulation, contrary to where ALPA as an organization stood on the matter. The United pilots saw deregulation as being in their best interests because it would allow the company to grow and increase its potential to dominate the industry. They saw that as very desirable. Parenthetically, there were no system board cases during this time. There were such positive relationships that the cases dwindled to practically nothing.

Aside from its impact on labor relations in this country, the PATCO strike in 1981 also contracted the industry at a time when the industry was looking for growth. The results were a cancellation of plane orders, a cutback in scheduling, and ultimately, bankruptcies and an industry recession. The result was a much different environment for everyone. It changed the system board attitudes as well.

Since 1983 the cases at United have gone off the board with over 200 cases now pending at United. We are scheduling into next year, and the relationship has turned sour. At Eastern even during the bad economic time, the parties used the four-member board. The cases have now increased astronomically, to where it is now impossible to get minor disputes resolved in a timely fashion. The backlog is enormous.

There has been a decided change from the sense of stability and trust and the ability to work together; everything has become very formalistic. I do not see the parties sitting down and resolving minor disputes. In fact, I see the parties using the arbitration process as just another part of their overall strategy, whether it is to aggravate, delay, and prolong the controversies, to buy time, or to protect issues for future negotiations. It is being used as a tactic involved in the overall labor relations strategy. It isn't a good sign, but it won't change until we see some stabilization in the industry, and that doesn't appear to be happening soon.

On a happier note, I can conclude with one last observation: there's a lot of work out there.

III.

JOHN M. HEDBLOM*

I came into labor law in 1985 at United Airlines to fight in arbitration cases. I come from an insurance litigation background where all you do is fight. I don't come in with a labor background. I agree that there is more legalization in labor arbitration. I don't see that as a negative necessarily, but I agree that we could do with a lot less acrimony. That has been a problem.

Yesterday I heard that one of the speakers described arbitrators' opinions as "father knows best" kind of opinions. If I could give my speech here today a title, it would be, considering that we're going into the 1990s, "expanded family knows best," because in the airlines we will continue to have a multiple board to work with. It is rare that we have solo arbitration cases.

Here is a quick overview of the boards I have worked on with United. We have five-member boards with both the flight attendants and the pilots. Since the 1960s, when we had a solo arbitrator, there have been only multiperson boards. On the ground side we do have some single arbitrators in discipline cases only; the board in ground agreements consists of three people, one from each side and the neutral arbitrator, who hear contractual disputes. That is the one limited exception. In the industry generally multiple-person boards are the rule.

I want to discuss first the negatives of the multiple-person board. The biggest negative is that it takes too long. For example, when a motion is made in a solo arbitration, the arbitrator rules on it immediately; but in our process there is argument on

---

*Senior Staff Specialist in Arbitration, United Airlines, Chicago, Illinois.

both sides, the board members contribute to the discussion on both sides, and then they ask for a caucus. Thus, there is a mini-executive session at various times during the hearing. Sometimes this takes 15 to 30 minutes. And if we don't finish the hearing in a day, we have to reschedule it for a later date. It's hard to get everybody together. So the case drags on.

Another area that is difficult from an advocate's standpoint is the presentation of witnesses. You all know with a solo arbitrator there are difficulties there. Testimony is let in "for what it is worth" frequently. Objections are generally overruled. I can't protect the witness in an arbitration hearing the way I would be able to in a court of law. If I object to hearsay, or the like, generally I will be overruled. Those problems with a board sitting are compounded by round-robin questioning. The arbitrator may have one or two questions; the board may have other items they consider important; that complicates matters.

When I bring in witnesses who have never been in such a proceeding, I tell them that testifying before a system board at United will be the most difficult job of testifying they will ever have to do, because of the additional problem of the board members being able to ask questions. I know I can object to board members' questions, but I also know I will not be sustained, and I will generally be looked at askance if I do object.

Another thing adding to the time delay is that transcripts go to all the board members. They have scheduled a later date for getting together in executive session to discuss the case and to fight it out all over again. There are few exceptions to this. This means there will be another round of fighting. Our skillful advocates will bring out all the technical considerations for the neutral's benefit. Then the neutral will draft an opinion and send it out to all the board members. They review that and send all their complaints, suggestions, recommendations back to the neutral, and hopefully it all gets worked out. All that takes a long time. Thus, you can see that anything that delays the process is a negative.

I'll touch briefly on expenses of the board, which I consider a negative. Those people who are employees of the company who sit as members of the board have their salaries paid during the time they spend on the board. With outside counsel, as on the pilots' board, that is an added expense for both sides. The most expensive item is coffee; with a five-member board, they drink plenty of it.

You might ask why we have multiple-person boards. We are not required by the Railway Labor Act to have multiple-person boards, or we wouldn't have the solo arbitrator sitting on the ground discipline cases. So that leads me to the positives of the multiple-person board.

First, it's a lot more fun for me. I'm convinced that a requirement for membership in the National Academy is that you all have to take a course in noncommital nodding and general inscrutability. If I present a case to a solo arbitrator, I get no reaction. But if I present a case to the opposite board members, I can bait them and get them to express their thoughts. Or if I say something out of line, I can get some facial expression from my own board members. So it's a lot more fun. Seriously, advocates for the airlines agree that we get better opinions from a language standpoint with a multiple-person board than we would get from a solo arbitrator. The board members have input during the process, during the executive session, in the opinions after the fact, and they may even work with their opposites on the board to tighten up the neutral's language. That focuses the award and prevents that part of the case not central to the issue from hurting either party by inadvertently reinterpreting some part of the agreement which has already been decided and which shouldn't be meddled with. I'm not saying we expect to have bad language with a solo arbitrator, but with the board we have more control.

The board also has pulled my feet out of the fire. If I have board members who know something about the case, they can ask the right questions; they can put the right thoughts in the neutral's mind; they can argue the right points in the executive session, whereas I might have missed something. Able counsel on the other side has done the same thing to us. The process adds more advocacy and may be more acrimonious, but it helps refine the board's decisions.

Another one of the big pluses of the multiple-board is that in the airline industry we are dealing with complex technological situations. Of course, sometimes we have very simple cases as well. One case I remember involved a ramp service man who was accused of driving a movable stairway too fast and overturning it on the tarmac. He insisted he was driving it carefully and described that he was air-drying it because it had just been washed. The neutral asked: "Wouldn't that leave spots?" We did not need a sophisticated arbitrator for that; we did need a practical one, and that's what we had.

As an extreme example, there is a device in the cockpit known as the INS, the inertial navigational system, which tells you where you are wherever you go. How it does that is far from simple; it seems to be magical. The current coordinates get plugged into the computer and it detects motion. It's in a lot of aircraft. What the machine does is simple, but how it does it is difficult. As an advocate trying to describe it to a single arbitrator, I could be certain that I would not be able to make it clear. But with a multiple board, I could rest assured that during the executive session, if the neutral had any questions, the other board members could answer them better than I could have during the hearing.

The contractual cases that we have are also complex. We have scheduling rules, particularly on our international operations, which are an absolute wasteland of gray areas, interpretations, practices, that no one knows everything about. Having a person on the board who knows about these practices is a real comfort to everyone involved, including the grievant. And the decision is a completely informed one.

In conclusion, the virtues of the multiple board outweigh the less expensive, more expedient, cleaner solo arbitration case. They're here to stay in the industry, and the bottom line is that if you arbitrate in the airline industry, you can expect company.

IV.

MARY CLARE HASKIN*

One of my job responsibilities is to coordinate the scheduling of the United Airlines System Board of Adjustment. United has 13,000 flight attendants who are represented by AFA, and we have 500 grievances presently pending before the system board. Some of our cases go back as far as 1971. This seems to be an incredible backlog, but we have a well-oiled machinery for expediting grievances at the arbitration level. I really don't find the

*Grievance Chairperson, Master Executive Council, Association of Flight Attendants, United Airlines System Board of Adjustment, Washington, D.C.

multiple board process as time-consuming as the previous speaker seemed to suggest. In scheduling, we try to pull out those cases which are likely to take a longer hearing time and schedule them accordingly. We don't find the board so time-consuming. In addition to arbitration, I also meet with the company several times throughout the year to review the pending cases and work toward settlements, if possible.

On case screening we don't have a formal system. But with the 500 cases, some get screened without being heard. Every grievant wants a day in court. We always give a document to the grievants to let them know that the case has been settled. While this is not as formal as a hearing before the board, we do try to satisfy each grievant.

Today, I'm going to focus on how our panel operates, specifically, where we get our mandate for our panel, how panel members are selected, factors contributing to cost effectiveness, our selection process of cases, and how our arbitrators interface with the system board and the advocates.

Our contract sets forth the establishment of both a five- and a four-person board. However, the four-person board has not been used for the last ten years or more. The contract also establishes that the parties will select at least 11 referees. This panel runs concurrent with the life of the agreement unless the parties mutually agree otherwise. Our contract further establishes that the cases will be heard during one week of each month. We schedule a minimum of 60 cases per year. Even though we may settle some cases, we use the time by scheduling back-up cases. We have had this practice for over 20 years.

For the past several years the company designees had scheduled all our cases with my concurrence. My turn came two years ago. To begin the process I start by assuming that all 11 arbitrators will accept service on our panel. So far that has proved true. Each arbitrator can be assigned five days plus one extra day for five arbitrators. I advise the arbitrators of the mutually selected dates for the year, and they in turn advise me of their availability for those dates. And that's when the fun begins.

It takes many hours to put faces on the schedule. Then the company and I negotiate about the schedule. While our cases are heard in Chicago, our arbitrators are from all over the country. Whereas in the past we may have had a different arbitrator for each of the five days, two factors have altered our scheduling practices when we schedule arbitrators for two to three consecutive days. A key reason is cost. Scheduling an arbitrator for consecutive days cuts down on travel expenses. The second reason is that our cases often require more than one day's hearing. It is far more expedient and cost effective to complete the case in one session, particularly since the arbitrator may not be rescheduled for several months. Every effort is made to hold executive sessions in the home town of the arbitrator because in the airline industry, company passes are available to employees for business-related travel whereas the arbitrator bills for expenses.

It is not unusual for arbitrators to find a conflict once the schedule is submitted. In that case we allow them to trade days. We rarely know prior to the month before what cases will be presented to a particular arbitrator. The union usually selects what cases will be heard. Our Master Executive Council policy mandates that we give discharge cases priority, and we rarely see a discharge case that is held in abeyance more than two months. The descending priority list involves the following matters: (1) MEC contract violations that affect the entire membership, (2) local grievances that may affect other domiciles, (3) individual cases of policy matters that may affect other flight attendants in the future, and (4) disciplinary cases.

Our boards know that we have a very technical contract, and hence there are numerous opportunities for contract violations. Also, we have a very educated membership who are quite capable of making their own interpretations. Then we have a practice of grieving every step of the disciplinary procedure involving such things as sick leave, to protect the grievant's rights in the future. It's hard to tell members not to grieve because when they get the oral warning, the written warning, then the suspension and they haven't grieved the previous action, they are bound by the determinations. We sometimes have to advise a grievant at the system board level that their case may be lacking merit, but it's hard to do that at the local level when a member feels it is very important.

The Railway Labor Act requires a system board for arbitration and, while we know that some airlines have a sole arbitrator for some cases, we have chosen a five-member board. Our board is unique in that we have participatory board members representing both the company and the union, who have served in this capacity for over 20 years. That is somewhat of a record. They know the contract as well as the precedents of the system board.

Another unique factor is that the board has established a set of rules regarding procedural and evidentiary matters, and all arbitrators must live with these. Continuity in contracts and consistency in board decisions is preserved by one of the rules, which states that prior contracts and board precedents shall be considered by the board at all times. The parties may direct the board's attention to any prior contract or any prior board decision without formal introduction into evidence.

I have attended all system board hearings in the past five years while I have had this job as grievance chairperson. I have observed continuity and consistency, but also a collegial atmosphere which exists between company and union board members and the neutrals. We feel our modus operandi is unique compared with the operations of other industries. We think that our system gives our membership expedient results on their grievances.

V.

MARTIN SOLL*

I will spend a few minutes on the subject Dana Eischen chose for me, namely, what could disinvite you from the system board panel provided that you should be chosen. I have presented cases for two airlines, on contract and noncontract issues, before three, four, five person boards. What might be acceptable to you and to the attorneys who present cases day in and day out may be totally unacceptable to the grievants who come to the board for the first time or to the management people, such as the manager of flight or the chief pilot, who are there for the first time and who have no knowledge about the arbitration process but may have quite a bit of clout in deciding who is chosen or who should remain on the panel. You have heard in prior discussion things you shouldn't do, but they continue to happen. I talk as a neutral myself, and I suggest that you listen because they happen in real cases.

The system board has many fronts. Here are a few pointers: A case may be political for whatever reason. Don't try to mediate.

*Labor Counsel, Manager of Flight Agreements and Contract Administration, Eastern Airlines, Miami, Florida.

The issue may be insignificant to you, but it is quite important to the grievant.

Another point is what goes on at the hearing, especially what goes on in executive sessions. In some cases we have had four days of hearing, with two hours of actual testimony and the rest executive session. What happens is that the arbitrator tries to appease one party or the other by listening and listening, but both sides get very frustrated when the arbitrator won't make a decision.

Another unacceptable fact is that the arbitrator lets the parties use the technical rule of exclusion. The attorneys can handle it, but the other members of the board have trouble with it. If the arbitrator becomes too legalistic, it does not serve the purpose of arbitration. In one case we even had to prove up the contract. The party who was prevailing in this point was just as angry at the arbitrator for allowing this to happen as the opponent. That person was not invited back.

Another problem involves the pleasantries that go on among the parties and the arbitrator. This may be wonderful at a social event such as this, but at an arbitration hearing the grievant and some of the management people who are there for the first time don't understand the in-jokes and feel that the process is working against neutrality. Be very careful. You are being judged by that grievant. If it is a disciplinary matter and a job is on the line, it is no joking matter.

Another example of this type of conduct occurred when an arbitrator during the course of the hearing made a disparaging remark about another union official. Unfortunately the grievant, hearing the remark, interpreted it as prejudicial to unions generally and to this case in particular. The union attorney was asked to require that arbitrator to recuse himself from the case. There was delay and increased cost, and it should not have happened.

If you want to have a one case tenure, don't bring the contract. Or bring the contract, but don't read the pertinent sections ahead of time, even when the parties let you know what the case is about. In a continuing contract, don't bring the file from the last session. Or bring the wrong file. Or with the system board of adjustment, show up at the right hotel but in the wrong city. Or have the board convene with everybody there except you, the arbitrator, and when you are called, say "I thought it was next week." I assure you that happens only once.

If you want to have only one case, fall asleep during the presentation of the case, or look like you're falling asleep. Tell one of the advocates "You don't have a case" during the hearing, by body language or otherwise. Don't issue the opinion for a number of months. We have one case where we submitted briefs three and a half years ago. The union's brief was seven pages, mine was five. We're going on four years since the case was heard.

If you really want to cause a lot of havoc and contribute to the cost of the board, add some footnotes that have nothing to do with the case but that give your opinion. We have been arguing one footnote now for 10 years. We've had 45 cases as to the meaning of the footnote, and we can't get a decision.

Decide other contract issues that aren't being grieved. Add to the contract and put in your own words. Send a draft copy of your award to the grievant or to the advocates.

With reference to backlogs, there are thousands and thousands of cases. We have been looking for ways to resolve this. We instituted an internship program at several universities with senior law students and permitted them to get the feeling of what the cases were, and they were going to be assigned minor disciplinary cases. Everybody was happy with the idea, but for some reason it didn't work out. We also went into a mediation-type procedure with an advisory opinion. I think it would have worked if we could have managed it.

CHAPTER 10

ARBITRATION IN THE FEDERAL SECTOR

I. A PANEL DISCUSSION

1. JEROME H. ROSS*

Collective bargaining was formally recognized in the federal sector in 1961, when President John F. Kennedy signed an executive order. "Paternalistic" is not too strong a word to describe the system of collective bargaining under that executive order. The system was run by the U.S. Civil Service Commission which was the personnel arm of the federal government at that time. Although a few contracts provided for arbitration of grievances, arbitration was virtually nonexistent in those early years.

In 1971 a second executive order was signed. It established the foundation of the present federal labor-management relations program. A Federal Labor Relations Council was created to administer the executive order, which required that collective bargaining agreements contain a grievance procedure. In the early 1970s arbitration began to increase following the negotiation of agreements which provided for binding arbitration.

In 1978 Congress passed the Civil Service Reform Act. "The program," as it is known by practitioners in the federal service, had finally gained status in law. The good news was that the law established an independent agency, the Federal Labor Relations Authority (FLRA). The law also provided that all collective bargaining agreements shall contain a grievance procedure with binding arbitration. The bad news was that the FLRA was empowered to review exceptions to arbitration awards filed by a party alleging that the award was contrary to a law, rule, or regulation, or on other grounds similar to those applied by federal courts in private sector arbitration cases.

Predictably in the late 1970s and into the 1980s, the number of federal sector arbitration cases increased; so did the frustration

*Member, National Academy of Arbitrators, McLean, Virginia.

of arbitrators. Arbitrators soon found out that their awards often were not final and binding following appeal to the FLRA. At the National Academy meeting in 1981, John Kagel presented a critique of federal sector arbitration, decrying the lack of finality in the process and the many complications in the system.

The 1980s have seen a continuing high percentage of arbitration awards appealed to the FLRA, and especially unfortunate, a high percentage of those appeals have been sustained, with many awards overturned in whole or in part. In recent years arbitrators have changed their position from one of protesting against the federal sector of arbitration to playing by the rules that govern the system.

From the arbitrator's perspective, too often the parties fail to provide the relevant law, rules, and regulations which must be considered in rendering an award. On the other hand, in the parties' view arbitrators often fail to apply the required standards or to consider the appropriate authority.

This workshop is intended to give both arbitrators and the parties the opportunity to share our differing perspectives with the aim of understanding each other's needs in the federal sector arbitration process.

Now I'd like to introduce the panel. There's no doubt that John Mulholland of the American Federation of Government Employees and Frank Ferris of the National Treasury Employees Union stand out as the two individuals in the union movement who have had the greatest impact in shaping federal sector collective bargaining agreements. Our panelists on the management side—William Dailey, labor relations consultant to the U.S. Department of Agriculture, and William Kansier, senior labor relations advisor to the U.S. Department of Health and Human Services—are two of the most respected and competent practitioners in the federal sector program.

2. WILLIAM R. KANSIER*

I've been involved in federal sector collective bargaining for some time. The difference between the federal and private sectors is that the federal sector is very highly regulated. You all

---

*Senior Labor Relations Advisor, Department of Health and Human Services, Washington, D.C.

know that. But we, the practitioners, owe our very existence to the law. We can't ignore the law, and we don't feel that arbitrators can ignore the law either.

With reference to the high percentage of arbitrations that are overturned, the Office of Personnel Management (OPM) estimates that there are between 600 and 700 arbitrations per year in the federal sector and that 20 percent of those are appealed. But only 4 percent of all awards are overturned. People appeal awards for all kinds of reasons. A lot of the appeals are very political. So we're talking about 24 to 28 awards being overturned each year. I wouldn't dwell on that 4 percent.

I think arbitrators are doing a great job and I applaud that. The federal sector is a labyrinth of laws, rules, and regulations. Most of the people who work for me couldn't look at 600 cases and in 574 of them fashion decisions that met all the requirements of law and regulation. Due to the newness of arbitration in the federal sector and the learning curve required of arbitrators, I think it's a great record.

Basically, arbitrators have to pay attention to four things. There are some more esoteric things, but these are the most important. First, if you look at the management rights clauses in 5 U.S.C. 7106(a), they're nonwaivable. Management has the right to do certain things. We can't dispute that. We didn't make the laws; we only live with them. The second important law involves the harmful-errors standard for review of disciplinary actions in Section 7701 of that same title. The third law (and this is most important in fashioning remedies) is the Back Pay Act, using the but-for test. Finally there are the rules regarding attorney's fees in the federal sector. If you look at those four laws and regulations and apply them, there should be no problem with having an award stand any test before the FLRA.

I know that most arbitrators don't have access to these laws, rules, and regulations. I realize that it's the responsibility of the parties to educate the arbitrators. But there is one thing arbitrators can do for themselves. The OPM publishes a newsletter for labor arbitrators. They have about 600 arbitrators on a master list. No. 12 is the newest issue. Any arbitrator who is not on that list should see to it that his or her name is added to the list. I can give you the address later. If you want back copies, just write OPM and they will send them to you. This newsletter lets you know what is new and current with reference to the impact of laws, rules, and regulations on arbitration.

The parties have responsibilities in this area. We have the duty to train our advocates to present our cases in a clear and concise manner. We shouldn't make complicated issues more complicated by neophyte advocates. The advocates should know the laws, rules, and regulations, as well as know the case. We have to educate the arbitrators. We don't start out with the expectation that they know all about federal sector arbitration. Some of them do because they came out of the federal sector themselves.

I also feel that it is the responsibility of the parties to begin using panels. Using panels helps arbitrators understand the law because of repeat cases in the federal sector. More important, it will help them to understand the organization. For example, my organization, the Department of Health and Human Services (HHS), has 125,000 employees scattered all over the country with about 70 different lines of management authority. That means there are 70 different ways that we deal with union organizations. It's very difficult to understand. I recently was involved in an administrative proceeding where it took us a day and a half to educate the hearing officer about how our Department was organized and how it works.

Further, I think it's important that the arbitrator spend enough time to fashion a proper decision. Most arbitrators don't like to charge the parties a lot, and we don't like to get big bills. But we also don't like to have awards overturned because an arbitrator thought it could be done in a quick and dirty manner, and neglected to study an important law, rule, or regulation which required that the decision be overturned. That doesn't help either party.

The parties have a duty to negotiate an expedited arbitration procedure, and use that procedure for relatively easy matters, such as short suspensions, leave denials, or official time disputes. These matters can be handled at a relatively low level with an informal hearing in four or five hours with bench decisions. We don't need to spend money on transcripts for matters that are easily resolved and easily understood.

There are some common aspects between federal sector and private sector arbitrations. In both sectors arbitrators are vested with full authority to make determinations concerning arbitrability issues, authority to control and conduct the hearing, and making all procedural and evidentiary rulings. Absent stipulations or joint submission of issues, arbitrators are free to frame the issues as they see fit. They are also empowered to make all findings of fact, to weigh evidence, and to interpret the contract using private sector standards usually drawn from the contract. Arbitrators are vested with broad authority to fashion remedies so long as they don't violate certain provisions of law or regulations, such as the Back Pay Act.

I've told you what I think the parties' responsibilities are. I believe that arbitrators have some responsibilities also. Arbitrators should take command of the hearing, not let the advocates go off on issues that are not on point. Arbitrators should control advocates, making them give the information needed to fashion an intelligent remedy. Arbitrators should lean on the advocates to provide specific laws and regulations. Ask about any issue you're not sure of, and require the parties to brief it. Have them provide the supporting documentation. It's the job of the advocates to educate arbitrators so that they can fashion proper decisions. Arbitrators should rely on previous decisions, and the parties should be required to cite them and furnish copies. Most arbitrators don't have access to the 33 volumes of the Federal Labor Relations Authority decisions. If the parties are going to rely on them, they should be required to append them to their briefs.

Finally, arbitrators need to spend enough study time to fashion proper awards. It doesn't help the parties when an award is overturned because somebody did a quick job under the mistaken perception that the parties couldn't afford much study time.

In addition to traditional arbitration, arbitrators are currently being used in contract negotiation and in EEO cases. We endorse the concept of mediation/arbitration. We have used it for four or five years. It is a type of interest arbitration. We suggest that mediation/arbitration be built into the negotiation process. That requires prior approval of the Federal Service Impasses Panel, but getting that approval is generally no problem. Mediation/arbitration is helpful to us in the federal sector because we don't have deadlines. There are no strike dates; people can't walk out; they have to keep working. So negotiations tend to drag on. In the absence of a deadline people are not likely to engage in serious negotiation. Therefore, having a mediation/arbitration schedule established and ready to go creates deadlines and causes the parties to face the issues and negotiate a contract. For us that reduces the cost of negotiations. It reduces the potential for negotiability disputes later on because the mediator/

arbitrator can ask the questions of the parties and fashion remedies that meet the standards of law, rule, and regulation.

We appreciate the fact that it is difficult for arbitrators to get
involved in interest arbitration because they have to schedule
large blocks of time. That's one of the reasons for deciding early
in negotiations that we're going to do it, so that we can get on an
arbitrator's calendar. We also understand that most interest
arbitrators require larger fees for those services because of the
number of hours and the energy it takes to perform this service.
We don't have a problem with that.

The last area I see growing is Equal Employment Opportunity
(EEO). In EEO we have regulations from the EEOC, entitled
1613, a really thick volume. It takes about 700 days on average in
the federal sector for a person who has an EEO complaint to
have that matter moved through the agency processes so that it is
appealable to the EEOC. That's a long time, nearly two years,
and that's the average. The Department of Health and Human
Services and the National Treasury Employees Union (NTEU)
have been looking at that, and we decided to begin a process
known as negotiated discrimination complaint arbitration procedure. Employees can elect this as an alternative to that two-
year 1613 EEOC procedure. The employee first sees an EEO
counsellor and files a formal complaint; then the parties meet to
develop the record and make an assessment about merit. If the
case appears to have merit, it moves on, and arbitration is
invoked at that time. We have a two-step grievance procedure
prior to the actual arbitration hearing. The expectation is that
we'll be able to do these cases within 180 days. As a quid pro quo
for the union's willingness to use arbitration for these cases,
management has agreed to pay 70 percent of the arbitrator's fee
while the union pays 30 percent. We think it's a good deal
because it costs a lot of money to have these complaints around
for two years.

Another requirement of this process that is creative is that the
arbitrator must spend the first day in a mediation effort. We
think mediation/arbitration works. An arbitrator who has the
authority to decide a matter becomes a very powerful mediator
when he or she begins to make suggestions for settlement.
Recently the EEOC signed a new law, 1614 (which still must be
published in the Federal Register for comment), forcing agencies to process complaints within 180 days, after which they will
be appealable to the EEOC. There will be more opportunity for

arbitration of these issues. It's one of the ways we can reduce the processing time from two years to six months.

3. JOHN MULHOLLAND*

My comments will focus on two areas of concern to arbitrators in the federal sector. First, what the union looks for in an arbitrator, and second, some of the things a federal sector arbitrator should look out for. In both areas the process of arbitration remains substantially the same as it is in the private sector, but there are some differences that you should be aware of.

Because the law does not permit an agency shop or servicing fee, the decision to take a case to arbitration means spending a significant part of a federal union's budget. Invoking arbitration is a weighty action, particularly when in an adversarial process the federal employer has unlimited amounts of money to spend. In fact, it is not unusual for federal employers to stonewall disputes just to force the union into arbitration. The federal employers can do that because they don't stand to lose any money since the taxpayers pay for the whole process. For example, the Social Security Administration (SSA) has filed over 2,000 grievances against the union just on the issue of official time. They refuse to consolidate these cases or otherwise streamline the process, and we anticipate a cost between $2 million and $3 million for the union and a similar amount to come from the Social Security fund.

Once a case reaches the arbitrator, it is likely to be a major issue for the union, so it is extremely important that the cost of arbitration be reasonable. Locals have complained that they were overcharged for their half of the arbitration costs because the arbitrator took eight days of study time on a case that took only a half day of hearing. This kind of billing is the quickest way to get a reputation that will make it difficult for the union to pick you in future cases. For example, on a recent case an arbitrator charged $13,400 to rule on just the threshold issue of arbitrability.

Another signpost of an arbitrator's desirability is whether the arbitrator defers to management only because it represents the

*Director, Field Services Department, American Federation of Government Employees, Washington, D.C.

federal government. Unions share information about how even-handed arbitrators appear to be, and an arbitrator who kisses the altar of management will have a hard time being seen as a candidate for impartiality. There is no reason to defer to management in federal sector arbitration, because the law provides that the federal employer is required to subject its actions to final and binding arbitration. The merits of the case, not the sacred cow of the mission of the agency or management rights, should dictate your approach in deciding the case. If you feel that the government should be immune or otherwise protected from the full reach of an arbitrator's remedial powers because of some inherent sovereignty, you should decline to hear federal sector cases.

As long as the Civil Service Reform Act (CSRA) contains a final and binding provision, and a statutory mandate that all collective bargaining agreements in the federal sector include such provisions, then the employer should not be treated as other than the union's equal. The employer must not be permitted to hide behind the undocumented defenses of management rights, management determination, management prerogatives, or other spurious refuge. The arbitrator who nods knowingly at a crucial point in the hearing to indicate that he or she understands how the bureaucracy works will be hard for us to hire in the future.

Agency-speak is the employer's deliberate tactic to avoid discussing the merits of the case. This ploy of deliberate confusion is so common that the first expectation a union representative has about an opposing case is that it will be heavy on regulations and light on merit. Your job as a neutral is to cut through this and to get to the essentials: Did the employer violate the contract? And if so, what shall the remedy be? With rare exceptions most of the regulations offered by the employer require no more deference than you would give a company's personnel manual. Agency regulations cannot, for example, be implemented in a manner that conflicts with the contract. In 95 percent of the cases agency regulations are subservient to the union contract.

A third characteristic that is important to unions is the degree of activism that the arbitrator demonstrates. There is nothing worse than a decision that hangs on the evidence the arbitrator wanted to have but didn't ask for. An activist arbitrator isn't afraid to make an inquiry, even if the parties did not examine that issue in the presentation. The point of the arbitration is to arrive at a neutral distillation of conflicting and strongly held versions of the facts. In a charged atmosphere it may be in the interests of one or both parties not to look under all the rocks. What is an obvious piece of evidence to the arbitrator may not be obvious to the union. In that situation it is the mark of arbitral professionalism to look for the evidence through your own initiative, if that's necessary. So don't hold back. Ask the parties and the witnesses the questions you think you need to have answered to reach the correct decision. The result will be a better base of evidence and a more reasoned outcome.

Let me give you some food for thought on what federal sector unions look for in an arbitrator. Here are a few tricks of the trade, also known as relevant case law that you should be aware of. Some were mentioned earlier, but I'll go into a bit more detail on them.

I mentioned one already, namely, the primacy of the labor contract over regulations that are issued after the date of the contract; the contract is already superior. There are three other areas where the differences between the federal sector and the private sector commonly arise—performance appraisals, back pay, and the award of attorney's fees.

Employee performance appraisal is one of the more important nondisciplinary areas of contract interpretation. In the federal sector employees may be fired, suspended, or kept from promotion lists on the basis of an erroneous performance appraisal. On an even more adverse level, employees' rankings for layoff are now included in the consideration of performance appraisals. An accurate and objective appraisal of an employee's performance is consequently most important.

Typically, employee performance appraisal disputes come before the arbitrator as either or both of two alleged contract violations: the union may assert (1) the management violation of contract language specific to the established performance system, or (2) a violation of more general language requiring that the employer administer personnel matters in accordance with applicable laws and regulations. In either case this is one area in which a correctly worded decision will withstand challenge.

Although it took the Federal Labor Relations Authority (FLRA) some two years to develop its approach to performance appraisal arbitration, the lead case was issued 18 months ago.[1]

---

[1]*Social Sec. Admin.*, 30 FLRA 1156 (1988).

In this case the FLRA clued the parties to the necessary elements of an arbitration decision which directed correction of an employee's performance appraisal. I read briefly from that decision:

> When the arbitrator finds that management has not applied the established elements or standards or that management has applied established elements or standards in violation of law or regulation or a properly negotiated provision of the parties' collective bargaining agreement, the arbitrator may cancel the performance appraisal or rating. If the arbitrator is able to determine on the basis of the record presented what the rating of the grievant's product or performance would have been under the established elements or standards if they had been applied or if the violation of law, regulation, or the collective bargaining agreement had not occurred, the arbitrator may direct management to grant the grievant a specific rating. If the record does not enable the arbitrator to determine what the rating should have been, the arbitrator should then direct that the grievant's work product or performance be reevaluated by management as appropriate.

Thus, the FLRA has ruled that arbitrators have authority not only to set aside an incorrect performance appraisal but also to direct the proper rating, provided that they can determine from the record what the correct level of performance should have been.

In other cases the FLRA has shown that it meant business when it established that requirement. For instance, in a more recent case also involving the SSA, the arbitrator determined that the grievant had not been appraised in accordance with the parties' collective bargaining agreement. So far so good. Then the arbitrator ordered management to change the performance appraisal to a specified rating level, unfortunately basing the relief on the general right of equity rather than the magic words "on the basis of the record of evidence." Therefore, the award was modified on exceptions to the FLRA, with the result that the employee was simply reevaluated by the employer. Even if the employee's appraisal were to be raised, which is not at all a sure prospect, the effect of the arbitrator's drafting error was to dilute his otherwise warranted decision as to what the employee's correct performance appraisal should have been.

A similar frustration of the process occurred more recently in a case where the arbitrator's meaningful remedy was successfully challenged because the decision said that management's capricious and arbitrary action violated the intent and spirit of the agreement, and again didn't use the magic words.[2] The award would have been immune from modification by the FLRA if the arbitrator had simply said that management did not apply "established elements and standards in violation of law, regulation, or a properly negotiated grievance provision," and that the arbitrator was determining "on the basis of the record" what the rating should have been.

Based on these cases, the FLRA has given every indication that it will not interfere with the performance-related arbitral decisions which are issued using the correct words and containing the necessary findings. When you get a performance-related case, don't make the mistake of using the wrong words if the grievant is entitled to a remedy.

On the other hand, the FLRA has put less rigidity in the form of the award in the area of back pay. The government has codified the whole authority of the Back Pay Act in Title V of the U.S. Code, and there are regulations implementing that law. All of these provide that back pay is applicable where there is "an unwarranted and unjustified personnel action." Those are the magic words. The net result is that arbitrators have appropriate authority to order back pay, assuming that the statutory and regulatory requirements are met to make such an award legal.

In a decision issued last fall involving the William Jennings Bryan Veterans Hospital,[3] the FLRA reiterated that the elements for a back pay award are (1) a finding that an agency's personnel action was "unwarranted and unjustified," (2) that such unjustified and unwarranted personnel action "directly resulted" in the withdrawal of the grievant's pay, allowances, or differentials, and (3) that "but for" such action the grievant would not have suffered the loss of these benefits. The Comptroller of the United States has ruled that a contract violation is as much an unwarranted and unjustified personnel action as a violation of any other rule or regulation.

Interestingly enough, the use of the magic words in the back pay area has become a bit more realistic, or at least in that case. The arbitration involved a suspension that resulted in a loss of pay for the grievant. The arbitrator found for the grievant and ordered back pay, but the employer claimed that the award lacked the necessary findings. In dismissing the employer's claim

---

[2]*Ft. Eustis*, 33 FLRA No. 50 (1988).
[3]*William Jennings Bryan Veterans Hosp.*, 32 FLRA 1223 (1988).

that the requisite findings were missing from the award, the FLRA allowed some paraphrasing. The arbitrator found that there was "insufficient evidence to support the agency's actions" in its disciplinary suspension. These findings were deemed by the FLRA sufficient to constitute a finding that the grievant's suspension was "an unjustified and unwarranted personnel action" within the meaning of the Back Pay Act. In addition, the arbitrator's order to management to remunerate the grievant for lost pay during the suspension was interpreted by the FLRA as meeting the remaining two criteria, namely, that the personnel action "directly resulted" in loss of pay and that "but for" the personnel action the employee would not have lost the money.

Why the rules for performance appraisals should be more strictly applied than those of back pay remains a mystery to me. The FLRA has yet to change its mind and reimpose more stringent wording requirements for back pay awards. However, if you are going to award back pay, the safest thing to do is to use those three criteria as they were enumerated in the *William Jennings Bryan Veterans Hospital* case.

The last matter is about attorney's fees, which has been undergoing some development in the federal sector. Since in these cases the determination will have been made that the case was handled by an attorney, I'm going to assume that representatives will present you with a basic listing of the elements necessary for attorney's fees. The lead case is the *Naval Air Development Center*,[4] decided in 1986. Another relevant case published the same year held that the employee must have prevailed in the case to collect attorney's fees. *Internal Revenue Service (Baltimore)*[5] stands for the proposition that partial attorney's fees are allowable if part of the personnel actions were unwarranted and unjustified and part were not. The arbitrator can dispose of different parts of the case in different appropriate ways, and order attorney's fees for that part of the attorney's time spent defending the employer's charges against which the grievant prevailed.

There are more recent developments in *Philadelphia Naval Shipyard*,[6] which was issued last summer. In that case it was decided that the arbitrator has continued jurisdiction under the

---

[4]*Naval Air Dev. Center*, 21 FLRA 131 (1986).
[5]*Internal Revenue Serv. (Baltimore)*, 21 FLRA 918 (1986).
[6]*Philadelphia Naval Shipyard*, 32 FLRA 417 (1988).

Back Pay Act to consider a request for attorney's fees that was filed within a reasonable time after the initial award became final and binding. That case followed the reasoning that it would be premature to decide requests for attorney's fees before an award becomes final and binding, since until that time it is not clear that the grievant prevailed and thus the essential element for awarding attorney's fees is missing. The decision does not preclude filing requests for attorney's fees before the arbitrator issues an initial award. But, underscore this, a postdecision request is not untimely.

The FLRA is taking the position that arbitrators can correct and clarify a final and binding award to a limited extent, namely, as necessary to correct a clerical error or a mathematical miscomputation; but unless both parties request it, an arbitrator lacks the authority to reverse an award which has become final and binding. This holding was recently issued in a decision involving the Overseas Federation of Teachers.[7]

The point of this discussion has been to provide a union perspective on what makes a good arbitrator, and to alert arbitrators to the nuances of a few common issues in the federal sector. In the final analysis, the quality of the decision and the efficiency of the hearing to provide a record of the proceedings are the duty of the arbitrator. Union representatives are happy if the arbitrator employs an activist method of operating, investigates the facts at the hearing, and treats the parties as equals. The arbitrator should be more comfortable knowing that the federal employer is not immune to carrying out meaningful remedies where the union or the employees prevail, and that the way a decision is written can affect whatever will be challenged before the FLRA.

4. WILLIAM DAILEY*

The previous speakers have highlighted some very important decisions of the Federal Labor Relations Authority (FLRA). Especially in the area of performance appraisal, they seem to be willing to take a decision and overrule it. In many contexts they have said that arbitrators cannot substitute their judgment for

---

[7]*Overseas Fed'n of Teachers (AFT)*, 32 FLRA 410 (1988).

*Labor Relations Consultant to the Deputy Administrator, Food Safety and Inspection Service, U.S. Department of Agriculture, Washington, D.C.

that of management. I'm an advocate; I don't mind going before an arbitrator and insisting, "Don't substitute your judgment for management," and I've done it. But the FLRA has said quite frankly that performance evaluation is a matter of judgment; it's very subjective. We all know that. You're a 3.0; you're a C; you're superior—whatever you call it in your system. In the last analysis, it's a gut reaction. You can sit around and try to quantify it and call it objective, and say that the federal government finally has a system that is close to what private industry does. But we all know that it's just as subjective in private industry as in the federal sector.

I think what the FLRA is beginning to say, or at least they've implied it, is that arbitrators have the authority in that area, if they use the rules that have been mentioned. If you play your cards right, walk your way through it, you can substitute your judgment and give grievants the rating you think they deserve just the way you can in applying the just cause standard.

If you think about it, in the area of just cause, there are no limits. In a discipline case it's your decision. Is the penalty going to be 15 days, 30 days, or are you going to put the grievant back to work with full back pay? So too, in the performance evaluation area, if I'm reading the Authority right, if you apply the rules, making a finding that the correct standards were not applied or that the agency applied the proper standards but did so in violation of law, regulation, or the collective bargaining agreement, at that point you can substitute your judgment for that of management if there's enough evidence in the record to make a finding, namely, the correct rating that should have been made if management had correctly applied the law, regulation, or the collective bargaining agreement.

As has been pointed out, the Authority is applying those tests, those criteria, and there have been several cases that have followed that lead decision. If you use those criteria, you can substitute your judgment for management's. So it's an opening.

I think it is even more important to look at the reasons the Authority gave for its reversal of the previous ruling. They're indicating that in the Civil Service Reform Act, Congress said there was to be binding arbitration, that grievance procedures would culminate in final arbitration. That was the law. If Congress said that, and if they also said that the scope of the grievance procedure could be negotiated (they took some 27 statutory appeal matters and made them subject to the grievance procedure), they must have known that arbitrators might substitute their judgment for management's. That's what it was all about. I think that's a positive.

Many of us who have had experience in the private sector continue to chafe over the constraints in the federal sector. I'm not going to criticize it as a Mickey Mouse operation because it's the law passed by Congress. It's nothing new; the executive orders did the same thing for some 18 years, if we go back to Executive Order 10988. We have to learn to live with it.

The substance of the rest of my remarks is from a critique of Dennis Nolan's article on the federal sector, in which he talked about the problems and the cures.[1] This was reproduced in a publication of the Montana Arbitration Association in the Fall 1988 issue. The point of the article was that there are things the parties should do to improve federal sector arbitration, most importantly to educate the arbitrator. The article also focused on poorly written arbitration decisions mentioning one court decision by Judge Harry Edwards of the U.S. Court of Appeals for District of Columbia, who wasn't kind, tactful, or polite in what he said about an arbitrator's decision. This has long been a problem in the federal sector. During my tenure at the Federal Labor Relations Council we studied some arbitration decisions and we saw some really bad ones.

I'd like to concentrate on what arbitrators can do to improve the process. Early on, there was the feeling that the federal sector ought to conform to what arbitrators wanted, that there was something about the federal sector that was strange, and that it ought to become more familiar by adapting to arbitrators whose experience had been confined to the private sector. That's not going to happen. All of us have had to adapt to the various state programs; so too you're going to have to adapt to the federal program. The overlay of law and regulation is there. Labor relations, when it came along as a structure in 1962, was required to accommodate itself to law in Title 5 and beyond, everything in regulations starting with the 5 CFR, the FPM, and beyond. And then you get into agency regulations. As was pointed out earlier, unless you can support your agency regulations by compelling need, a lot of that is negotiable.

---

[1]Nolan, *Federal Sector Labor Arbitration: Differences, Problems, and Cures*, in Grievance Arbitration in the Federal Service (Huntsville, Ala.: Fed. Personnel Mgmt. Inst., 1987).

Unions have been asking agencies to sit down and negotiate regulations that touch on personnel matters, and in my agency we do negotiate a lot. Our internal regulations have been worked out with the union and are just as binding as the collective bargaining agreement. But the reality is that the system is not going to change; it was superimposed on this long history of law and regulation. And in interpreting the collective bargaining agreements, arbitrators in the federal sector have to remember that the law and the governmentwide regulation must prevail.

To illustrate my point, let me tell you about two experiences we had with arbitrators—one was a good experience; the other was a bad one. The good one was a case that we lost. We had a two-day hearing. It dealt with a midweek schedule change, a tour-of-duty change. We came in on a Wednesday and told employees that tomorrow they would have to work the afternoon shift instead of the morning shift. We felt we could do that, and we weren't prepared to accommodate the employees in any way. So they filed a grievance, not confronting our right to make the basic change or to determine when they would work, but to require that they be paid premium time for what we did to their work schedule. Since our action had interfered with their plans for that afternoon, they wanted 16 hours' pay for 8 hours' work.

After the hearing there were posthearing briefs; there were the law, governmentwide regulations, agency directives, interpretive decisions, legislative history. We really laid it on. Seventeen study days later, 43-page opinion, $10,000 fee—the arbitrator threw it all back in our faces and sustained the grievance. But what we got was an opinion that we could apply in the future, and it has become part of the fabric of the collective bargaining agreement. From day to day we refer to this decision; it continues to guide us.

However, another decision—the bad one—we won; the arbitrator denied the grievance. It dealt with management's right to select certain employees for a training assignment during which they would train their fellow employees. We felt we had to reach out and pick the very best employees for the job. We weren't willing to share that judgment. The union wanted to set up some sort of equitable procedure for that assignment.

It went to arbitration in the context of a refusal to bargain because we were refusing to negotiate on that issue. The union would not present a proposal because we would have called it nonnegotiable. We had numerous decisions in our favor, and they didn't want to give the FLRA a chance to uphold management's position. So there we were before a private sector arbitrator, trying to convince him that there was no duty to negotiate because of our superior management right.

This case probably should not have been in arbitration; it should have been before the Authority as an unfair labor practice charge or as a negotiability issue. We really laid a record on the arbitrator of FLRA decisions. He gave us 14 study days, an 8-page decision, $8,000+ fee, and it's garbage. The union admits it; we admit it; there's nothing there that we can apply in the future. We didn't get anything back in return, whereas in the earlier case with the 43-page decision we have something we can apply in the future.

The lesson I draw from all of this is that the second arbitrator should have stayed out of the case. He was ill-equipped to operate in the federal sector. The arbitrator should be an attorney or somebody who can think like an attorney. I'm not talking about the personal-injury type attorney or the sort who hangs around the criminal courts. I'm not talking about the workers compensation attorney. I'm talking about the corporate type, the trust department type, the careful kind of attorney who can handle that overlay of law and regulation, or somebody with those skills, careful analytical skills. There is no substitute for this. Dennis Nolan says this too, so read that article.

In the federal sector there's hardly any case that is a nuts-and-bolts contract interpretation type. They just aren't there. In all of them you have to look at law and regulation. Although the advocates are there to educate you, they're not beyond steering you a little askew. We need arbitrators who can sift through all of that, just like in the first case. He took the study time, he wrote the 43-page decision, and we got the answer we could use.

Another thing is that the Federal Mediation and Conciliation Service (FMCS) could do something here. The FMCS will let anybody with five cases get on their arbitrator list. That's not enough. I'm not saying that arbitrators should take the same examination that an administrative law judge has to take, but at least you ought to be required to show federal sector decisions. The FMCS could create a meaningful examination. If the arbitrators can't screen themselves, we urge FMCS to do that, to get people who are qualified and capable of handling the federal sector, who are prepared to roll up their sleeves and work to adapt to the federal sector.

5. FRANK FERRIS*

I would like to talk to you today about a small corner of federal sector arbitration, i.e., interest arbitration. I focus on this area in that there is good news, especially for the people in this room. In 1988 we had more negotiation impasses in the federal sector than in any previous year. Moreover, those people who keep track of the numbers tell us that this next year is also going to be another record-setting period. This is hardly good news for anybody else in the labor relations field. It certainly does not reflect well on the practitioners in the field; however, the reaction among arbitrators such as yourselves is probably somewhat akin to that among a group of orthopedic surgeons on the brink of the football season. Moreover, given the changes associated with the new political administration in Washington, the next few years should continue to be very active ones in the growth of interest arbitration. Because the Federal Service Impasses Panel has been very liberal in approving the use of outside neutrals in connection with interest arbitration, I think members of the Academy should give some thought to how they should operate in these types of disputes.

As is so often the case with any good news, there is also bad news. Though the federal sector parties are going to need experts such as yourselves more and more, you need to be aware that these same parties tire very easily of neutrals who like to make decisions for the parties, especially those who are quick to make decisions. Even though those of us in federal sector labor relations say we are looking for a few good "interest arbitrators," I think we are actually in search of a few tough mediators to help us make our own decisions. Like other negotiators, we want to avoid having an outsider make decisions for us.

I am not saying that someone who comes in and makes interest arbitration decisions is not going to be successful. I have seen many different styles of arbitration work. Indeed, one arbitrator entered a dispute, went through a list of the issues, and then taking them one by one told us how he would decide the substan-

---

*National Treasury Employees Union, Washington, D.C.

tive dispute before he had even heard the positions or arguments of the parties. We did not formally object to the final outcome; indeed, the relationship remained intact and continued to be healthy. However, I must point out that this type of arbitrator behavior is rarely rewarded, even where a good contract is produced. We never used this arbitrator again and this little story quickly spread through the labor-management community alerting our colleagues to the dangers of using this particular arbitrator. By way of emphasis, let me say that arbitrators can close interest arbitration disputes by using many of the same decision-making techniques they use in grievance arbitration. Yet it is unlikely that these approaches will be rewarded by the parties. As I said earlier, we are looking for mediation skills rather than arbitration skills.

Consequently, I will concentrate the remainder of my talk on the ability of an arbitrator to function largely as a mediator. From my perspective, this is a criticially important skill. For example, NTEU just finished negotiating its largest contract. The dispute went to impasse with over 150 issues between the parties. However, even though we gave the interest arbitrator only five days to resolve the dispute, he wrapped up the entire contract without having to make one substantive decision. Now, how do you go about doing the same in your arbitration practice? What follows are my thoughts about how to be a successful interest arbitrator in the federal sector.

I think you have to abandon the reluctance grievance arbitrators normally have about questioning witnesses. The substantial concern in your mind flows from grievance arbitrators taking the initiative to examine or cross-examine witnesses on issues the advocates did not touch or fully explore. There is always the worry that if you conduct your own inquiry you will unfairly help one party over the other and thereby win the undying wrath of the advocate who lost because of your questioning. You must know that in my experience this type of reaction from the advocate isn't likely in interest arbitration. The negotiations dispute is typically as much a communication breakdown as it is a dispute about formal rights. The parties generally are looking for a neutral to get involved in their discussions and help them look at the issues differently or more fruitfully.

Let me give you an example. In a typical case, we will put a proposal on a specific subject, such as performance appraisal, in

front of you, spend a short time explaining how our proposal
works, and then give you some documentary evidence or testimony to support the need for our proposals. The opposing
party will respond in kind. This is hardly the level of communication necessary to produce an agreement. Your job is to make
sure the parties consider the actual, causal problem as well as
alternative solutions. You can only do this by getting involved
and questioning the parties as well as the witnesses. Do not just
ask what the issue is, but also why it is an issue between the
parties. Then, force them to list alternative ways to solve the
problem and explain why they chose the particular approach
contained in their proposals. By getting involved with the parties
through questions such as these, you can begin to send subtle,
and not so subtle, hints as to the weaknesses in each proposal and
the more productive or fruitful approaches the parties should be
taking to solve the problem.

Although it is hardly a secret in the labor-management community at this time, the best seller, *Getting to Yes*, written by Roger
Fisher and William Ury, contains excellent advice to the parties
on how to move through interest arbitration in a problem-
solving manner. The interest arbitrator needs to read this book
as if it were entitled *Helping Others Get to Yes*, looking for various
ways to improve communications and practice multiparty problem solving.

The second suggestion I would give you as part of any effort to
improve the mediation skills among the members of the
National Academy of Arbitrators is that you begin looking over
your shoulders at the fast growing occupation known as "facili-
tator." Generally these people are in the full-time employ of
management and are trained in group dynamics as well as problem solving. In the federal sector they were originally used as
part of efforts to improve the management of the quality of the
work produced by the government, where they have generally
done an excellent job of building confidence in their problem-
solving techniques. Today, they are used more and more by the
parties to solve all sorts of workplace problems. For example, in
one recent contract we negotiated, the parties came extremely
close to replacing arbitrators with facilitators in those disputes
that traditionally go to expedited arbitration. Our thinking was
that all too often there is no contract answer for the types of
problems encountered in grievances that go to expedited
arbitration. As a result, we should not use an arbitrator to search

for the answer, but employ a problem solver who can help us create an answer.

Facilitators have been able to build up this kind of following not only because they use problem-solving techniques rather than the principles of contract construction, but also because the labor-management community is quickly realizing that the workplace is changing so quickly that we are less and less able to rely on answers in a labor agreement negotiated months or years earlier. The best solution is to look at the problem as it exists today, in light of the traditions of the past, and create new solutions tailored to this specific problem. This requires mediation and facilitation, not arbitration.

Facilitators are predisposed to helping the parties create experiments to test several different solutions to a problem. In contrast, arbitrators try to find the one best answer based only on evidence of what happened in the past. In other words, arbitrators restrict problem solving efforts rather than energize them.

Facilitators are respected because of their ability to go beyond the stated issue to help the parties search for the root of a problem. In contrast, arbitrators are comfortable agreeing to stay within the artificially created limits of a stated issue even before they have heard the facts or had an opportunity to assess the disputing parties.

A third piece of advice would be that if you feel compelled to continue to act as decision-making arbitrators, you at least delay imposing a substantive decision as long as possible. Perhaps the least harmful decision you can make is to help the parties decide what the problem is. If they come to the bargaining table thinking a particular issue has to do with the institutional rights of two parties and you can help them discover that it is much more simply a matter of determining how to deal with a law or regulation that stands in the path of a solution, then you have done them a great service. Moreover, you have probably put them on the way to solving their own problem.

If, however, the dispute takes more than providing a decision as to what the root problem of the disputed issue is, then I would suggest that you resort to the next level of decision making by merely giving the parties a direction in which they should go to seek their own solution. For example, if they are arguing over how many steps should be in the grievance procedure and who should attend at each step, you might want to think about advising them to search for a grievance procedure that permits all levels of management and union officials to participate at some point while assuring that the process takes no longer than X number of days to conclude. This sort of direction will often enable the parties to focus more clearly on a resolution and the potential to create package offers, which often settle many issues at once. Finally, when you do provide a decision on the substance you might want to look for ways to give the parties, orally and informally, a choice of a particular resolution. If you do, you will often learn something from their reactions and you may find that once their choices are narrowed to two or three alternatives, at that point they can make the decision themselves.

Federal sector interest arbitration is an extremely interesting area of practice for an arbitrator. You could walk into an agency which has over 100,000 employees and through your efforts, redirect the direction of that agency and government. You can have some impact on the values of the workplace, not just the language of the simple contract clause, and you can promote the building of long-term, mature, labor-management relationships that yield benefits long after you have closed out the dispute. This type of arbitrator is the one that has real impact in the workplace, the one who is frequently rewarded with additional work, and the one who can truly enjoy the practice of arbitration.

Questions from the audience—

Q: In med/arb cases involving interest arbitration, when do you decide that you are no longer a mediator and become an arbitrator?

A: In a recent case we gave the mediator/arbitrator five days from Monday morning to Friday midnight to handle the case. He hadn't decided one issue by 11:30 Friday night, but by one or two in the morning we had it done. Some arbitrators I've dealt with will take the small issues and give the parties some nudges and early decisions to let them know he's there. Others have said: "I will not make a decision. If you want a contract by midnight, go get it." That scares me but it's starting to work. Arbitration has developed in this country as a decision-making process, and we're going to have to find people who think that making a decision is an exception in interest arbitration.

Q: If that's the case, why do you need an outsider at all?

A: Well, we get locked into positions during negotiations. Often we can't see the forest because we have all these trees around us. Somebody else objectively looking from the outside often can help us find our own path through the woods. Sometimes they can't because we're locked into position politically because that's where we have to be. If helping us see those options doesn't work, I would expect that the mediator/arbitrator would begin to use the authority of the office, maybe without saying what the ruling will be, but suggesting to either party that some of the issues are losers. I react to such signals. If I need to get more authorization in that area, that's what I'll do rather than lose the issue. I'll get the authority to change my position to negotiate my way through. When it's clear that mediation is not working, the arbitrator can start calling the shots, which he or she always has the right to do. Those who are successful don't make decisions unless it is unavoidable, but sometimes it's unavoidable.

Sometimes the arbitrator's main job is to get the parties to look at the problem. They are more in love with their language than they are able to see a problem.

Q: What do you do about a whole pile of FLRA decisions and FPR interpretations when you don't have a chance to read any of them to ask questions about them at the hearing? Then when you get home and start writing the decision, you see all kinds of things that seem to apply, but the parties haven't mentioned them during the hearing. What do you do about that?

A: I'd say that the parties before you did not do their job very well. They didn't take their responsibility of educating the arbitrator seriously enough. We come in with expert witnesses who talk about all these things and lay it all out for the arbitrator so that what you say happened, doesn't happen. Since the personnel in labor relations in the federal sector work with law and regulation every day, they sometimes take for granted that the arbitrator knows as much as they do, which is usually a mistake.

The governmentwide regulation applies if it was in effect before the contract was negotiated, and the parties must bring that to the arbitrator's attention. You're entitled to adjourn the hearing for a few minutes or to take a half hour to read all the material and make sure that you comprehend enough of it at the time to ask the right questions about it.

The union has the obligation to make it very clear when some regulations do not apply in a particular case or are overruled by provisions of the agreement and what relation the various documents have to the dispute at hand.

Q: The FMCS currently does not make provision for an arbitrator's listing mediation experience on the bio form. What can be done to let the parties know about an arbitrator's mediation experience?

A: I think the FMCS would be interested in having this information. I know management and union advocates share this information. As I told you, we avoid arbitrators who try to decide everything immediately in interest arbitration instead of trying to mediate. That is probably an excellent suggestion because alternate dispute resolution (ADR) is chipping away at arbitration.

I think that's something that the Academy could communicate to the Mediation Service, to have some place on that bio sheet for ADR and mediation experience and background.

Q: I have a problem interfering in the parties' presentation of their cases. I don't think that they want a so-called activist arbitrator in the grievance cases I handle even in the federal sector.

A: I didn't mean that the arbitrator should take over the case handling and examine and cross-examine witnesses. But when an agency wants to dump 15,000 pages of regulations into the record, and the arbitrator doesn't challenge that, I have a problem with that. I had an arbitrator ask: "Do I really have to read all this stuff? It really doesn't seem to be relevant to the case." The arbitrator should control the process so that it doesn't get out of hand. Government agencies are expert at doing that. With all the regulations they have, they'll do everything they can to prevail in that case. Arbitrators should not let that happen. But I don't expect them to put on our case.

Q: How do management advocates feel about activist arbitrators? I just came from a workshop where the management people opposed that sort of thing.

A: I like to have management advocates who can put on their own case without the arbitrator's help. People are all different; some are better than others. But we work very hard to train our people to present cases in a clear and convincing manner. But in the federal sector often we understand some things that you as arbitrators are totally unfamiliar with, and in those cases you should certainly ask questions. But as a general rule, the parties put on the case; so let them put on the case.

I personally welcome questions from the arbitrators because that's a sign that they understand the case or at least know where we're coming from.

Q: My impression is that federal sector arbitration cases take much longer than those in the private sector. It seems to have something to do with the process and the method of presentation. Is there something that can be done about this?

A: Maybe we can negotiate it into the arbitration clause in the agreement, if there is something that can be done.

I don't think that's a problem we can do anything about. It's a function of the skill of the people putting on the case. Less is better, in my judgment. The more you clutter up the record, the worse the presentation. As more and more regulations go in, I have to improve my defense against a long litany of regulations.

Q: I've found that federal sector advocates try to put in every piece of paper they can get their hands on, and they use 16 witnesses to testify to the same thing. I request in federal sector cases that they jointly docket materials with me in advance of the hearing so that we don't have to start off by wasting an hour for presentation of exhibits. There's got to be a better way to do it.

A: There is a better way. I talked about overcharges in arbitration cases and I also talked about abuses of the system. When I get complaints about exorbitant fees, I tell my constituents, "Well, you put all these documents into the record and insisted that the arbitrator read them. What did you expect?" After that we got more training for the advocates on how to better present a case because they caused their own problems.

Q: Where are all these interest arbitrations taking place? In Washington, D.C., or in other places?

A: They are taking place all over the country. Wherever there is a local impasse, it's ripe for interest arbitration.

Q: How are panels formed?

A: We have a number of panels on expedited arbitration in AFGE and they are working quite well. When people want to get on the panel, they send me a bio, and we sit with management and go over the names and select them. Most of my referrals come from the state central labor bodies. When we need names in a particular area, we call the central labor body of the AFL-CIO and ask them to send names.

II. FLRA REVIEW OF ARBITRATION AWARDS

JAMES M. HARKLESS*

From the beginning of the Civil Service Reform Act (CSRA) in January 1979 to January 1, 1988, there were 1,371 exceptions to federal sector arbitral awards filed with the Federal Labor Relations Authority (FLRA). This averaged about 150 per year. Unions filed 828 of them, about 60 percent. Agencies submitted 528, about 38 percent, and individual employees filed 12, about 1 percent. The FLRA sustained approximately 60 percent of the awards (829), modified or set aside about 18 percent (254), and determined that some 14 percent were untimely filed. Other dispositions were made in the remaining 7 percent (92). These primarily were due to lack of jurisdiction, or the matter was not subject to the filing of exceptions.

Of the union-filed exceptions, the FLRA sustained the awards in 70 percent (582) and dismissed another 20 percent (169) as untimely filed. The FLRA set aside or modified the award in only about 2 percent (19) of union-filed exceptions. By contrast, the FLRA sustained less than 50 percent of the arbitration awards involving agency-filed exceptions (47 percent (248)). It modified or set aside 44 percent of awards which agencies challenged (232) and found that about 5 percent of them were untimely filed.[1] A similar pattern occurred in the 156 decisions which the FLRA issued in calendar year 1988 on exceptions to arbitration awards.

This is a disturbingly high percentage of FLRA reversals in cases where agencies appeal arbitration awards. These figures, however, should be placed in perspective. All these exceptions, whether by agencies, unions or employees, represent a relatively small portion of arbitral awards in the federal sector. As far as I know, there are no hard data on the number of federal sector arbitration decisions. Based on the number of these cases which the Federal Mediation and Conciliation Service processed in FY

---

*James M. Harkless, Vice President, National Academy of Arbitrators, Washington, D.C. This paper was presented at the Academy's Continuing Education Conference in Milwaukee, Wis., October 30, 1988.
    [1]Kenneth L. Smith, a Labor Relations Specialist in the Office of the Deputy Assistant Secretary of Defense (Civilian Personnel Policy), Washington, D.C., compiled these statistics.

1986 and 1987, and the fact that FMCS does not handle all of them I estimate some 1,000 to 1,500 federal sector awards are issued annually.

A considerable number of modifications or reversals of arbitration awards fall into two broad categories: (1) those involving the Back Pay Act, 5 U.S.C. 5596(b), and (2) where the FLRA found that arbitrators had intruded on management's statutory right to direct and assign employees, 5 U.S.C. 7106 (a)(2)(A) and (B). The latter occurs frequently in performance appraisal cases. To a great extent these reversals or modifications reflect the failure of many arbitrators to appreciate that in the federal sector relevant statutes, rules, and regulations are an integral part of the common law of the shop.

During the past year there have been no new developments in FLRA decisions in connection with the Back Pay Act. However, it is somewhat surprising that the FLRA continues to modify and set aside awards of arbitrators including Academy members, where the arbitrators have not met the requirements of the Back Pay Act in awarding remedies to employees. George Birch of the FLRA legal staff reviewed these requirements at the 1987 NAA Continuing Education Conference in Cincinnati. In order to award back pay an arbitrator first must find that an agency personnel action with respect to a grievant was unjustified or unwarranted. The arbitrator also must conclude that this resulted in the withdrawal or reduction of all or part of the grievant's pay, allowances, or differences, and that "but for" such unwarranted action, the grievant otherwise would not have suffered such withdrawal or reduction of pay. Arbitrators also should know that the Back Pay Act was amended in December 1987 to provide for payment of interest on awards of back pay to federal employees.

In the performance appraisal area the FLRA issued two significant decisions in the past year. The first, *Newark Air Force Station*,[2] was decided in December 1987. It involved the arbitrability of a grievance alleging management violated applicable law when it established the grievant's performance standards and elements. The grievance was filed before management had evaluated the grievant against the standards. Applying then existing FLRA case law, the arbitrator determined the matter was not arbitrable. The union had claimed

---

[2] 30 FLRA 616 (1987).

before the arbitrator that the performance standards were vague and nonobjective in violation of 5 U.S.C. 4302, which requires that performance standards, to the maximum extent feasible, must permit the accurate evaluation of job performance on the basis of objective, job-related criteria and must be defined in measurable terms.

In *Newark Air Force Station,* the FLRA noted the broad definition of a grievance under the CSRA, and stated the congressional intent that all matters under the provisions of law can be submitted to the grievance procedure unless the parties specifically agree that certain matters are not covered by it. Earlier in 1987 the federal circuit court of appeals had already decided that an arbitrator, in a removal action for unacceptable performance, has jurisdiction to review whether the performance standards comply with law.[3] The FLRA had previously held that, in a grievance alleging an employee had been adversely affected by management's application of performance standards, an arbitrator could sustain the grievance on the basis that management had applied the standards in violation of law or regulation.

Therefore, in *Newark Air Force Station* the FLRA reconsidered its prior decisions and held that a grievance alleging that management violated applicable law when it established the grievant's performance standards and elements is arbitrable. This is so, even though management had not yet evaluated the grievant, unless the parties had excluded such a grievance from the scope of the grievance procedure. The FLRA could see no reason why an arbitrator should not have the same power to examine the content of performance standards and elements for consistency with law *before* an agency takes action against an employee, as an arbitrator does *after* the agency imposes an adverse action based on poor performance.

The other important performance appraisal case is *Social Security Administration,*[4] decided in January 1988. There the FLRA reconsidered the remedial powers of arbitrators in resolving disputes concerning performance appraisal matters. The FLRA held that where certain conditions are met, an arbitrator may direct management "to grant employees the performance ratings they would have received if they had been appraised

---

[3] *Rogers v. Department of Defense Dependent Schools, Germany Region,* 814 F.2d 1549 (1987).
[4] 30 FLRA 1156 (1988).

properly." The FLRA reemphasized its holding that proposals offered by unions in collective bargaining "which improperly interfere with management's rights to identify elements and establish standards are nonnegotiable." The FLRA said this continues to apply for arbitration awards to which exceptions are filed, if they "alter or determine the content of established performance standards." The FLRA also noted its recent decision in *Newark Air Force Station*.[5]

Against this background the FLRA concluded in *Social Security Administration* that an arbitration award requiring an agency to change a grievant's performance rating does not necessarily violate management's rights under Section 7106 (a)(2)(A) and (B) of the CSRA to direct employees and assign work. The FLRA observed that disputes relating to the application of established elements and standards to an individual employee are grievable and arbitrable. The FLRA accordingly held that arbitrators may sustain such a grievance, if they determine that management has not applied the established elements and standards, or that management has applied them in violation of law, regulations, or a properly negotiated provision of the collective bargaining agreement. When such a finding is made, the FLRA stated:

> The arbitrator may cancel the performance appraisal or rating. When the arbitrator is able to determine on the basis of the record presented what the rating of the grievant's work product or performance would have been under the established elements and standards, if they had been applied, or if the violation of law, regulation or the collective bargaining agreement had not occurred, the arbitrator may direct management to grant the grievant that rating. If the record does not enable the arbitrator to determine what the grievant's rating would have been, the arbitrator should direct that the grievant's work product be reevaluated by management as appropriate.[6]

In applying these principles to the facts of the case, the FLRA concluded that the arbitrator impermissably altered the content of the established standards in issuing his award. The award was modified to provide for reevaluation of the grievant.

Another notable FLRA decision occurred in *Overseas Federation of Teachers*.[7] In that case the FLRA held that an arbitrator lacks authority to reopen and reverse an award which has

---

[5]*Supra* note 2.
[6]*Supra* note 4 at 1160–1161.
[7]32 FLRA 410 (1988).

become final and binding. There the arbitrator had denied a grievance alleging that the agency had violated a provision of the collective bargaining agreement. The union filed exceptions to the award, which the FLRA dismissed as untimely. After that, the union submitted a motion to the arbitrator, requesting him to reopen the award for the purpose of correcting his allegedly erroneous interpretation and application of FLRA precedent. The agency opposed the motion on the ground the arbitrator had no jurisdiction to reopen the matter.

The arbitrator concluded that he had jurisdiction to correct the award to bring it into conformance with FLRA precedents, since the record in the initial arbitration proceeding was incomplete due to the failure of both parties to submit an accurate statement of the law to him. The arbitrator thereupon issued an award reversing his prior award and sustaining the union's grievance. The agency filed exceptions to the corrected award.

The FLRA found in *Overseas Federation of Teachers* that the corrected award was inconsistent with Section 7122(b) of the CSRA and exceeded the arbitrator's authority. The FLRA ruled that the authority of an arbitrator to clarify or correct an award after its issuance permits the correction of clerical mistakes or obvious errors in arithmetical computation, but does not empower an arbitrator to reopen and reverse an award which has become final and binding. The FLRA said the award became final and binding when no exceptions were filed with the FLRA within the time period established in 7122(b), and the parties were bound by it.

The FLRA also remarked that failure of both parties to cite applicable law does not provide a basis for an arbitrator to assert jurisdiction and correct an award to bring it into conformance with precedent. The FLRA ruled that in the absence of a joint request from the parties, the arbitrator had fulfilled his role and was *functus officio* when he issued the corrected award. The FLRA stated:

> The responsibility to identify applicable law is one which is jointly shared by the arbitrator and the parties to an arbitration proceeding. The failure of the parties to identify applicable law may make an arbitrator's task more difficult, but it does not confer jurisdiction on an arbitrator to change an award in an attempt to make the award consistent with the Statute.[8]

---

[8]*Id.* at 415–416.

This contrasts with the FLRA decision in *Philadelphia Naval Shipyard*.[9] In that case the FLRA decided that the Back Pay Act confers jurisdiction on an arbitrator to consider a union request for attorney's fees after the issuance of the arbitrator's decision awarding back pay. The FLRA held that in those circumstances the doctrine of *functus officio* did not apply, as long as the request was filed within a reasonable time after the award was issued or became final and binding. The FLRA indicated that it is permissible for such requests to be submitted during the course of an arbitration proceeding, but that nothing in the CSRA or applicable regulations requires this.

The final noteworthy FLRA decision is *Federal Aviation Administration, National Aviation Facilities Experimental Center*.[10] In that case an arbitrator decided that the agency had not proved the grievant was negligent in performing his work or gave false information to a supervisor. The arbitrator vacated the three-day disciplinary suspension and awarded the grievant three days' back pay. However, the arbitrator denied the union request for attorney's fees on the grounds that: (1) the agency had reason for bringing the charges against the employee, and (2) the agency could not have known in advance that it would "lose in arbitration." The union excepted to this denial on the basis that its request was warranted "in the interest of justice," and because the grievant was determined to be "substantially innocent."

The FLRA held that the arbitrator failed to apply the correct standards under 5 U.S.C. 7701(g)(1) for determining whether the union's request was warranted "in the interest of justice." The FLRA indicated that such a request is warranted under 5 U.S.C. 5596 and 7701(g)(1), when the result of the appeal shows that: (1) the agency's action was "clearly without merit" or "wholly unfounded," or (2) the employee was "substantially innocent" of the charges. The FLRA vacated the award and remanded it for resubmission to the arbitrator for "a fully articulated, reasoned decision" addressing both these standards, as well as reasonableness of the amount of the fees, if they were to be awarded.

---

[9]32 FLRA 417 (1988).
[10]32 FLRA 750 (1988).

In the federal sector it is incumbent on arbitrators to keep abreast of FLRA decisions and other legal precedents. Arbitrators must be sure in each case that any applicable statutes, rules, or regulations are carefully considered. Otherwise, the rate of FLRA reversals or modifications of arbitration awards to which agencies file exceptions will continue to be unacceptably high. This will tend to call into question the competence of arbitrators to resolve successfully labor-management disputes in which some law, rule, or regulation may have an effect. Of course, an arbitrator cannot prevent modification of an award, if the FLRA chooses to reverse its own decisions. However, this has not been the reason for the great bulk of the FLRA's modifications or reversals of arbitral awards.

CHAPTER 11

ARBITRATION IN SPECIFIC ENVIRONMENTS

I. THE STEEL INDUSTRY

1. ALFRED C. DYBECK*

This is a somewhat unique session because I have the privilege of being both moderator and speaker. I started arbitrating as an assistant to Syl Garrett at the Board of Arbitration in the steel industry, and I've been associated with that umpireship ever since. In January 1979, I became chairman of the board. We have two commentators here: Jared Meyer of United States Steel and Robert Kovacevic of the United Steelworkers of America. Since 1981 Jared Meyer has been General Manager, Labor Relations, Arbitration and Administration, for what is now the USS Division of USX. Robert Kovacevic is head of the department that manages wage, coordinated bargaining, and arbitration for the United Steelworkers.

We're talking about permanent umpireships in the steel industry. The other day we had a session on problems in permanent umpireships. Aside from the oxymoronic nature of the term permanent umpireship, one of the speakers divided umpireships into minor and major umpireships. Most of the time we'll be talking here about a major umpireship, but I have held a minor umpireship. In 1968 when I had an opportunity to hear cases outside the U.S. Steel-Steelworkers relationship, I got a call from a company in Tupelo, Mississippi. Both parties were on the phone asking me whether I would be permanent umpire under the contract. I was delighted, but I feared that this would be such a major undertaking that it might interfere with my obligation to the steel industry umpireship. So I asked them how many cases they arbitrated in a year, and after a long silence one of them said, "Well, maybe four," and the other one said, "No, maybe

---

*President-Elect, National Academy of Arbitrators; Chairman, United States Steel-Steelworkers Board of Arbitration, Pittsburgh, Pennsylvania.

three." And I said, "OK, write me in." Three years passed and I never went to Tupelo, but I got another phone call, and they asked me if I would mind being written into the contract again as the permanent arbitrator for their relationship. I don't know what has happened to this umpireship because I haven't heard from them since. Either they're now writing me in without asking me or somehow I lost my acceptability without ever hearing a case.

My experience has been with only one of the companies in the steel industry, namely U.S. Steel, but for many years there have been permanent umpireships involving the Steelworkers and other steel companies, such as Bethlehem, LTV (which should be divided into the J&L and Republic relationships), Inland, Armco, and since 1978 the iron ore industry. Of the major companies that were last in the coordinated collective bargaining relationship, only National Steel has not had a permanent umpireship arrangement (although it did have one at its Great Lakes facility and may still have one there).

At U.S. Steel the parties first established their umpireship in 1945. Prior to that there may have been some arbitration (nobody's very sure), but if there was any, it was on a purely ad hoc basis. In that year the parties established the Board of Conciliation and Arbitration, composed of three members—one designated by the company, one by the union, and the third member (the chairman of the Board) selected by the parties. The Board was authorized to obtain suitable offices in Pittsburgh, Pennsylvania, and to employ the necessary personnel to meet its requirements. Since 1945 the Board offices have been located in Pittsburgh, Pennsylvania, separate from either the company or the union.

When the parties included the term "conciliation" in the Board's title in 1945, they meant exactly that. The Board was expressly instructed in the agreement to "endeavor to conciliate the grievance in a manner mutually satisfactory to the parties." Should such effort fail, the Board was to proceed to arbitration of the grievance. So much for the concept of "med-arb" being some sort of new idea. I am told by reliable authority that the Board took the conciliation duty seriously, so seriously in fact, that the initial Board members agreed among themselves that, if conciliation should fail, all arbitration decisions would be unanimous.

Within a relatively short period of time, however, this attempt at statesmanship failed. The 1947 agreement contained no instruction to conciliate and, indeed, by the early 1950s the Board seldom, if ever, attempted conciliation. In essentially every case, one party representative or the other dissented, many times with written dissenting opinions. (I don't believe, however, that the system reached the point where the neutral wrote a decision and both parties dissented, as I have been informed occurred in a tripartite system at one of the coordinating steel companies.) I should note that the parties have moved so far from the original conciliation concept that strong objection has been voiced when any of the arbitrators overtly attempted mediation of a grievance dispute.

In 1951 Sylvester Garrett was selected as chairman of the Board, a post that he ably filled until the end of 1978. Shortly after his appearance on the scene, the parties decided to remove the partisan representatives from the Board concluding apparently that, since the neutral chairman made the decision in any event, no need existed to continue the tripartite arrangement.

Although the term Board of Arbitration (note the dropping of the word "conciliation"), has continued to be used to this date it has not been a tripartite board and all authority has rested with the chairman of the Board. At about this time in 1952 the relatively new chairman, Sylvester Garrett, was aware that shortly he was about to face extremely difficult and complex issues, such as incentive issues, problems involving the application of the local working conditions provision, and job description and classification problems under the new CWS system. Resolution of these issues, Garrett concluded, required practical input, which only the parties' representatives could provide but which might not always be revealed at the arbitration hearings.

This type of consultation could, perhaps, be provided by a tripartite system. Remember, however, that the parties had just removed the partisan representatives from the Board. This resulted in Chairman Garrett's consulting with the parties and receiving their agreement to what was then a unique procedure in arbitration. The parties agreed that, before any award issued, it could be submitted to a designated representative of each party for comment. These designated representatives were also available for consultation with the chairman prior to the preparation of a full opinion. This procedure worked so well that a tentative draft on virtually every case was being submitted to the designated representatives shortly thereafter. Since 1979, however, the parties have agreed that discipline and vacation scheduling cases are not to be entered into the procedure unless a given case involves a unique question of law or contract. More recently, after the parties agreed in 1987 to new contracting-out provisions, including a very expedited procedure for the processing of such cases, we have not yet utilized the review procedure in such cases, largely because of the time constraints.

The introduction of the review procedure in effect preserved one of the attributes of a tripartite system—namely, the limited participation of the parties in the decision-making function—while discarding the much less beneficial aspects and even detriments of the system.

Over the years the steadily increasing caseload required the chairman of the Board, with the parties' agreement, to use special arbitrators on an ad hoc basis to hear and decide cases subject to his approval. In the early 1960s the parties agreed to hiring the first full-time assistant to the chairman, and within several years two more full-time assistants were employed. In the mid-1970s the complement rose to four, and in 1980 a fifth assistant was employed. Through the 1980s the complement has remained at five. Nonetheless, the caseload remained at such high levels that in addition to the assistants a number of other arbitrators have been used on a case-by-case or ad hoc basis.

Early on, it was concluded by the parties that the assistants hired at the Board need not be experienced arbitrators. Initially at least, all of the assistants were trained from scratch at the Board. After the advent of expedited arbitration in 1971, three of the assistants subsequently hired at the Board had some experience in expedited arbitration.

Several significant patterns have been followed:
1. All the assistants employed are lawyers.
2. Their employment is agreed upon in writing by the parties for a fixed term at a negotiated salary.
3. For at least the first two years of employment, the assistants are expected to devote all of their time to the Board.
4. After two years they may negotiate with the parties the right to hear a limited number of cases outside the Board, subject to the discretion of the chairman.

In terms of grievance resolution output, the Board, from January 1, 1979, through the first quarter of 1989, has averaged 95 grievance resolutions a quarter or about 380 resolutions a year. But this is not the only service provided by the Board. It is involved in a grievance from the date it is appealed to arbitration. Under the agreements administered by the Board, the union has 30 days to appeal a grievance to arbitration from the date of receipt of the company's written answer in third step. This appeal is made directly to the Board, where it is docketed and subsequently scheduled for hearing. An administrative assistant handles the docketing and scheduling, and arranges for hearing rooms in the vicinity of the plant involved, reporter services, and the like. Over half the cases appealed are withdrawn prior to hearing. There are postponements. All of this paperwork is handled by the Board, not by the parties. These services, the arbitrators' salaries and expenses, and the maintenance of a Board staff cost the parties about $900,000 a year.

I have attempted to evaluate the system in a neutral fashion, while admitting to a bias in favor of an umpireship. While the system established by the steel companies, particularly USX, and the Steelworkers is not viable for all relationships, in part at least, it has survived over the years because of the sheer pressure of grievance numbers appealed to arbitration. In the 1980s over a thousand cases a year were appealed to arbitration. Can you imagine the administrative problems the parties would incur if they attempted to handle this number of cases on an ad hoc basis? Even the use of a rotating panel without the administrative work being handled by a third party would be an administrative headache. Thus, I am under no illusion about why the parties have been forced to continue the type of umpireship I have described.

However, there are other reasons for continuing the system. First and foremost is predictability of results. Each party wants to have fairly firm guidance from the Board of its interpretation of the contract. The Board is expected to follow the precedent established over the years. Indeed, I would expect that it is in that context that they negotiate new or changed provisions of the agreement every three or four years. The opinions of arbitrators outside the Board are not considered as precedents, although it is not unheard of that one party or the other will cite an outside case, depending on whose ox is being gored at a given time.

As indicated earlier, another benefit to the parties is the administration of the arbitration system. The Board receives all the appeals, dockets the cases, and schedules the hearings. The particular arbitrator to hear the case or cases is usually selected by the Board from among the assistants or associates at the Board or from the agreed-upon ad hoc arbitrators. Here again continuity is significant. As the arbitrators hear more and more cases, they become acquainted with the steel operations at the plant. All the arbitrators presently at the Board have visited the company's steel-making plants on numerous occasions. So the parties know that, if a case involves a blast furnace operation, the full-time arbitrators know what it is all about and, more importantly, the parties know that the arbitrator knows.

I have observed that it takes about twice as long to hear a case where a relatively new arbitrator is involved compared with an experienced arbitrator at the Board hearing the case. If the parties feel that the arbitrator understands their operation in the mill, they can more efficiently present their case. We also, of course, do not hesitate to engage in a plant visit on a given case, sometimes at the suggestion of one party or the other but sometimes when neither party makes a request.

In a permanent umpireship the parties, in conjunction with the umpire, can by agreement put into place procedures that might not be feasible in an ad hoc relationship. At the Board the parties have agreed to rules of procedure that are available to all staff personnel presenting cases. Aside from some of the purely administrative matters discussed above, these rules require, for instance, prehearing briefs filed 14 days prior to the hearing. In its brief the company is required to include as an appendix the complete record of the handling of the case through the grievance procedure. This record is highly beneficial to the Board, enabling the arbitrator to be apprised before the hearing of the critical facts and issues that gave rise to the grievance. Many times as a result of this knowledge, it is possible to arrive at stipulations at the hearing, reducing the need for receiving evidence that would merely repeat the facts that the record reveals are agreed upon. Only in exceptional cases do we have posthearing briefs.

I would be remiss if I did not also read to you what I believe to be one of the most statesman-like procedural provisions ever agreed upon by competing parties in dispute resolution. This provision deals with the conduct of the hearing as follows:

> A. Hearings will be conducted in an informal manner. The arbitration hearing is regarded by the Board as a cooperative endeavor to review and secure the facts which will enable the Board to make equitable decisions in accordance with the requirements of the

provisions of the labor agreement. The procedure to be followed in the hearing will be in conformity with this intent.

B. Consonant with the dignity and order of the hearing, minimum use will be made of formal and legal procedures. The Board will have a liberal policy in entertaining evidence.

It may be that most arbitrators, in fact, proceed on the basis set forth above. There is a clear advantage, however, when the parties themselves agree to such procedure.

I am not going to claim that the Board is always current in scheduling, hearing, or in deciding the appealed cases. However, with the responsibility placed on the Board for scheduling the cases appealed, there is a constant flow of grievances on the docket into hearing. We normally try to schedule 80 to 100 cases a month depending on arbitrator availability. This means that as many as 15 to 20 cases a week may be scheduled for a given plant. Obviously we cannot hear all of these, but most times, if the plant is not scheduled this heavily, inefficiencies arise because there is at least a 50 percent withdrawal rate before the hearing dates.

The problem with scheduling and hearing arbitration cases where companies with a relatively high grievance load are appointing arbitrators on an ad hoc basis is exemplified by the iron ore experience. In the Masabi Range and northern Michigan there existed in the late 1970s some eight companies or partnerships in the business of producing iron ore pellets, whose employees were represented by the Steelworkers. In 1978 these companies all agreed with the union to establish a permanent umpireship, termed the Iron Ore Industry Board of Arbitration. For some seven months in 1979 I was chairman of that Board. Prior to 1978 seven of the companies and local unions had used ad hoc arbitrators and seldom, if ever, scheduled a series of cases for a given week.

You can imagine the cultural shock that occurred when the IOI Board scheduled as many as eight cases in one week. It was unheard of in those relationships. But, over a period of time the IOI Board convinced the representatives that it was possible to hear two grievances in one day and hold more than one day of hearing in a week.

Obviously the arrangement described above is not viable unless a large caseload demands it. It is expensive, but I am not sure the caseload we experience could be handled efficiently in any more economical fashion under any other dispute-handling system. It has occurred to me that perhaps the very existence of the Board may tend to generate the caseload. I have no way of proving or disproving this thesis. Certainly cases are appealed to the Board that should not be appealed. Many of these, however, are currently being withdrawn or settled after appeal but before hearing. There remains the possibility that were it not for the permanent umpireship making it relatively easy to appeal cases to arbitration and rendering unnecessary the selection of arbitrators on an ad hoc basis, fewer cases would reach arbitration. But that is for the parties to decide, and I am now going to turn the session over to Jared and Bob for their comments and reactions.

2. Jared H. Meyer*

As Al [Dybeck] said, I assumed my present responsibilities in 1981. I therefore had nothing to do with establishing the Board of Arbitration; I inherited it, so my function today is more like that of a fiduciary or trustee, having received from my forebears, like John Stevens, Webb Lorenz, and Bruce Johnston, this institution to manage for a period of time. At some time I will turn it over to other people. I accordingly can take no credit for this institution, for which I have the highest regard. The best I can hope to do is use reasonable care as a fiduciary to preserve the institution, improve it, and pass it on.

As a company man (and I am most comfortable as an advocate), what can I say about the Board. First, you need some necessary preconditions to have a Board of Arbitration. Every business or every company could not efficiently utilize this mechanism. Some of these are up-side attributes of a Board of Arbitration, and some are down-side.

First, you need a high case load. As Al said, the Board costs the parties about $900,000 per year. This is not a large amount of money, when you consider that a continuous castor will cost you $220 million, but it is a significant amount of money. Remember that U.S. Steel is not in the arbitration business; it is in the steel business. Therefore, the Board represents pure cost. From a business point of view no operation can be efficient and sustainable unless it has a high throughput. Your fixed costs eat you up.

*General Manager, Labor Relations, Arbitration and Administration, U.S. Steel Division of USX, Inc., Pittsburgh, Pennsylvania

Regretably we do, and that in turn gives us efficient output and reasonable costs per case.

The second prerequisite is that you have to have a stable of good arbitrators, because you're married to these folks for some significant period of time. It has to be a stable group of arbitrators. That means that you are asking professionals to tie their careers for some period of time, either short or long term but essentially full time while they do it, to only two parties. In many cases that means that the arbitrators' professional career development might suffer because they will have to forgo professional, academic, or other party representation, or other tasks that might be assumed as ad hoc arbitrators.

Although I have criticized decisions of our arbitrators and will no doubt do so in the future, I can say that we have been blessed at U.S. Steel, both before my time and during my time, with an exceptionally able group of arbitrators. I think these people are at the very first rank among Academy members. I feel much more comfortable saying that, having just renegotiated all of their contracts, knowing they won't be asking for salary increases.

Third, you need a large number of plant sites, all of which are union represented. If you don't have that precondition, you cannot maximize the efficiency of the Board, because you cannot schedule in depth. By scheduling in depth I mean that if you have six arbitrators, you don't want to schedule one arbitrator each week for six consecutive weeks. You want to use three or four during the same week. To do that, you need three or four locations that require their services. If you have only two plants, you cannot efficiently use six arbitrators.

If you lack these three preconditions, this seminar is not for you, and you won't hurt our feelings if you move to another. Those are the prerequisites you have to have. There may be others, but in my judgment those are baseline requirements.

In U.S. Steel we have a high caseload; we have multiple union-represented locations (although by a strange coincidence, ever since I arrived in U.S. Steel, we've been shutting down more plants than we've been opening), and we have a stable of arbitrators who I think are in the first rank.

What are the advantages of this arrangement to the company? First, the Board, by reason of its stability, creates precedents that the company can rely on in making its business decisions. That's very important. We don't like to manage in a sea of uncertainty.

We're much more comfortable managing where we know what's going to happen. It's a lot easier to do business. So certainty is very important. The Board provides predictability. In fact, in our labor agreement there are whole sections which are really codifications of arbitration decisions. Syl Garrett in effect wrote our vacation scheduling language. The quality of predictability has actually flowed into the labor agreement, and that's an advantage to the parties.

Second, the Board has the ability, on short notice, to dispatch arbitrators where they are needed if we need to put out a fire. We don't have to call a member of the Academy and be told we can have a hearing date in three months. These arbitrators work for us. We used this asset recently when we had to dispatch an arbitrator to Fairless because there was a fire down there that got into federal court. So you have a resource here that you can command rather than persuade, cajole, or purchase.

Third, the Board provides an opportunity, one that is highly unusual, for executive level review by both parties of proposed decisions, permitting us to head off gratuitous or bad advice. We can address that issue without affecting bottom line results.

I want to make it very clear that this is not a way for the international union and management to get together to conspire against the working man or the plant manager. It's simply that many writers don't follow Lord Chesterton's admonition: "I wrote a long letter because I didn't have time to compose a short one." On occasion, we help the Board with its composition so that the resulting award will serve our needs with minimal damage. That is not the result we are likely to achieve if the first time we see an award is when we open our mail and say: "Oh my God, what are we going to do about this!"

Fourth, a Board is especially effective if the parties have a high withdrawal rate. I assume all Academy members are confronted with this cancellation problem. You commit yourself to time, you schedule a hearing, and one week before the hearing the parties call and say they've settled the case. We in U.S. Steel have a 50 percent withdrawal rate on a thousand grievances a year, so just handling *not arbitrating* would be a very difficult task without an administrative office to manage that for us. This mechanism serves a very good purpose because, if that activity was not going on at the Board, it would be going on at my desk. I have enough to do now.

Those are what I call the distinct advantages of a Board. I commend them to any industry that has the preconditions to use this mechanism.

Now, are there disadvantages? In my judgment there are. Al and I disagree on this. In theory, if I take 1,000 grievances to 1,000 different members of the Academy, I could win 1,000 straight cases because each of you would be deciding one or two cases without knowing what your colleagues were doing in other isolated cases. Realistically, this outcome is not possible with a Board. There is an institutional dynamic which requires both parties to win some cases. That doesn't mean that Fairless can't lose all its cases, but what that plant wants to do is to dump Fairless' losers on Gary or some other location. Within the closed system, however, there's an institutional necessity for this mixed result to occur. In theory, that tendency would penalize the party that is more faithful to the contract because, although sometimes we lean toward the margin of the contract and sometimes we walk down the middle, the net results don't necessarily even out in both directions. I'll leave it to your judgment as to which party benefits from this dynamic.

In addition, as the reciprocal of predictability, but on the down-side, when we get error into the system, we are stuck with it. In U.S. Steel, we adhere to the minority view that we cannot discharge somebody merely for not coming to work, no matter how infrequently that employee comes to work. We have kept some employees that were literally coming to work 50 percent of the time. One of our problems in health care is that we have a few employees who are unique. When one gets sick, usually one of two things happen—one recovers or one dies. In U.S. Steel we have some employees who just stay sick. Yet we were told we could not remove such an employee from employment without just cause, which means you have to catch the employee at the hockey rink, or tending a bar (and we have done just that on occasion) to get rid of them, but on occasion that has been insufficient.

Steel is a very craft-oriented business with work jurisdictions set by arbitration. Our basic labor agreement is about 260 pages. You could take it home to your nine-year-old child, and he could read the whole thing, and he won't find anywhere in that agreement anything about craft jurisdiction. (In the future he will because we had to reverse some of the Board decisions through negotiation.) But in the past craft jurisdiction was not in there.

It's solely an arbitral doctrine. It may even have been a good doctrine back in 1950, but it's a terrible doctrine in 1989.

These are just a few examples of problems which can be aggravated by having a permanent umpireship—once you get a ruling, you're stuck with it. We have been required to change the basic labor agreement to deal with these and some other problems as a vehicle to get us out of some doctrines that we were only into in the first place as a result of arbitral decisions.

Finally, it can happen that any one arbitrator going to any one location can sustain or deny a string of cases at that one location (and I sympathize with the arbitrator on this one), thereby becoming very unpopular at that location through no fault of his own even though he is thoroughly acceptable at all other plants. This does not happen much in the ad hoc world because there an arbitrator sees a party maybe once or twice a year and is gone. Our arbitrators are very capable, as I have already stated, and I have an institutional responsibility as well as a desire to protect them insofar as I can from unwarranted criticism that they are pro-company or pro-union or crazy or what have you. Nevertheless, I think, to the degree that this occurs, it occurs more often in a permanent system because with permanent umpires you have people who have been five to ten years with one relationship, and over time are bound to alienate some people. We have arbitrators who have been with us longer than many people stay married these days.

Some arbitrators long for the good old days, but no one can turn back the clock. With that as background it's very difficult for any manager to tell you that anything in today's world will be permanent. Those born and raised in Pittsburgh, as I have been, can remember when steel mills were permanent. There was no such thing as an employee quitting the steel industry. That was unheard of. It was assumed that when a person got a job with a steel company, it would be permanent. Recently all but 6 of 31 electricians we recalled from strike at Fairless quit the steel industry. That would have been unheard of in the old days.

For 1989 and the foreseeable future, the Board realistically, adequately, and with distinction serves the parties for all the reasons I mentioned. The Board provides us with a service which meets a very real business need. Given U.S. Steel's and the steel industry's other real problems—foreign competition, costs, quality, environment problems—it would be a foolish manager who would go looking for nonproblems to solve when real problems confront him. I had a Yale law professor who taught me: "If you're going to shoot moose, go where the moose are." Similarly, if you want to solve problems, go where the most problems are. Don't solve the ones that are nonproblems. So, for the foreseeable future, from company perspective, this Board will continue to serve us today as it has served us in the past. I therefore would anticipate that this particular dispute resolution mechanism will survive many more labor agreements. However, that said, nothing would please me more than to use the service less.

3. ROBERT KOVACEVIC*

I was interested in Jared's comment about who was more faithful to the terms of the contract—management or the union. There are thousands of grievances filed by our members against the company, and I can't think of a single one the company has filed against the union. So I leave it to you to decide who has abided by the agreement more.

While Jared's experience has included work with the Iron Ore Industry Board as well as the steel industry Board of Arbitration, I have had a somewhat different experience in that I deal with various systems, even with ad hoc arbitrators, since our union has contracts outside the steel industry. We have different systems in aluminum, tin can, and even in the various companies in the steel industry. U.S. Steel is unique. This is the only Board of Arbitration in which we pay the arbitrators a salary and they work for us. In Bethlehem and Allegheny Ludlum, for example, we have different systems. At Allegheny Ludlum we have no permanent umpire, but there is a pool of arbitrators that we draw from, and we rotate that board. At Bethlehem we have a permanent umpire, and he uses several other arbitrators that we call upon, and he dispenses them wherever they may be needed. At LTV we need only one arbitrator for the Republic side and one for the Jones and Laughlin (J&L) side. It could be concluded that the grievance load is less than it is at U.S. Steel or Bethlehem where we have several arbitrators. This type of system would not be logical for any other company except maybe Bethlehem Steel.

---

*Director, Collective Bargaining Services, United Steelworkers of America, Pittsburgh, Pennsylvania.

For those of you who don't know about the steel industry system, we have a draft system, whereby we review the decisions prior to their issuance. We use that procedure in only three systems—the Iron Ore Industry Board, the U.S. Steel Board of Arbitration, and LTV. At one time we kept that a secret so that nobody would know we were reviewing the cases. We're not reviewing the cases to change the bottom line, although the bottom line may have been changed in one instance. But we review them to make certain that the arbitrators do not issue decisions that could totally disrupt our relationship and the collective bargaining process.

My problems are quite different from those that the Board of Arbitration deals with. I not only have to involve myself in those cases, but I also have to deal with other umpires and with other arbitrators in the other systems and at other companies. Familiarity breeds contempt in this business as in others. That is one of the weaknesses of this type of Board. Arbitrators get overexposed. The Board sends an arbitrator back to a location—particularly one who is able to pump out a lot of decisions, very effective, very efficient—but because of this somewhere down the line I will end up with an irate member or local committeeman, who will say: "Don't send that arbitrator back here again," and I've had that happen. I've heard management people say the same thing. They complain about losing cases because they're violating the contract. When local union people tell me to fire the arbitrator, I tell them that you can't fire the arbitrator every time you're unhappy with the decision. Although some arbitrators say that the union has to win some and the company has to win some, I don't think that you have to play a numbers game. I think that there are cases that can go either way, and when that happens, some arbitrators reflect on whose turn it is today.

The point is that I may not be upset about a certain decision, but that same decision may totally upset the local union people because of their personal involvement, because of political pressures. The company has the same problem. The managers say: We'll violate the contract because you should not have negotiated that provision; if the union files a grievance, you defend our action. When they lose, they want to fire the arbitrator.

I have been fortunate in dealing with a lot of permanent umpireships in that the consistency of decisions are such that we have not been subjected to a lot of the pressures. That's not to say that some arbitrators do not seem to fall into a pattern. When they do fall into that pattern, hostilities are bound to arise. With mystery novels, I have a habit of looking at the back to see whether the butler did it. Likewise I always look at the award to see whether we won.

I don't like surprises. I can pretty much predict what a particular arbitrator will do in a given case. When I get a decision I can't understand, I try to look for a reason. Arbitrators must have stability. That's the only way the U.S. Steel Board of Arbitration can survive. The day I have to yield to local union people or Jared has to yield to local management to fire an arbitrator under this system will only generate a tit-for-tat attitude: you fired one so now I'll fire one. We can't bend to that. When you start firing people, you have difficulty finding replacements. We have great arbitrators.

My counterpart at LTV once said: "There's no such thing as a good arbitrator." This was said in presence of an arbitrator, and what he really meant was that it depends on what decision comes out; somebody wins and somebody loses. I don't agree. A good arbitrator pays attention to the contract and is consistent.

About five years ago I became somewhat disillusioned about the arbitration process. The steel industry was in such terrible shape, and I began to feel that arbitrators were reading the newspapers instead of contract language. If the steel industry is in bad shape, let the union deal with the concessions that we may have to make at the bargaining table. I don't want an arbitrator saying that it makes good business sense to rule a certain way. I was on the telephone pretty fast about that decision.

You can't dispense your own brand of industrial justice. You must interpret that agreement and render a decision that is logical and that has the proper rationale to be acceptable. I don't mind losing cases. I presented eight cases before an arbitrator and never won one, but in my opinion that arbitrator is a top professional. So I don't look for a won-lost result.

If people ask me whether someone is a good arbitrator, I have to base my answer on the past record. A local union person called me the other day and asked about an arbitrator. I told him I thought the arbitrator was pretty good. The local union person asked, "How is he on discharges?" People expect arbitrators to be different on different types of cases.

I don't agree that arbitrators should make a case for either party, but they have an obligation to get the facts. If that means asking questions, they should ask them. I don't expect questions because I present a pretty good case, but in our business we have some weaker staff people. If arbitrators know a question should be asked and they don't know the answer to it, but refuse to ask it on the ground that one or other of the parties would benefit, I think they are not performing in a manner that is consistent with the way in which this Board operates. The arbitrator owes it to the parties to get the facts.

Sometimes arbitrators on our Board of Arbitration will interrupt and ask about eight questions, all of which I intended to ask. But at that particular time it may be important to the arbitrator to get those facts in a preliminary manner to help with understanding so that the questions will not be forgotten. That's what I like about the Board. Our arbitrators are trained properly to get the facts. I don't have that opportunity with ad hoc arbitrators or in other systems. We have conferences and get a chance to tell them what we don't like about a proposed decision, which we don't do with other arbitrators.

What do I look for in an arbitrator? Integrity first of all. The numbers game is not important. Integrity is the supreme obligation that arbitrators have to themselves and to the parties. If arbitrators have character and integrity, I won't worry about whether they should be fired. Our arbitrators are very experienced, but at one time they weren't. Maybe they're still learning. Experience is something you can acquire, but intelligence and integrity you are born with. In our system experience is what you get while you're being paid, whereas in some other situations experience is what you have when you're too old to get the job.

In our system the Board reviews every decision, whereas in ad hoc arbitration you send in the decision and somebody says, "Boy, did you blow that one!" and you don't know why. With our system arbitrators get not only the input of the chairman of the Board but also our input. It's pretty much a screened decision-making process, but it's one that we feel we can live with. We get the benefit of more than one mind.

Nothing turns out right unless somebody takes on the job to see that it does. We have been very fortunate in the chairmen we have selected—Al Dybeck and before him, Syl Garrett. They make that board run. Regardless of the quality of the arbitrators under them, if you didn't have someone capable sitting as chairman, the system would fail. We're going to have this system with us for a long time. Jim Wright, former speaker of the U.S. House of Representatives, said it all when he stepped down, quoting Horace Greeley: "Fame is a vapor; popularity is an accident; riches take wings; and those who cheer today will curse tomorrow. But one thing will endure and that's integrity." As long as we have arbitrators with character and integrity, this system will endure.

Questions from the audience—

Q: Under your current contract, do you have prearbitration screening?

A: What we have is a review procedure. What occurs is that someone from my department and the company representative weed out cases because we have such a heavy caseload. In some plants we have 600 or 700 grievances, but at Fairless we're talking thousands. Once these two weed them out, we bump them up to a neutral arbitrator to review. The neutral will tell the parties who is likely to prevail or that to get the facts will take arbitration. He'll take another shot at getting the garbage out of the system. If it goes to arbitration, however, he will not be the person to hear that case. We've decided on this as a permanent part of the system. It's not a brand new provision; there are similar provisions in other steel agreements, but they have not been implemented.

We're using one person now. If it works well, we may agree on other arbitrators to do it.

Q: One speaker said that craft jurisdiction was not in the agreement but was invented by arbitrators. The parties years ago negotiated the CWS system, and the maintenance operation was then run by management in accordance with those classifications with the custom of using crafts for certain jobs. Didn't the arbitrators merely implement what management had been practicing for years?

A: The CWS system, which was put in before I came with U.S. Steel, was part of a two-pronged process which dealt with wage-rate inequities; the other half dealt with incentives. That process ran aground like the Exxon Valdez. The only part of the process that the parties came to grips with was the CWS half. I view that program principally to create equitable classifications on the job and to replace negotiated job rates. That does not necessarily imply that a welder who does not weld for some period of time cannot be reassigned to welding. We find that we've lost that opportunity because now that's part of the millwright job.

Q: The parties could negotiate into the contract language that would totally take away arbitral discretion. If not, do you factor that in?

A: In 1961 I worked at U.S. Trust Company in New York. I was taught that in drafting there is no gold star for brevity. The gold star is for clarity. I've tried to adhere to that standard. I have tried to draft provisions that are perfectly clear. Of course, in collective bargaining there are times when you have to knowingly leave provisions ambiguous. If I achieve that objective of clarity, however, I expect that language to be applied. Any language is inherently ambiguous and there is obviously arbitral discretion because if it was all that clear, we wouldn't even need the agreement. It is very dangerous for an arbitrator to guess what's going on behind the scenes. You usually will guess wrong, and you may find the case is really one the union wants to lose. When you go too far down the road of arbitral discretion, what you are doing is thinking in terms of what the objectives might be and are acting on incomplete information, thereby producing a result which may be exactly contrary to what the parties intended. With your equitable decision you may cut the legs off a management or union representative, who has told the local people to eat this one but has gotten overruled by much brighter people.

Q: Does the arbitrator like to have decisions reviewed by the parties? Is there any application of this to ad hoc arbitration?

A (Dybeck): Yes, I like it. Not because I'm all that happy about people telling us how wrong we were, but even that's educational. We have a proclivity for sticking our feet in the collective mouths of the parties. On occasion both parties on the same sentence in the draft will say, "Do we really need that to get the same result?" It could be used in ad hoc work only if the parties agree to it. In some tripartite situations you find the advocate members on the board saying, "Just write up the opinion, and one of us will concur and one of us will dissent." But I've seen times when the board really had to work. That way you get input that you don't ordinarily have. I use tripartite boards; I literally ask them to use the system for a constructive purpose.

If I were an ad hoc arbitrator, to maintain acceptability I would try to get the parties to agree to that review procedure because I think it would be in everyone's interest. I don't know how far you can comfortably go in suggesting this, however, because if the suggestion is not taken, at some point you inevitably have to drop it.

Q: Would you recommend that the parties put that review procedure in the arbitration clause in the contract?

A (Jared): I don't think it should be in the contract. At one time in U.S. Steel this process was quite secretive because if the wrong person found out about it, he could make an issue of it by claiming that the company and the union were getting together and fixing the grievance. That is not what happens, of course, but to put it into the basic labor agreement enhances that risk. In terms of sitting down and negotiating a grievance procedure, however, it is certainly something to talk about. If it fits in with your arbitration arrangement, you could put it in a side-bar letter. We have several side-bar letters with the Steelworkers that are not published but are binding.

Kovacevic: One of the problems of the review procedure is that when the decision finally comes out, whether it's for management or union, people think that we had the power to change the bottom line decision. If they don't like the decision to begin with, they say, "How did you let that decision come out? You're the one who reviewed that decision." The purpose of the system is not to arrive at a decision any different from what the arbitrator would have. It is only to review the manner in which the rationale is handled or to take something out that is not necessary or may be damaging to the parties at a later time. It has to be handled quite delicately, so I would certainly advise against putting it in the contract.

Dybeck: There is another advantage. We don't always have transcripts in our cases. As a matter of fact, there is a rule that we have them only in incentive and discharge cases. I can have them in other cases at my discretion. But the review system is also educational for the parties, primarily for the union, because the representative, in reviewing a case, might find that facts didn't go in or arguments weren't made so that later he can go back to the local people and help them improve their presentation skills.

II. The Postal Service

J. Earl Williams*

It is an understatement to suggest that the United States Postal Service (USPS) is a large and complex organization. It is one of

*Member, National Academy of Arbitrators, Houston, Texas.

the largest employers in the world, approaching 750,000 employees at the present time. Every geographical area is represented; there are more than 30,000 post offices in 50 states, Guam, Puerto Rico, and the Virgin Islands.

About 90 percent of the employees are unionized. The two major unions are the American Postal Workers Union (APWU) and the National Association of Letter Carriers (NALC). Between them they represent more than 500,000 members. A third union is the National Post Office Mail Handlers, Watchmen, Messengers and Group Leaders Division of the Laborers International Union of North America AFL-CIO, which represents about 50,000 sorters and handlers. The fourth union is the National Rural Letter Carriers Association, representing more than 75,000. The Mail Handler arbitration load is minimal compared to the first two unions, and the National Rural Letter Carriers case load is extremely small, to some extent almost nonexistent. Add to this some 30,000 managers, and you have the basis for a very complex organization.

Arbitration in the USPS has labored under a handicap to some extent, since the grievance and arbitration procedure was late in developing. Even though unions represented employees in the Postal Service as early as the late 1800s, it was not until a 1963 presidential executive order that a procedure for advisory arbitration was set up. This resulted from an agreement between the former Post Office Department and six organizations certified as exclusive representatives at that time. The arbitrator's award could be appealed by any party to the Assistant Postmaster General for Personnel, whose decision was final. No one suggested that this was truly final and binding arbitration.

This changed dramatically in 1970 with the passage of the Postal Reorganization Act, which placed postal labor relations under the private sector National Labor Relations Act. Starting in 1971, there have been seven national agreements between the parties. All of them provided for final and binding arbitration. While there are those who suggest that, somehow, arbitration in the Postal Service is different and not quite the same as arbitration in the private sector, this is a misconception. Every conceivable kind of issue that can arise in the private sector (and perhaps a number which would not arise in the private sector) arise in the Postal Service. Consequently, from the beginning the problem has been how to manage the large number of grievances and arbitrations that arise from so complex an organization.

In 1971 the parties operated under a one-tier level of grievance arbitration, with all cases, regardless of the type, being heard in the same forum by one of the arbitrators on a small, mutually agreed-upon panel or occasionally by a mutually agreed-upon ad hoc arbitrator. All cases were scheduled from headquarters by a mutual letter, which caused such delays that there developed an ever-increasing backlog of cases.

Realizing the problem, the parties, in their 1973 negotiations, adopted an expedited arbitration procedure for hearing minor disciplinary cases beginning on January 1, 1974. This was a traditional kind of expedited arbitration, in that the hearings were to be informal with no transcripts or briefs. Decisions were to be short, noncitable, nonprecedential, and issued within 48 hours. Thirty panels of arbitrators were established throughout the country to hear these cases, and the panels have been enlarged continuously until today, when there are more than 150 arbitrators who hear only expedited cases.

Getting back to the 1971 agreement, it also stated that the contract was a complete agreement of the parties, and that neither party had any obligation to bargain about anything else during the life of the agreement. This did not bode well for an organization as complex as the Postal Service. So, the parties changed Article 19 in the 1973 agreement to allow for continuous revision of contract obligations through handbooks and manuals. This increased the need for expertise on both sides of the table, as well as the need for increased expertise on the part of arbitrators.

To meet this need in the ever-increasing case load, and based upon a subcommittee's recommendation, the parties changed the grievance arbitration procedure in the 1978 labor negotiations. Scheduling was to be done by regions on a first-in, first-out basis, and submission letters were eliminated. Parties were encouraged to settle cases at the lowest possible level. The national parties also agreed that arbitrators would serve for the life of the contract plus six months. It was felt that this would give more stable expertise to the various panels. Finally, there were to be regular and expedited arbitration panels within each region. This included regional panels for removals, as well as contract cases, and a panel for impasses when the parties negotiate at the local level. These were in addition to the expedited panels.

Despite the variety of panels and the introduction of computerization for scheduling, the backlog continued to grow. By the time of the 1981 negotiations, it was evident that the unions, during the life of the 1978 agreement alone, had appealed almost 40,000 cases to arbitration and 19,000 were backlogged. When you compare this to the fact that the Federal Mediation and Conciliation Service gets only about 30,000 requests for arbitration panels per year from all types of industries, the size and complexity of the postal grievance arbitration procedure is evident.

It appeared that cases were not being settled at the lowest possible level. In an attempt to reduce the backlog, the expedited system was expanded, in that certain contractual issues could be referred to expedited arbitration. In addition, an expedited backlog procedure with a separate panel was developed in agreement with the APWU and the NALC. The APWU procedure allowed the use of written fact sheets, containing facts and contentions, to be put before the arbitrator, and witnesses were to be used only for credibility purposes. While this procedure, over a couple of years, greatly reduced the number of backlog contract cases, the advocates were not happy with the system, because they had to rush through the hearings with little time for research and preparation, and the arbitrators, who felt that it was just another form of expedited arbitration, were not carried away with the system either. Consequently, the parties went back to the old system of sending all contract grievances with a few exceptions to full arbitration at the regional level.

From 1981 on the parties have experimented with a number of ways to stay on top of the arbitration case load. In recent years, for example, it was not at all unusual for at least 40,000 cases to be certified to arbitration at any given time. The problem is complicated by the fact that the sheer volume makes it difficult to relate to many of the cases until the last minute. As a consequence, as early as the period 1978 to 1981, only 47 percent of the discipline appeals and less than 7 percent of the contract appeals actually were arbitrated. It doubtless is true that less than half of each is arbitrated at the present time.

One of the ways the APWU and the Postal Service used to stay abreast of the case load was known as the "blitz." This brought together in one location a number of arbitrators and parties from all over the region, and arbitration might go on all day for up to a week. Hundreds of cases were scheduled, and hundreds of backlog cases, in the event that any was resolved at the last minute. While this seemed to have an appreciable effect on the case load, it was extremely burdensome on the parties, for the sheer volume was too much to digest in a week's time.

Other procedures have been tried. For example, efforts have been made to set up a panel for a major city, such as New Orleans. In trying to cut down on expenses, the parties used only local arbitrators, many of whom were not qualified in Postal Service arbitration. Other cities are considering having a panel of arbitrators for their city chosen from the regional panels. In addition, a wide range of programs has been worked out between the parties in an attempt to settle grievances before they reach arbitration. Some of them have borne substantial fruit.

While this has been an extremely brief overview, the complexity of the labor relations organization and the enormity of the case load are obvious. However, as late as 1971 the parties in Postal Service labor relations were at essentially the same place as labor relations in the rest of the United States in the 1930s. They were starting from scratch. They learned their lessons well, and advocates have been continually trained. As a consequence, I feel that they have moved faster and more professionally than almost any labor relations group in the United States. At the same time, there are a number of inherent problems, which continue to make it difficult to stay on top of the case load and to find ways to reduce the number and cost of arbitration. Some of the problems are:

1. *Selection of arbitrators.* An overconcern with box scores of arbitrators, mixed with a little politics, has often affected the selection of arbitrators to regional panels. As a consequence, if an arbitrator greatly favors one side over the other, that side tends to shepherd and protect the arbitrator through thick and thin. This has had some effect on the quality of arbitrators and feelings about the system.

2. *Scheduling of arbitrations.* Arbitrations are scheduled by computer, which matches arbitrators with dates they have given in advance and locations. However, arbitrators are asked to give dates six months in advance, and they have no idea where the postal cases will be. Consequently, they are often boxed in with other cases, when they ultimately find out where they are scheduled on a certain date. In addition, the computer is not programmed for economy. As a result, one arbitrator may make a trip of a thousand or more miles each way, four times in a month, when the cases could be put back-to-back, saving the parties thousands of dollars. Since many of the postal arbitrators are

full-time arbitrators and can be flexible in their schedules, real economies could be realized, if the parties contributed to the salary of one person, who would call the arbitrators as their case loads came out of the computer and would work out travel schedules and back-to-back hearings. The monthly savings would more than offset an annual salary.

3. *Top management instability.* It is well known that many changes have taken place at the top levels of the Postal Service from the Postmaster General down to postmasters and regional positions. This has made it difficult to maintain consistency of policy to the extent that lower level management would like.

4. *Details.* For the stated purpose of giving postal employees a broad experience over a number of areas, a great deal of detailing to other jobs is done in the Postal Service. Unfortunately, the net result, for example, may be that a very stable labor relations staff at a large post office is decimated by details out and inexperienced details in. On one occasion a few years ago I went to the Houston post office for cases and discovered that all the labor relations representatives were new details, and none of them knew the union representatives with whom they would be arbitrating that day. This obviously affects arbitration case loads.

5. *The political nature of unions.* While unions by their nature are and should be democratic, this results in problems for all unions. There often is a turnover of stewards and local presidents. A large number of cases must be arbitrated because of the political position of grievants and/or possible lawsuits or EEO complaints if they are not. A Supreme Court decision in *Bowen v. United States Postal Service*[1] held the APWU liable for damages in a breach of the duty of fair representation because the union had declined to take the grievant's case to arbitration. This has expanded the number of cases going to arbitration.

6. *Training.* Given the thousands of supervisors and shop stewards, it is an almost impossible job to train to the extent necessary to keep all of them abreast of the contract, workbooks and manuals, rules and regulations. This inevitably leads to a greater number of grievances and arbitrations.

7. *Expedited arbitration.* Experienced arbitrators generally are not interested in a steady diet of minor discipline in contract cases. No study time is allowed, and the cases are noncitable and nonprecedential. For the most part the expedited system is

---

[1]459 U.S. 212, 112 LRRM 2281 (1983).

where neophyte arbitrators are trying to break in. In a speech at
the 36th Annual Meeting of the Academy in 1983, the General
Manager of the Arbitration Division, Labor Relations Department, U.S. Postal Service, pointed out that many of the awards
did not have a sound contractual basis. This mixture of noncitable, nonprecedential cases and dissatisfaction with many
awards leads to arbitration of more and more cases. This problem is exacerbated when contract issues, such as denial of employee requests for miscellaneous leave, are thrown into the
expedited system. This issue became a major regional issue and
eventually went to the national arbitration level. Its inclusion as
an expedited case encouraged local people on both sides to keep
throwing the issues into the expedited system. Finally, as the
manager said, the lower costs of expedited compared with regular arbitration panels encourages grievances, and people at the
local level throw more and more expedited cases into the mill, so
that the total cost is even more than it might be otherwise.

8. *Experiments with local panels.* In a few cities experiments
were tried in the hope of reducing arbitration costs. Local panels
were set up composed only of arbitrators living in the local area.
In New Orleans, for example, none of them were postal arbitrators. Therefore, there was great dissatisfaction with the quality of the awards. This encouraged the thinking that there are no
standards regarding most issues, causing ever-increasing arbitration. I understand that, at least in New Orleans, this problem
is being corrected.

9. *Handbooks and manuals.* Like all federal agencies the Postal
Service has myriad handbooks, manuals, rules, and regulations.
Clearly some of them are needed because everything cannot be
put into the national agreement. However, the problem is the
lack of availability of these handbooks and manuals. At a recent
National Academy regional meeting, a member chairing a postal
panel discussed this problem:

> I remember the first time that the parties cited the Employee &
> Labor Relations Manual to me, and I said, "Well, let me have a copy
> of the manual." There was a pause followed by hysterical laughter.
> "This guy wants a copy of the Employee and Relations Manual, hoo,
> hoo, ha, ha!" I tell you, people, I would stand a better chance of
> getting an autographed copy of The Satanic Verses from the Ayatol-
> lah Khomeini. I have concluded that there is only one complete copy
> of the Employee and Labor Relations Manual, and it is locked up in a
> platinum chest in a missile silo under Cheyenne Mountain.

The net result is that arbitrators know only what is handed to them from the manuals on a case-by-case basis, and the parties spend a great deal of time searching through manuals trying to find additional justification for arbitrating a case that they think they will lose based solely on the national agreement.

10. *Language in the national agreement.* While the local parties have no control over the language in the national agreement (and this is not unusual in labor relations), some of the language contained in the national agreement leads to grievances and arbitration. For example, an article in the national agreement is devoted to the assignment of light-duty work to ill or injured employees. It is the most liberal language related to light duty that I have ever seen. As a consequence, this tends to encourage employees to grieve every time light duty is requested and denied. On the opposite side, the language related to shortages in fixed credits is the toughest that I have ever seen. In fact, postal arbitrators generally hold that the very fact of a shortage in fixed credit is a rebuttable presumption that the employee has not exercised reasonable care and, therefore, is guilty of the shortage. It goes without saying that every employee who is disciplined and/or ordered to pay a fixed credit shortage files a grievance and pursues it to arbitration.

11. *Technical approaches.* Although the parties probably did not plan to be technical, they have wandered into technicalities, which appear to increase grievances and arbitration, as a result of detailed language and/or procedures. Some of them are:

(a) The language as to how one goes from Steps 1 to 3 in the procedures which must be followed, is extremely detailed. It includes making known all facts, contentions, provisions, and exchanging relevant papers and documents. Consequently, a favorite approach of some advocates is merely to say, "The information presented by the other side is not in my file. Therefore, it cannot be considered." Advocates from both sides have told me, "It is a game we play."

(b) At any time either party can conclude that an interpretive issue under the national agreement, or some supplement thereto, may be of general application and send the case to Step 4 of the grievance procedure. More often than not, Step 4 is used for strategic and political purposes rather than bona-fide national interpretive issues. This prolongs and duplicates the process.

(c) There is a national level arbitration panel, which was set up for the purpose of hearing cases with interpretive issues of general application. Yet, this essentially is what Step 4 does. So, there is duplication of effort here. There is also confusion among the parties and the arbitrators as to the precise role of the national interpretive arbitration panel. I have taken the position that the parties established the panel for the purpose of making a final and binding decision to be used by all regional arbitrators regarding interpretive issues. However, until the parties and all regional arbitrators accept this role of the national panel, many issues will continue to be arbitrated unnecessarily. There needs to be a clarification.

(d) Then, there is the battle of awards. Since regional awards are citable and precedential, most regional arbitrators receive an avalanche of awards. I have received as many as 15 or 20 from each side in a single case. In an attempt to develop order out of chaos and to have standards, which say, "This is where we are on this issue," I have written a number of standards. However, even if the evidence on a particular issue is clear in that most arbitrators decide one way, this has not stopped the other side from throwing in its handful of winning awards. Fewer grievances would be pursued to arbitration and much money saved, if the parties could find a way to recognize standards in terms of certain issues.

(e) Finally, the procedure appears to be that for every kind of issue there should be a separate grievance. For example, employees absent from work who are not excused may suffer two penalties. First, they will not receive paid leave for the absence, and, second, they may be subject to discipline for unauthorized absence. But, the employee will have to file two separate grievances, which may go to two separate panels for two separate arbitrators to decide essentially the same fact, that is, whether the employer should have approved the employee's request for leave. The same is true on a wide range of issues, such as AWOL/discipline or disciplinary action (including fights or drugs), in which five, eight, ten, or more are involved in the same situation. Yet, there might be five, eight, or ten different grievances and the same number of arbitrators.

Summary

Despite the many problems, in terms of case load and the complexity of the system, many arbitrators feel as I do that the

Postal Service and its advocates and arbitrators form a family. We don't like to be criticized by outsiders, and we are working on our problems constantly. Consequently, this has been a short summary of some of the problems one member of the postal arbitration family feels other members of the postal arbitration family should consider. If working together we can find ways to resolve some of these problems, as well as to implement the innovative measures that Postal Service advocates are currently proposing, great progress will be made in the reduction of the case load and the cost of arbitration.

[*Editor's note:* Those who participated in the panel discussion of Postal Service arbitration, besides Williams, were: William J. Downs, Director, Office of Contract Administration, U.S. Postal Service, Washington, D.C.; Thomas A. Neill, Industrial Relations Director, American Postal Workers Union, Washington, D.C.; Thomas B. Newman, Regional Manager, Labor Relations, Central Region, U.S. Postal Service, Chicago, Illinois; and Lawrence Hutchins, Vice President, National Association of Letter Carriers, Washington, D.C.]

III. THE RAILROADS

MARTIN F. SCHEINMAN*

Our topic today is arbitration in the railroad industry. To give you some familiarity with this unique area with long experience in arbitration, I will begin with a historical overview.

Most of the conferences on railroad arbitration have focused on the problems of the process—the delays in hearings, the delays in rendering decisions, inadequate funding, excessive resort to the grievance procedure, failure of the organizations to screen grievances, failure of the carriers to provide due process in discipline, objectives perceived by the parties as antiquated and no longer relevant. I expect we will hear more of these complaints today.

However, I believe that there is another side, and I think we should start with that. Many of the basic tenets of arbitration that we know about, such as just cause in discipline, relationship between language and practice, local practice versus systemwide

---

*Member, National Academy of Arbitrators, New York, New York.

practice, fluidity of the recognition clause (or as we call it, the scope clause), issues of how to deal with veracity and honesty of witnesses—all trace their origins to the railroad industry. This may come as a surprise to those who have cases in the railroad industry and then go out to arbitrate cases in other industries for the first time, to find out just how much applicability there is. This industry is dominated by decisions of individuals who are perceived as giants in the arbitration practice. Many of the founders of this Academy, many who are the greats in the profession, have had some relationship with the railroad industry. The same names keep coming up.

In railroads we have two kinds of arbitration—voluntary and mandatory. Voluntary arbitration applies to interest disputes. Pursuant to Section 7 of the Railway Labor Act of 1926, as amended, in major disputes the parties upon agreement may have their disputes submitted to binding arbitration, that is, interest arbitration. This procedure has been used throughout the years, but not as extensively as some may imagine. In his detailed study of this aspect of arbitration, Benjamin Aaron reported that 350 cases were filed for interest arbitration from 1935 and 1975; 152 terminal and railroad companies and 60 labor organizations were involved. In 1988 we discovered that there were six railroad proffers of arbitration, some of which were accepted, primarily in the commuter railroads. I recommend Aaron's study to those who want to look more closely into this matter of voluntary interest arbitration.

If arbitration is not accepted, the disputes are resolved either through negotiation or through the emergency board procedures set forth in Section 10 of the Railway Labor Act. These are actually factfinding boards and therefore outside the scope of this particular seminar. I mention it because the terminology is familiar to many of us, and many have had some involvement with presidential emergency boards, congressional advisory boards, and the like. In 1988 we had five presidential emergency boards, but there were no congressional advisory boards.

In these interest disputes, the panels are normally tripartite, payment of the partisan members is made by the parties selecting them, and payment of the neutral is made by the National Mediation Board. This is a unique aspect of this type of arbitration, which raises some eyebrows.

The main type of arbitration we are going to talk about this afternoon is called arbitration of minor disputes, mandatory arbitration, grievance arbitration, rights arbitration—contract interpretation and application, time claims, seniority claims— the run-of-the-mill disputes that labor arbitrators and parties deal with. In most arbitrations outside the railroad industry, one does not begin arbitration without discovering the arbitration clause, by which the parties have agreed that certain issues will be resolved by the machinery called a grievance procedure with the final step being arbitration. This is unnecessary in the railroad industry.

The railroad industry is the only one where Congress has prescribed as mandatory the administrative machinery for resolving minor grievance disputes, and has provided further the payment to resolve these disputes. In 1934 the Railway Labor Act was amended to add Section 3, establishing the National Railroad Adjustment Board, statutorily required to be in Chicago, Illinois. It is composed of four divisions, each containing equal labor and management members, who sit as a sort of supreme court, an appellate body. These are not de novo cases. These cases are decided on the basis of paper, so-called ex parte submissions, documents, briefs, which are based on the evidence, information, witnesses, and facts established on the property. This is a very unusual process which does not exist outside the railroad industry.

As John Dunsford mentioned yesterday when he was talking about just cause, when Carroll Daugherty wrote his seven tests of just cause, he was speaking about an appellate review in the railroad industry. That's one of the reasons some of us have had difficulty with the notion of investigation before the discipline. That is required in railroad cases but may not be applicable to other industries.

Deadlocked cases are given to an outsider who is called the referee, appointed by the National Mediation Board, normally with the acquiescence of the particular parties in the particular division. There are four divisions: (1) operating employees represented by the Locomotive Engineers and the United Transportation Union (UTU), although mergers have caused some changes; (2) shop crafts, represented by the International Brotherhood of Electrical Workers (IBEW), the Carmen, the Sheet Metal Workers, the Fireman and Oilers, and the Machinists; (3) nonoperating employees, represented by the Transportation Communications Union (TCU), Signalmen, and the like;

and (4) a catch-all covering any other employees not represented in the other divisions.

Cases are argued in a unique way, namely, in small panels
where there is one union Board member, one Board management member, and the referee. Occasionally parties are permitted to travel to Chicago to have so-called referee hearings, where
they have an opportunity to tell their story in five, ten, or fifteen
minutes (but not to present new evidence), based totally on what
has transpired on the property as articulated in the ex parte
submission. Nonreferee hearings (five or ten a day, according to
my experience) are normally conducted with ten to fifteen minutes for each side to present the case. There are no discussions of
credibility or of the kinds of things that most labor arbitrators
spend their time doing outside the railroad industry.

I remember one of my first cases, where I drafted an opinion
and indicated that I had no right to make an assessment about
the "misdemeanor" of a witness. Of course, it should have been
"demeanor," but I guess that was a Freudian slip about the
honesty of the witness.

In fiscal 1988, 1,353 cases were handled by all four divisions;
219 were withdrawn; 297 awards were issued without referees;
and 837 had refereed decisions by the Adjustment Board.

The 1934 amendments to the Railway Labor Act established
the right to have special boards of adjustment. Most of the
current ones involve disputes about specific issues, such as protection of employees under merger. In 1966 Congress passed a
law permitting boards to be established between particular railroads and particular unions on the property. These are the so-
called public law boards, which may be set up without the
requirement of mutuality. Either side can petition for it. These
PL boards are now the largest source of grievance arbitration in
the railroad industry. In fiscal 1988, 6,074 cases were resolved by
PL boards; 1,005 were withdrawn, and 4,569 were decided by
arbitration. We're talking about an industry of about 350,000
employees, or about one arbitration decision for every six
employees.

The members now are called neutral members, rather than
referees. PL boards are appellate; the cases are based on the
evidence in the record and should not be supplemented by new
evidence or even new arguments. That is another big difference
between railroad arbitration and other arbitration. In nonrail-
road arbitration most of us have to contend with new evidence,

even surprise evidence; in a hearing it is virtually never the case that a new argument cannot be raised. But specifically under the Railway Labor Act with public law boards and the Railroad Adjustment Board, this is not permitted. Occasionally if a public law board feels that it is missing a piece of evidence, since the source is located just down the street, they can ask for it. This is not true of the Railroad Adjustment Board, however.

In summary, the salient differences between railroad and other arbitration are: (1) This process is appellate; it is not a de novo hearing; there are no live witnesses. (2) The fees and expenses of the neutral (not the expenses of the parties) are paid for by the federal government. (3) There is strong reliance on precedent; neutrals are bound by stare decisis. From 1934 to 1988 there were 200,000 awards issued, and there is no index for research purposes. (4) Arguments and evidence are frozen on the property; no new evidence, no surprise evidence, no new argument is permitted. (5) Time frames are different; a grievance that is not denied in a timely fashion is considered granted as presented. (6) The incredible level of usage is unique. One explanation is that since the parties don't have to pay, why not go for it.

[*Editor's note:* Those who participated in the panel discussion of railroad arbitration, besides Scheinman, were: Kenneth R. Peifer, Assistant Vice President, Labor Relations, Southern Pacific Transportation Company, San Francisco, California; William Miller, West Coast General Chairman, Transportation-Communications International Union, Rockville, Maryland; Robert G. Richter, Vice President, Labor Relations, Illinois Central Railroad, Chicago, Illinois; and Fred A. Hardin, President, United Transportation Union, Cleveland, Ohio.]

NATIONAL ACADEMY OF ARBITRATORS
OFFICERS AND COMMITTEES, 1989–1990

Officers

Alfred C. Dybeck, President
Howard D. Brown, Vice President
Martin A. Cohen, Vice President
Marcia L. Greenbaum, Vice President
James L. Stern, Vice President
Dallas L. Jones, Secretary-Treasurer
Howard S. Block, President-Elect

Board of Governors

Michael H. Beck	Harold D. Jones, Jr.
C. Chester Brisco	Nathan Lipson
Gladys Gershenfeld	William S. Rule
Gladys W. Gruenberg	Jack Stieber
I. B. Helburn	Mark Thompson
David M. Helfeld	Marlin M. Volz

Thomas T. Roberts (Ex-Officio)

Executive Committee

Alfred C. Dybeck, President

Howard S. Block	Dallas L. Jones
Martin A. Cohen	Thomas T. Roberts

National Coordinator of Regional Activities

Frances Bairstow

Annual Proceedings Editor

Gladys W. Gruenberg

Past Presidents

Ralph T. Seward, 1947–49	David L. Cole, 1951
William E. Simkin, 1950	David A. Wolff, 1952

Edgar L. Warren, 1953
Saul Wallen, 1954
Aaron Horvitz, 1955
John Day Larkin, 1956
Paul N. Guthrie, 1957
Harry H. Platt, 1958
G. Allan Dash, Jr., 1959
Leo C. Brown, S.J., 1960
Gabriel N. Alexander, 1961
Benjamin Aaron, 1962
Sylvester Garrett, 1963
Peter M. Kelliher, 1964
Russell A. Smith, 1965
Robben W. Fleming, 1966
Bert L. Luskin, 1967
Charles C. Killingsworth, 1968
James C. Hill, 1969
Jean T. McKelvey, 1970

Lewis M. Gill, 1971
Gerald A. Barrett, 1972
Eli Rock, 1973
David P. Miller, 1974
Rolf Valtin, 1975
H.D. Woods, 1976
Arthur Stark, 1977
Richard Mittenthal, 1978
Clare B. McDermott, 1979
Eva Robins, 1980
Edgar A. Jones, Jr., 1981
Byron R. Abernethy, 1982
Mark L. Kahn, 1983
John E. Dunsford, 1984
William J. Fallon, 1985
William P. Murphy, 1986
Arvid Anderson, 1987
Thomas T. Roberts, 1988

Standing Committees

Membership

Margery F. Gootnick, Chair

Reginald Alleyne
Tim Bornstein
Raymond L. Britton
Raymond Goetz
Herbert L. Marx, Jr.
Richard H. McLaren

Harvey A. Nathan
David A. Petersen
James J. Sherman
Carlton J. Snow
Gil Vernon
Donald H. Wollett

Law and Legislation

Ronald F. Talarico, Chair

Bennett S. Aisenberg
Ellen J. Alexander
Louis Aronin
Paul Barron
Richard B. Bird
Barry C. Brown
John F. Caraway
Milo G. Flaten
Mark J. Glazer

Barnett M. Goodstein
Theordore K. High
Jacob D. Hyman
Arthur T. Jacobs
Thomas F. Levak
Alexander Macmillan
Stanley H. Michelstetter, II
W.B. Nelson
Ivan C. Rutledge

Professional Responsibility and Grievances

Arthur Stark, Chair

Benjamin Aaron	Richard Mittenthal
Richard I. Bloch	Alexander B. Porter
John F. Caraway	Francis X. Quinn
Shyam Das	Charles M. Rehmus
Alex Elson	Milton Rubin
David E. Feller	Alan Walt

Auditing

Mark L. Kahn, Chair

William J. Fallon	George Nicolau

Research

Mario F. Bognanno, Chair

Arthur Eliot Berkeley	Marcia L. Greenbaum
Steven Briggs	William H. Holley, Jr.
Arlen Christenson	Joseph Krislov
Charles J. Coleman	Clifford E. Smith
Donald P. Crane	Irvin Sobel
David A. Dilts	Hoyt N. Wheeler
Joel M. Douglas	Perry A. Zirkel

Continuing Education

Jay E. Grenig, Chair

Mei Liang Bickner	Michael Jay Jedel
Tim Bornstein	James P. O'Grady
Steven Briggs	Samuel S. Perry
Thomas F. Carey	Lois A. Rappaport
Edna E.J. Francis	Josef Rohlik
Bruce Fraser	John M. Stochaj
William H. Holley, Jr.	W. Gary Vause
Sharon K. Imes	William M. Weinberg
Timothy D.W. Williams	

Nominating

Milton Rubin, Chair

Arvid Anderson	James M. Harkless
Gladys W. Gruenberg	Thomas T. Roberts

Special Committees

Arrangements—1990 Annual Meeting

Kenneth A. Perea, Chair

Frederick H. Bullen	Marshall Ross
Walter N. Kaufman	William S. Rule
Arthur A. Malinowski	L. Lawrence Schultz
Robert G. Meiners	Joseph M. Sharnoff
Charles M. Rehmus	Thomas H. Vitaich

Program—1990 Annual Meeting

Anthony V. Sinicropi, Chair

Innis Christie	Marvin F. Hill, Jr.
Shyam Das	William S. Rule
Tia Schneider Denenberg	Clifford E. Smith
John J. Flagler	Herman Torosian
Joseph F. Gentile	Leo Weiss
I.B. Helburn	Helen M. Witt

Arrangements—1989 Education Conference

Edward Parker Archer, Chair

Harry Berns	Barbara W. Doering
Steven Briggs	Patrick J. Fisher
	Fred Witney

Future Meeting Arrangements

Nicholas H. Zumas, Chair

Fred L. Denson	Michael David Rappaport
Mark L. Irvings	Barbara Zausner Tener
Harold H. Leeper	Dallas M. Young

Legal Affairs

George R. Fleischli, Chair

John A. Bailey	Arnold Ordman
Robert A. Creo	Herman Torosian
Gerry L. Fellman	Ted T. Tsukiyama
Joseph F. Gentile	P.M. Williams
Joseph P. Girolamo	Sol M. Yarowsky

Legal Representation

Nathan Lipson, Chair
Timothy J. Heinsz, Chair-Elect

David L. Beckman   Mark L. Irvings
Elliot I. Beitner   Ida Klaus
Mario Chiesa   Harold H. Leeper
Howard C. Edelman   Robert E. Light
Albert A. Epstein   Bert L. Luskin
R. Wayne Estes   John F. Sass
Barnett M. Goodstein   John Paul Simpkins

Carlton J. Snow

Academy History

Gladys W. Gruenberg, Chair

Byron R. Abernethy   Dennis R. Nolan
Paul Barron   William S. Rule
Gerry L. Fellman   Irvin Sobel
Sharon K. Imes   James L. Stern
James R. McDonnell   Marian Kincaid Warns

Robert G. Williams

New Member Orientation

John E. Dunsford, Chair

James R. Beilstein   Lois A. Rappaport
John J. Mikrut, Jr.   Andrew L. Springfield

International Studies

J. Joseph Loewenberg, Chair

George E. Bowles   Ida Klaus
G. Gail Brent   Dennis R. Nolan
John Van N. Dorr, III   Robert V. Penfield
Claude H. Foisy   George S. Roukis
Alvin L. Goldman   John C. Shearer
William B. Gould, IV   David Ziskind

Designating Agency Liaison

Clare B. McDermott, Chair

Thomas G.S. Christensen   Sylvester Garrett
Peter Florey   Edward E. McDaniel

Rolf Valtin

Public Employment Disputes Settlement

Walter L. Eisenberg, Chair

Robert J. Ables	Donald B. Leach
Sara Adler	Thomas F. Levak
Barry J. Baroni	Leonard E. Lindquist
David R. Bloodsworth	James L. Litton
Bruce R. Boals	Alexander Macmillan
Mollie H. Bowers	Sherwood Malamud
Leonard H. Davidson	Allan S. McCauslan
Irwin J. Dean, Jr.	Richard H. McLaren
Stanley T. Dobry	Stanley H. Michelstetter, II
Howard G. D'Spain	Anne Harmon Miller
Howard C. Edelman	Edward J. O'Connell
Milton T. Edelman	Oscar A. Ornati
Paul J. Fasser, Jr.	Edward A. Pereles
Charles H. Frost	Philip Tamoush
Barnett M. Goodstein	Jeffrey B. Tener
Harry Graham	Louis Mills Thomson, Jr.
Mark K. Grossman	Arthur T. Van Wart
Lawrence I. Hammer	Martin Wagner

The Chronicle

C. Chester Brisco, Managing Editor
Editors

Sara Adler	Sharon K. Imes
Reginald Alleyne	Edgar A. Jones, Jr.
Jonathan Dworkin	Geraldine M. Randall
Janet L. Gaunt	Carlton J. Snow
Joseph F. Gentile	Arthur Stark

Barbara Zausner Tener

Publications

Gladys W. Gruenberg, Chair

James P. Begin	Jay E. Grenig
Howard G. Foster	Ernest E. Marlatt

Perry A. Zirkel

Tribunal Apeals

Patrick J. Fisher, Chair

Howard A. Cole   William E. Rentfro

Professionalism Programs

Walter J. Gershenfeld, Chair

Frances Bairstow   Mark L. Irvings
Daniel F. Brent   Andria S. Knapp
Dana E. Eischen   J. Joseph Loewenberg
Barbara Zausner Tener

New Directions and Functions of The Chronicle

Edgar A. Jones, Jr., Chair

Reginald Alleyne   Tia Schneider Denenberg
Arvid Anderson   John E. Dunsford
C. Chester Brisco   Mark L. Kahn
Dallas L. Jones

Review of Intercommittee Relationships and Functions

Howard S. Block, Chair

Richard I. Bloch   William P. Murphy
Theodore K. High   Milton Rubin
Dallas L. Jones   Theodore J. St. Antoine
Edgar A. Jones, Jr.   James L. Stern

Honorary Memberships

William P. Murphy, Chair

Richard Mittenthal   Arnold M. Zack

Regional Chairs

1. New England   Mark L. Irvings
2. New York City   Lois A. Rappaport
3. Eastern Pennsylvania   Barbara Zausner Tener
4. District of Columbia   Ira F. Jaffe
5. Southeast   Jack Clarke
6. Upstate New York   James R. McDonnell

7. Canada	Howard D. Brown and John F.W. Weatherill
8. Western Pennsylvania	David A. Petersen
9. Ohio	William F. Dolson
10. Michigan	Mario Chiesa
11. Illinois	Barbara W. Doering
12. St. Louis	James M. O'Reilly
13. Southwest	Harold H. Leeper
14. Rocky Mountain	Daniel M. Winograd
15. Northern California	Geraldine M. Randall
16. Southern California	Donald A. Anderson
17. Pacific Northwest	John H. Abernathy

COMMITTEE ON PROFESSIONAL RESPONSIBILITY AND GRIEVANCES*

OPINION NO. 19

Subject: Advertising and Solicitation

Issue: Would an arbitrator's conduct, in the circumstances set forth below, violate the provisions of Code Provision Part 1-C-3 which state:

    C. Responsibilities to the Profession

        3. An arbitrator must not advertise or solicit arbitration assignments.

Circumstances: The arbitrator, who is a professor, had for many years used his office at the University for all mail regarding his arbitration practice. When he retired, he continued to maintain a unversity office but decided to conduct his arbitration practice out of his home. At subsequent hearings, he had to advise the parties of his new arbitration address. Instead of getting business cards for this purpose, he purchased ballpoint pens imprinted with his name and address. During all subsequent hearings he handed a pen to each of the parties' representatives with instructions to send their post-hearing briefs or letters to him at the address listed on the pen. He also handed the pens to others present at the hearing as souvenirs.

Opinion: There is nothing improper about an arbitrator handing a business card to the parties' representatives at a hearing.[1] Subsequent communications may be necessary and the parties' representatives have an obvious interest in learning or being reminded of the arbitrator's address. The ballpoint pens in question obviously conveyed this same information. But they

---

*Code of Profesional Responsibility for Arbitrators of Labor-Management Disputes: Opinion recommended by the Committee and approved by the Board of Governors, National Academy of Arbitrators, May 28, 1989.
[1]But see Opinion No. 18, with respect to the general distribution of business cards, *Appendix C*, in Arbitration 1988: Emerging Issues for the 1990s, Proceedings of the 41st Annual Meeting, National Academy of Arbitrators, ed. Gladys W. Gruenberg (Washington, BNA Books, 1989, Item No. 11, at 376.

also constituted a useful writing tool which, to the extent it was thereafter used, would serve as a continuing reminder of the arbitrator's availability. These characteristics convert the pens into a form of advertising or solicitation prohibited by 1-C-3. Although that may not have been the arbitrator's intention, it is the necessary effect of his actions and, accordingly, this distribution is barred under the Code.

AUTHOR INDEX—1988–1989*

---

*For the Cumulative Author Index covering the period 1948 through 1987, refer to
Arbitration 1987: The Academy at Forty, Proceedings of the 40th Annual Meeting, National
Academy of Arbitrators, ed. Gladys W. Gruenberg (Washington: BNA Books, 1988).

279

TOPICAL INDEX

A